The history of Hawke's Bay

Second edition

MATTHEW WRIGHT

Intruder Books

This book is copyright and subject to international treaties.
No part may be copied, reproduced, or otherwise duplicated by any means, without prior permission of the copyright holder.

Copyright © Matthew Wright 2019

The moral rights of the author have been asserted.

ISBN-978-0-908318-24-7 (Intruder Books)

First published by Intruder Books, Wellington, 2017
Second edition, 2019

Cover art copyright © Matthew Wright 2019
Cover photography: Myra Skinner (front), Matthew Wright.
Matthew Wright photographs copyright © Matthew Wright
Matthew Wright Collection photographs copyright © Matthew Wright
Other photographs copyright as credited.

www.matthewwright.net
www.mjwrightnz.wordpress.com
www.facebook.com/MatthewWrightNZ

Front cover: Puketitiri district, early 1930s. Myra Skinner, author collection.
Back cover: Tom Parker Fountain, Napier. Matthew Wright, author collection.
Author photo by Ken Dwyer.

Contents

Introduction ... 5

1 Land and people ... 7
2 Cowboy frontier ... 27
3 The land of the shepherd kings ... 45
4 Iron horse towns ... 91
5 Farmer backbone's engine ... 121
6 Suburban paradise ... 163
7 Metropolitan province ... 191

Notes ... 213
Bibliography ... 242
Index ... 254

Introduction

Hawke's Bay has a remarkable history, brief by world standards, yet filled with colour, pace and life.

In coming pages we will consider the sweep of Hawke's Bay's past, the wider tale of people and their ideals. We will glimpse the pre-European history of the district, explore some of the themes and ideas of Hawke's Bay's rumbustious settler era, and ponder the ideals of ordinary, everyday urbanites in Napier and Hastings. We will look at how the wars of the twentieth century framed district life. And we will see how district society responded to the roller-coaster ride of the late twentieth century before emerging, re-invented and matured, in the twenty-first.

This book, slightly revised for this new edition, offers a way of understanding the broadest patterns of Hawke's Bay's past. It is intentionally an overview, designed to explore changing social shapes and patterns of district history, focusing on the pivots and places where key social change occurred. I have deliberately not narrated every event at every geographical locale. That is not my purpose.

It is an illustrated history, and this second edition brings a slightly revised and expanded selection of images. Photographs and artworks add a dimension; they are historical documents of themselves, telling us how the inhabitants of our past liked to see themselves. Images are principally from the Alexander Turnbull Library and the Hawke's Bay Museum, while others come from private collections. All are captioned according to information provided by the relevant libraries or donors.

I am grateful to the successive librarians of the Hawke's Bay Museum: Annette Fairweather, Joy Axford and Gail Pope. Chris Johnson, Archivist with the Hastings District Council, provided invaluable assistance and guidance over the years. Roger Smith of Geographx kindly supplied the hypsometric textures underlying the maps— which I have edited a little to account for pre-1931 geography. I am grateful to the Alexander Turnbull Library and to the National Library of New Zealand for their assistance; and to Laura Vodanovich of MTG (the Hawke's Bay Museum) for confirming use of photographs from their collection. And I extend special thanks to Glen Balks for his drone photography, taken for this book and used in this second edition.

Matthew Wright

Chapter One
Land and people

In the deep mists of time, so legend tells us, Maui drew Te Ika a Maui — the North Island — from the oceans on his hook, Te Matau a Maui.[1] The hook became coastal Hawke's Bay, its point Te Kauae o Maui — Cape Kidnappers.[2]

This tradition is a powerful metaphor for the origins of Hawke's Bay, which did indeed rise from the waters. It did so under the impact of mighty forces over thousands of centuries, and it did so not once but several times, in the fashion of a great fish being fought by a legendary hero. Hawke's Bay was seabed during the great ages of the dinosaurs. Continental drift sheared ancient New Zealand— Zealandia— from ancient Gondwanaland during the late Cretaceous era, some 70 million years ago.

Cycles of uplift and erosion, as the Indo-Australian plate rode up over the Pacific, brought the district into view and buried it again. Hawke's Bay was mostly underwater again some five million years ago,[3] and a new cycle of uplift began, eventually thrusting the Kaweka, Ruahine and Kaimanawa Ranges into the skies.

Dinosaur-era forest in Hawke's Bay: this is Ball's Clearing, a relic of the Puketitiri Bush.

Matthew Wright

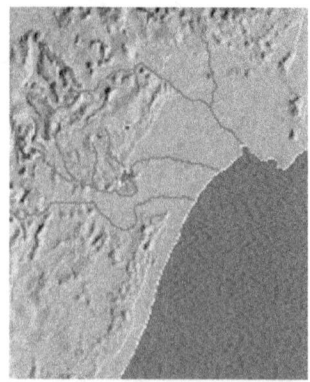

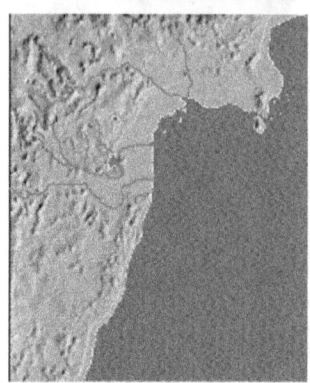

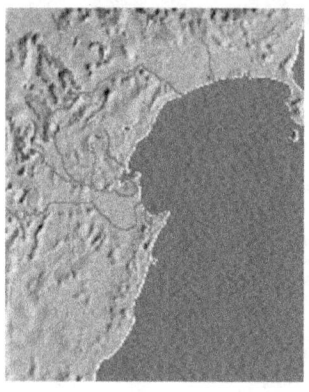

Conceptual impressions of the Hawke's Bay coastline as it changed from the effects of sea-level rise after the end of the last glaciation. Top: 14,000 years bce; centre, 7500 years bce; bottom, nineteenth century.

Matthew Wright, Matthew Wright Collection.

New Zealand kept its original biota almost unchanged until humans arrived in the mid-late thirteenth century. The plant and animal life of the Hawke's Bay district — like the rest of New Zealand — was essentially late dinosaur-era, further evolved through time: a fragment of late-Cretaceous flora and fauna in which birds — which were formally reclassified in the late twentieth century as a specialised type of dinosaur — ruled supreme. Many had lost the ability to fly, for there was nothing to threaten them on the ground. The only native mammal was a species of bat. In many ways, New Zealand was truly the 'lost world' of science fiction.

This environment generally survived both the rigours of tectonic movement and erosion, and the slow cycles of natural climate change.[4] Around two-and-a-half million years ago that this climate change became more severe, as an era of ice ages dessicated the world, although we are wrong to imagine a prehistoric Hawke's Bay swathed in snow. Average temperatures across the district were perhaps two degrees cooler, at most, than during the twentieth century. But it was a wider land. Ice, principally at the poles and in the northern hemisphere, locked up so much of the world's water that sea levels fell dramatically. At glacial maximum, 20,000 years before the present, grassy plains extended from Cape Kidnappers in a kinked line beyond the Māhia Peninsula.[5] Ironically, the main shaping force was not ice but fire; Hawke's Bay was within range of the volcanic fields of the central North Island, particularly Oruanui and Taupō. Some 26,000 years ago a colossal Taupō eruption devastated the central North Island, coating Hawke's Bay with up to half a metre of ash and debris.[6]

By around 12,000 years ago much of the district was forested in conifers and broadleaf. Other areas were shrub-land, populated by moa, swan and duck.[7] Rising seas flooded the low-lying alluvial plains and reached the hills west of modern Napier. Throughout these ages the ranges slipped and crumbled, sending shingle rolling down the Tutaekuri, Tukituki and Ngaruroro Rivers, and building wide alluvial plains. Broadleaf and conifer forests proliferated.[8] Around 1800 years ago another Taupō eruption showered debris as far as the Kaweka Range, salting the upper airs with ash and giving the northern hemisphere spectacular sunsets, recorded in China and by the Romans. Earthquakes had other effects, including a major event around 1460 that created Ahuriri lagoon.[9]

Polynesians entered Hawke's Bay's world of mountain, scrub, forest, bird and swamp from colonies elsewhere in New Zealand. Precisely when they arrived took years to determine. Nineteenth century researcher S. Percy Smith's notion of a 1350 canoe migration was cast aside during the mid-twentieth century in the face of new techniques for dating samples on the basis of carbon isotope decay. This suggested a quite early date for New Zealand settlement — and for Hawke's Bay. Sites at the mouth of

Te Mata Peak: graphic evidence of massive uplift, revealing some of the geological forces that shaped Hawke's Bay over millions of years.
Glen Balks

the Maraetotara River, for example, were dated to the tenth or eleventh centuries.[10] By the 1980s there was a general consensus that New Zealand had been settled between 700 and 1300 AD.[11] However, many of the earlier dates were then questioned on the basis that carbon dating demands proper calibration and even then gives only date-ranges. Some samples even contained 'old' carbon, giving a wholly misleading date.[12]

Subsequent work in the 1990s and beyond refined the Polynesian arrival to the more recent end of the range.[13] There was no evidence of human occupation in northern New Zealand below a Tarawera ash layer, initially dated to 1260,[14] later around 1314.[15] While the earliest arrivals may have been too small to be archaeologically visible, they could not have much pre-dated the fourteenth century.

Smith's timing, in short, had been about right after all — which was not surprising, given that he obtained it by assigning time-spans to whakapapa. The conclusion was inescapable; New Zealand was the last habitable land mass in the world reached by humans.[16] A dating method using moa eggs suggested that people were in Hawke's Bay, in numbers, by the fifteenth century;[17] and there is evidence of burial sites near Ahuriri being caught up in the mid-fifteenth century earthquake.[18]

This was the age of Tamatea the traveller, the 'roller-up' of the land,[19] the mighty explorer-hero who led the *Tākitimu* canoe and pioneered the landscape, commemorated in Hawke's Bay by the longest place-name in the country, a hill near Porangahau whose epithet is rendered in English variously with 85 or 92 letters. He remains intimately connected to the district through whakapapa, and was reputedly the father of Kahungunu.[20]

Hawke's Bay's first human population spread like a tempest through virgin landscape. Pollen analysis has pinned waves of deforestation to the fourteenth and fifteenth centuries,[21] highlighting people expanding into virgin territory, cropping bird life that fuelled a population explosion which some analysts have put as high as 3.7 percent per annum.[22] Moa, kākā, kākāriki and kākāpō were hunted during this period; Hawke's Bay was one of several moa hunting regions,[23] though afterwards their remains were difficult to find. William Colenso 'diligently sought after' bones of this 'immense domestic cock' for years.[24]

This was a golden age for people used to the limits of coral islands, but it did not last. Moa and other birds were eaten faster than they could be replaced— estimates suggest up to 35 bird species were hunted to extinction in short order.[25] Natural climate change added to the pressure. Polynesians arrived at the end of the 'Waihīrere warm period',[26] but the 'cool Spörer minimum' that followed was less favourable. It has also been argued that tsunami in the fifteenth century, following major earthquakes, prompted coastal settlements to be abandoned.[27] While none of these factors should be considered individually decisive, a period of upheaval and social change followed, leading to a new indigenous culture characterised by new artwork and gardening patterns— Māori.[28]

The first major Māori groups in Hawke's Bay included Ngāti Hotu and Ngāti Mahu.[29] Exactly when they arrived is not clear. There seems to have been a good deal of migration around the country by canoe during this period. While it has been shown that this was not responsible for spreading cultural ideas,[30] it has been argued that such voyages gave rise to Smith's ideas about mass migration from an ancestral home.[31] Arrival by coastal canoe certainly seems to have been true for Hawke's Bay; apart from the *Tākitimu* tale, another tradition recounts how Whatonga, a prominent ancestor of Rangitāne and Ngai Tara, brought the *Kurahaupō* waka into Nukutaurua, near the Māhia Peninsula.[32] Whatonga then moved to a plain to the southwest, building a house which he called Heretaunga.[33]

Exactly when this happened is unclear: but the specifics of date in European terms are less crucial than the sequence of events. The fact remains that by perhaps 1550, or thereabouts, Ngāti Awa and Ngāti Orotū were settled around the Te Whanganui-ā-Orotū lagoon, a resource centre protected by pā at Otatara, on the hills above modern Taradale; and at Heipipi, near modern Bay View.[34] Rangitāne dwelt on the Heretaunga plains north of the Ngaruroro River, based around the pā of Tānenuiarangi, on the banks of the Ngaruroro. Further south again, Ngai Tara lived around the resource centres of Lakes Poukawa and Roto-a-tara. Their society was based principally on the hapū, a grouping of whānau (extended families).[35] It has been argued that hapū emerged as a key socio-political unit in part as a function of resource management; they could collect enough food without straining what was available. Seasonal resources also demanded movement, which did not suit larger scale political structures.[36]

Māori flourished in Hawke's Bay. Surveys in the late 1970s identified 78 pā and 212 settlements from all phases of the pre-European period.[37] They drew from a range of resources including gardens, bird life, and fisheries. Midden heaps and hangi pits have been found near Waimarama, showing that pipi were an important part of the local diet. Fern roots and hinau were gathered. Other resources were less important; the only known sealing occurred at Māhia. The local economy was brisk, and even inland groups travelled to the coasts for shellfish.

Despite idealistic post-colonial images of Māori at one with the land and its bounties, indigenously 'green' in a way that environmentally unfriendly pākehā colonists were not, the reality is that Māori too had an impact on the environment. Because resources were limited, that impact was controlled by custom: Māori were careful not to over-exploit any resource, particularly the swamps on which they relied for eels and fish. But they still had an effect, and it was sometimes spectacular, particularly when it came to forest fires.

Deforestation has always been the lynch-pin of the argument over the environmental impact both of the Polynesian settlers and later, of indigenous Māori. In Hawke's Bay there was no doubt that bush had been burned before Europe arrived; the argument, as elsewhere, was always over the balance between natural causes and human intervention.[38] Archaeological work has shown that volcanoes, climate, storms and droughts all had effect.[39] These generated deforestation identified in Hawke's Bay around the tenth century, before Polynesians arrived.[40] The

> "Hawke's Bay's first human population spread like a tempest through virgin landscape."

Ruataniwha Plains were apparently already clear when the first Polynesian explorers turned up, and natural fires continued to occur.

However, the new settlers also lit fires, initially to flush out game, later to clear bush for gardens. Te Awanga, for instance, was clear by the sixteenth century.[41] James Cook observed both bush and the smoke of fires when he sailed past in 1769,[42] and early European settlers such as Colenso and later H. Guthrie-Smith found evidence of recent deforestation.[43] The land around Rissington in the early 1860s was covered with fern, tutu, flax and grasses, indicative of regeneration.[44] The problem Māori had was when such fires ran out of control, scorching much wider areas than were intended.

This process went on through the entire period and the timing is clear. To imply, as one post-colonial historian proposed, that New Zealand's deforestation was instead due to Māori lighting fires to signal passing pākehā ships — in effect, levelling the blame on the colonial process — smacked more of an attempt to present that process in emotionally polemic terms than as a layered reality. The fact was that Hawke's Bay's flora and fauna, like that of all New Zealand, was subject to complex human and natural processes that played out over centuries, during which humanity placed its stamp across the wider patterns of nature. Māori and pākehā alike were both parties to it.

The arrival of Ngāti Kahungunu

Around the turn of the seventeenth century the life of Ngāti Awa, Ngāti Orotū and the other peoples of Hawke's Bay was changed by the arrival of Ngāti Kahungunu.

Exactly how these people arrived and what that arrival meant has been widely debated. It was known from the Māori oral record, and early pākehā historians often portrayed the migration as an invasion.[45] This idea grew in part from evidence given by Ngāti Kahungunu to the land courts in the mid-nineteenth century, reinforcing claims to particular pieces of land by conquest. Settlers also persisted in viewing Māori warfare in terms of battle-to-death, an idea that — as John Keegan has shown — was actually a product of Western thinking.[46]

In such circumstance the settler-age stereotyping of Māori as a people of 'quaintness, poetry, and ferocity'[47] was as inevitable as it seemed rational, and a migration such as Taraia's was easy to re-paint as a military effort. Early missionary William Colenso lamented the 'bloody, desolating wars' of New Zealand's pre-European period, and his assessment of war as the 'life and genius' of Māori society captured settler thought. Colenso's qualification — that the 'famed and civilised' nations were

'just as bad'⁴⁸ — did not reduce the persistence of the stereotype. The apparent prevalence of pā — between 4000 and 6000 have been identified nationally, mostly associated with horticulture and resource regions⁴⁹ — reinforced the idea. Even a late twentieth century analysis of the 'musket wars' referred to Māori as having a 'warrior lifestyle'.⁵⁰ There were even suggestions that this could be explained by genetics.

In reality, classic-era Māori warfare differed both from the nineteenth century settler concept of war, and from the industrialised 'total war' of the twentieth century that framed the post-colonial historical views.⁵¹ We have to draw distinction between the military role of pā and the nature and place of warfare in Māori culture.⁵² For Māori, fighting was one aspect of a complex skein of social mechanisms that established both individual place within a community, and rights between communities. All aspects of that system tended to feature in the oral record, which was designed to capture a sense of place and relationship. Warfare was only a part of the whole. Fighting was also often abstracted. At times, slaves were killed as proxies; and while many battles were pursued with deadly intent, others — as J. D. H. Buchanan suggested in regard to Hawke's Bay — were culturally more akin to 'football matches'.⁵³ This did not reduce their intent: but as Keegan points out, posture-fighting is common to

Otatara and Heipipi were hilltop fortifications, pā, overlooking Ahuriri and the Heretaunga plains, dating back at least to the fifteenth century. Although the archaeological site was effectively destroyed by quarrying during the colonial period, it was recognised and partially preserved by the early twenty-first century. Sample palisades were erected to create the impression of what had once been.

Matthew Wright

Tānenuiarangi pā, seen here in 1859, was one of the oldest continuously occupied Māori habitations in Hawke's Bay.

Henry Stratton Bates, watercolour, Alexander Turnbull Library, NON-ATL-0008

many subsistence societies,[54] and for common reasons; the cost of warfare in terms of resource. Māori were certainly resource-limited;[55] Warriors (toa) were also the labour force. Fighting was simply one of many tasks, including farming, fishing and hunting, that were integral with the social system.[56]

Settler-age ideas about how Māori interacted persisted for decades. It was not until the 1960s that Buchanan went beyond the prevailing picture to consider some of the social dynamics associated with large-scale migrations such as Taraia's arrival in Hawke's Bay. More complex forces were at work than invasion; Buchanan instead saw a sophisticated interplay of limited warfare, negotiation, re-settlement and inter-marriage.[57]

Exactly when this happened is another matter. The Ngāti Kahungunu heke (migration) was originally dated anywhere from 1500 to 1625.[58] Archaeological studies subsequently revealed significant pā building around Te Whanganui-ā-Orotū between about 1575 and 1700; and around Te Rotoatara between about 1575 and 1650.[59] This very likely reflected the dynamic of change as Ngāti Kahungunu arrived, mingled, and re-settled. The picture is supported by whakapapa. Nineteenth century Ngāti Whatuiāpiti chief Te Hāpuku, born around 1797,[60] counted eight generations of direct descent from Taraia's sister Taiwha.[61] Archaeological analysis has shown that Māori women first concieved around age 18-19 and continued to do so at three or four-year intervals, typically having three or four children.[62] On this basis, Taiwha probably flourished around 1600-1640.

Environmental evidence adds a tantalising pointer to the same period. Oral traditions attribute the Ngāti Kahungunu migration from Māhia to an argument over resources;[63] and there was an apparent confluence of resource-related pressures across Hawke's Bay in the early seventeenth century. An estimated magnitude 7.5-8.0 earthquake around Māhia about 1600 produced significant uplift of the east coast,[64] and with it a temporary disruption of local food sources such as shellfish beds.[65] These were left high and dry, much as beds were off Kaikoura after the magnitude 7.8 quake of November 2016.

To this was added the pressure of wider climate change. The 'little ice age' reached new depths in the first decade of the seventeenth century, pushed in part by the early 1600 eruption of Mount Huanyaputina in Chile.[66] This spewed ash and carbon dioxide through the upper airs, disrupting weather patterns and agricultural yields across the world.[67] New Zealand was generally cooler from the outset of the seventeenth century,[68] and while natural disasters and climate change should not be considered

John Pearse sketched this pā near Poraiti during the 1850s. Europe's influence is already evident, but in other ways the scene reflects life in pre-European times. The importance of the adjacent lagoon is clear.

John Pearse, monotone wash, Alexander Turnbull Library, E-455-f-024-06

the sole or direct cause of human events, we cannot rule them out as contributing factors. Population growth may have added pressure.[69]

On this evidence it seems likely that Ngāti Kahunguna arrived in Hawke's Bay in the early years of the seventeenth century, give or take a decade or so. But while we cannot pin the date of migration down more closely, the events are better known. Ngāti Kahunguna originally came from Turanga (Gisborne). Elements under Rakaihikuroa moved to Nukutaurua, on the Māhia Peninsula, after a dispute over chieftainship. Initially they were allowed in by the chiefs Kahuparoro and Hauhau; but a struggle followed with Kahuraparoro on the pretext that he had obtained the bones of the Ngāti Kahungunu chief Tupurupuru and was using them as fish hooks. Ngāti Kahungunu then ambushed Hauhau and his people while the latter were digging fern root for them.[70] Ngāti Kahungunu did not stay in the district, instead moving to Wairoa where they asked the local hapū to provide canoes for a crossing to Ahuriri, led by Rakaihikuroa's son Taraia.

Ngāti Kahungunu reached Hawke's Bay with a related group under Te Aomatarahi,[71] mistakenly called Taraia's 'captain' in some accounts.[72] The heke landed first at Aropaoanui, north of Ahuriri, then went to the mouth of the Ngaruroro River mouth. Here a force went south under Te Aomatarahi, while Taraia tackled the pā around the Te Whanganui-ā-Orotū lagoon.[73]

What followed, as Buchanan has observed,[74] was as much a function of intermarriage as warfare. The immediate result was the emergence of socio-political groupings around the main resource centres. The northern group, dubbed Te Ika a Raurahanga, dominated the Te Whanganui-ā-Orotū lagoon and Tutaekuri river River as far south as Lake Oingo. Further south, Te Ika a Papauama settled around Lake Poukawa and Te Rotoatara. These 'polities' drew descent simultaneously from the earlier inhabitants and the newcomers.[75]

Such descent highlighted a reality that did not become obvious to Western scholarship until towards the end of the twentieth century. Nineteenth-century settlers — and some later analysts[76] — often lumped Hawke's Bay Māori together under the blanket term Ngāti Kahungunu, identifying separate kin-groups as 'factions'.[77] Such thinking betrayed a general settler failure to bother with the reality of Māori society and politics; hapū and iwi structure were instead sieved through the lens of period British thinking, with its focus on larger identities and a tendency to ignore subtleties that differentiated smaller groupings.

However, it has been argued that the predominance of Ngāti Kahungunu was partly a response to pākehā contact.[78] What actually emerged as the dust of Taraia's arrival settled was a diverse collection

European goods such as blankets, pipes and tobacco are evident in this late 1859 view of Pakowhai pā, a typical Hawke's Bay kāinga of the period. However — apart from that European intrusion, the appearance is not too different from that of kāinga a generation or two earlier.

Henry Stratton Bates, watercolour, Alexander Turnbull Library, NON-ATL-0099

of nominally independent communities living alongside each other.[79] New hapū and groups of hapū appeared as kin groups changed, some eponymously named after their founding ancestor.

Hawke's Bay during the 'musket wars'

The 'musket wars' swept through Hawke's Bay from the 1820s. They came on the cusp of European settlement and — thanks largely to the focus on 1840[80] — remained a historical desert for years. It was 2000 before a full narrative account emerged,[81] followed in 2003 by an academic attempt to intellectualise the wars out of existence,[82] and in 2011 by a further book pointing out that they had, in fact, happened.[83]

These wars were among the most significant ever to befall New Zealand in its human history. The net outcome of more than 500 battles, migrations and a near-total upheaval over a generation was strain on existing Māori socio-political systems, leading in one case a new form: the loose 'empire' of Te Rauparaha.[84] The legacy of these wars echoed

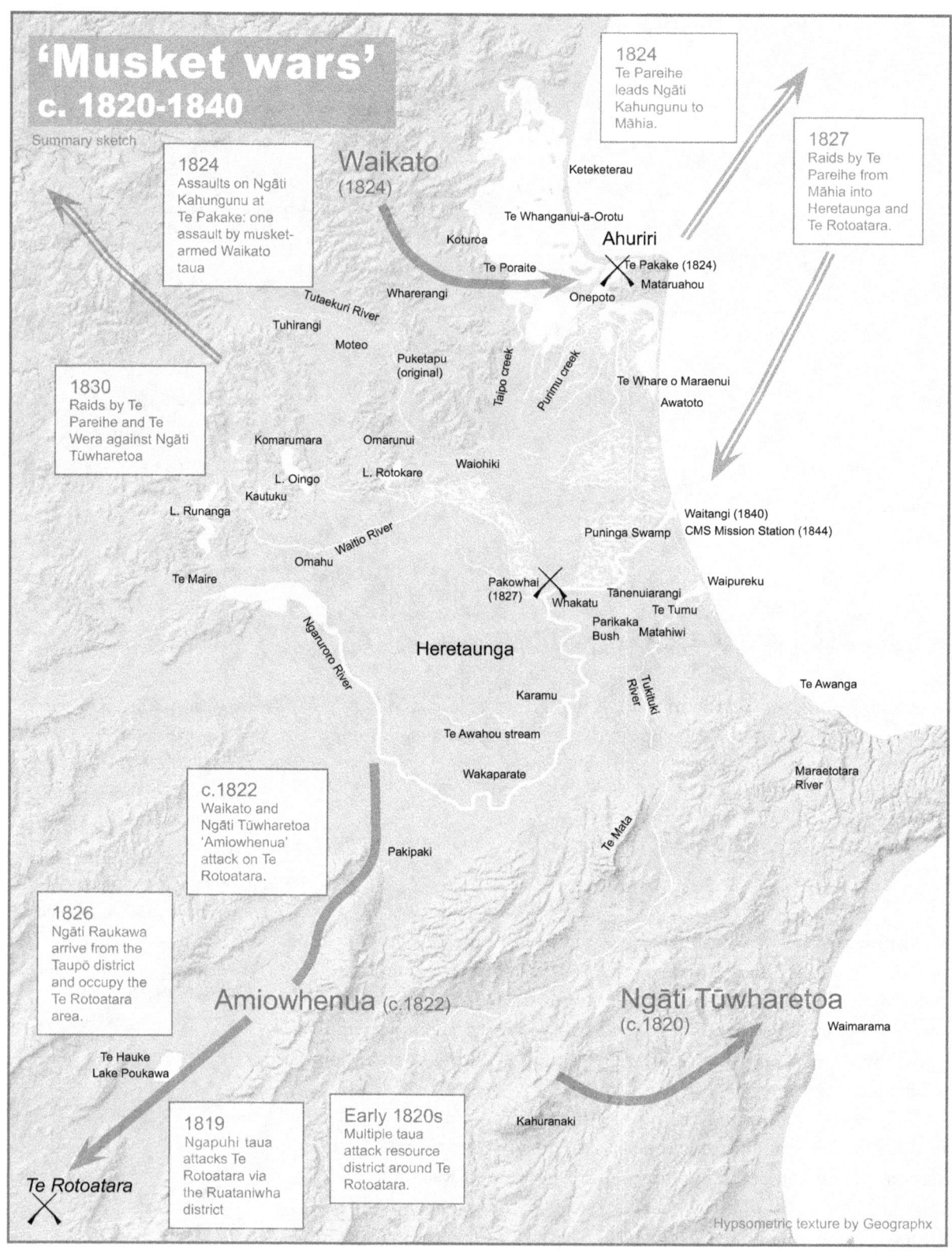

Lake Poukawa— a significant resource centre for Māori, and focus of multiple raids and sieges during the early 1820s. By the time Charles Decimus Barraud painted this picture in 1877, Europe had already made itself felt. The lake was drained a few years later, against Te Hāpuku's wishes.

Charles Decimus Barraud, chromolithograph, Alexander Turnbull Library, PUBL-0016-22.

through the settler period and beyond, shaping the Māori response to the New Zealand wars of the 1860s;[85] and echoes were still resounding in the twenty-first century, because the upheavals created new patterns of land-holding that had not shaken down when government agents began negotiating purchase, creating issues that were often not fully addressed when a final settlement process relative to the colonial process finally began in the late 1980s.[86]

Observers at the time, and the settlers who followed, inevitably filtered the 'musket wars' through the nineteenth century lens. The Hawke's Bay experience highlights some of the mythology, including the period tendency to blame the causes of these wars solely on the Māori acquisition of European guns,[87] an idea that was still being presented, as if true, as late as 2000.[88] In fact— with the exception of Ngāpuhi— muskets played only a small part at tactical level until the late 1820s.[89] Even then, as the Hawke's Bay experience reveals, muskets did not always feature; one account records an assault pursued by a taua— war party— with 20 muskets against defenders with none.[90] Even when muskets were widespread, they gave surprisingly little advantage in battles where

Te Pakake pā, where the last known cannibalism occurred in Hawke's Bay in 1824, is centre right in this 1850s watercolour The district had changed little by this time from its 'musket wars' shape. Later, the island was engulfed by pākehā reclamation. By the early twenty-first century the site was occupied by a business park.
Joseph Rhodes, watercolour, Alexander Turnbull Library, A-159-033

hand-to-hand weapons were also deployed. The reason, primarily, was the combination of a slow rate of fire, combined with relatively short range, which meant that combatants only had time to get a shot or two off before the hand-to-hand battle was joined. The issue had particular effect in the New Zealand environment because the home-made powders and makeshift bullets that Māori usually had to hand further reduced the hitting power of the muskets. Arguably the more important driver was the general range of European products being sold or made available to Māori, including potatoes. These transformed the Māori economy and with it the labour calculation, making warfare relatively cheaper; and at the same time practically fuelling the long-range raids that made the 'musket wars' so different from what had gone before.[91] It was this long-range aspect that particularly affected Hawke's Bay.

On this basis the issues Māori faced essentially flowed from the collision with an industrial society that was itself in turmoil. For all that, the interaction between the arrival of Europe and the sudden upswing in warfare among Māori during the early nineteenth century has been extensively debated, inevitably being drawn into the general issues of culture-contact and colonialism. The waters were often muddied by the fact that some of the immediate triggers for warfare in the 'musket age' drew on deeper socio-cultural precedent and dispute that pre-dated Europe. Certainly this was so in Hawke's Bay where older disputes became reason for new warfare.[92] That allowed some observers of the settler period, such as Donald McLean, and some historians later, to argue that the 'musket wars' had little to do with the arrival of the colony.

> "The Hawke's Bay experience typified the way that the 'musket wars' generated a range of Māori responses, which echoed directly into the colonial period...."

In fact the wars were a symptom of the collision between Māoritanga and British industrial society — and on many levels. That collision did not, as some historians supposed, break Māori society. On the contrary, traditional values remained paramount, and even the new long-range aspects of the 'musket wars' were framed within older social systems and structures.[93] However, the arrival of British industrial-age goods and foods transformed the power of Māori society to do things — just as industrialisation had transformed Britain's own power just a generation or so earlier. One immediate result was an ability to expand the scale and range of warfare. Until the early nineteenth century, Māori warfare had been limited by economic factors: toa (warriors) were also gardeners and fighting always took place at the expense of resource gathering. That changed in the face of European technology and goods, which acted as a multiplier for traditional Māori systems and methods.

What this meant was that in the early nineteenth century, distant kin groups became allies and distant resource centres became targets. The old self-limiting systems were still in place, but the limits had shifted

Part of the reason for the shift was coincidental: British industrial-era trade arrived at a time when Māori social systems were under pressure from a range of factors. Some were internal. Populations appear to have been rising, an issue further complicated for a resource-limited society by the external pressures imposed by the often sharp climatic shifts of the late eighteenth century, as the 'little ice age' went through further spasms.

Both factors likely added complicating pressures to a Māori economy that had always had to face the challenge of a generally inhospitable environment.[94] Tree-ring evidence has specifically identified cooling in the 1760s and 1790s,[95] and wars were certainly fought in the Waikato over resources in the 1790s— which provided utu justification for raids during the 'musket wars'.[96] There was another cooling period around 1800 and, when coupled with evidence that Māori were expanding their gardens about this time, a picture builds of a people pushing against their resource base. Further climate-related pressure came in 1816 — which for those in the northern hemisphere was the 'year without a summer' — triggered by the eruption of Mt Tambora, east of Java.[97]

> "Muskets in numbers added lethality to battle, and with other British industrial products gave new endurance to warfare that remained framed by traditional social values..."

All these issues, in combination, raised tensions between Māori groups; but they would probably have done little of themselves without Britain's industrial products and technologies rushing into the mix and transforming the production base. Hawke's Bay was drawn into the new world that followed around 1819,[98] after long-standing opposition between Ngāti Whatuiāpiti and Ngai Te Upokoiri erupted into fresh conflict.[99] Details vary between sources,[100] but the struggle ultimately involved some of the rangatira who became prominent a few decades later in the settler era, among them Te Hāpuku, Takamoana, Tareha, Kawepo and Te Moananui: the latter often known as Kurupo Te Moananui in the settler period, to differentiate him from Tareha, who adopted the same name after Te Moananui's death. The outcome helped define rights across Hawke's Bay in the settler period. The mana gained by Takamoana during the 'musket wars', for example, contributed directly to his status when the settlers arrived.[101] The Hawke's Bay experience typified the way that the 'musket wars' generated a range of Māori responses which echoed directly into the colonial period which overlapped the end of the 'musket wars' era. Hapū and iwi that had not been wholly devastated or displaced by the wars— such as Waikato— tended to resist the pākehā arrival a few years later.[102] Those at the receiving end of defeat and migration — such as the Te Ati Awa who settled in the Wellington district during the 1830s — subsequently welcomed pākehā as protectors.[103] The Hawke's Bay's experience fell between the two, generating a quest for security and independence that framed local race relations through the settler period.

The wars came to Hawke's Bay through local causes, primarily the rights to the resources of Lake Rotoatara,[104] a 'land of hillocks'.[105] This area had traditionally been disputed, but the argument gained a new dimension when Te Uamairangi of Ngai Te Upokoiri was defeated by Ngāti Whatuiāpiti, and in response sought allies outside the district.

Ngāti Tūwharetoa of Taupō were Te Uamairangi's relatives, via his mother; but toa from as far distant as Whanganui joined the taua and inflicted a drubbing on Ngāti Whatuiāpiti at Mangatoetoe. Ngāti Whatuiāpiti prevailed in a second battle near Waipukurau,[106] but Ngai Te Upokoiri responded with an attack on Te Aratipi pā, which fell; whereupon Te Pariehe was made war-leader of Ngāti Whatuiāpiti. This was another new phenomenon; Te Pariehe was junior to hereditary rangatira such as Te Hāpuku and Te Moananui, but his military victories gave him status.[107]

Both sides continued to invite distant relations into the district during the early 1820s, and over the next few years Hawke's Bay was riven by a succession of taua. There was an effort by a Ngāti Awa taua to take the Ngāti Kahungunu pā at Te Pakake, on the edge of the Ahuriri harbour — later the Napier woolstore district and, by the early twenty-first century, the site of hotels and apartments. Ngāti Awa were not musket-armed to any extent — but although, as we have seen, this was more effective as a morale and status weapon at the time, the attack failed.[108] Nonetheless, Hawke's Bay had clearly become a target. The next raid, by Ngāti Porou and Ngāti Maru under Tangiteruru, came from Inland Patea, defeated Ngai Te Upokoiri, then took the pā at Te Roto-a-Tara and another at Maungawharau, near Waimarama.[109]

Local politics intervened. Te Wanikau of Ngai Te Upokoiri, who had withdrawn to the Ruahines, clashed with Te Whatuiāpiti over access to the resources of Lake Poukawa, this time over a tangi feast for Te Nahu.[110] In response, Te Wanikau called for aid from Ngāti Tūwharetoa. If an evident correlation between tales can be accepted,[111] this apparently drew Hawke's Bay into the great Amiowhenua ('encircling of the land') launched by Waikato and their allies — including Ngāti Tūwharetoa — around the southern half of the North Island in 1821–22.[112] The assault into Hawke's Bay was given additional dynamic for the Ngāti Tūwharetoa leader Te

Te Hāpuku (c1797–1878), paramount chief of Ngāti Whatuiāpiti. Promoted by Donald McLean as a key seller of land in Hawke's Bay, he was one of several major figures in the district. Samuel Carnell took this photograph late in Te Hāpuku's life.

Samuel Carnell, S. Carnell Collection, Alexander Turnbull Library, G-22221-1/4

Heuheu Mananui by the death in battle of his brother Manuhiri,[113] and the taua besieged Ngāti Whatuiāpiti in the pā at Te Rotoatara, probably early in 1822. Ngāti Whatuiāpiti were eventually forced to withdraw. The assailing taua then moved to the Ruataniwha Plains, attacked a pā there, and pushed through to the Manawatu.[114]

Meanwhile, Ngāti Raukawa— from the Maungatautauri region— arrived in Taupō, and their chief, Te Whatanui, went on to Hawke's Bay in the hope of finding succour and refuge for his people.[115] Te Pariehe eventually defeated the Ngāti Raukawa taua in a valley at the head-waters of the Waipawa River. However, a new threat appeared; Te Wera of Nga Puhi had settled at Te Māhia, and moved to Mataruahou (the Napier hill) in response to a request by a Mohaka chief to avenge the death of his son. The eventual result was an attack by a combined taua on Ngāti Hawea, a hapū living near the Tukituki river River mouth, after which Te Wera settled into the Tānenuiarangi pā on the banks of the Ngaruroro.[116] Here he was confronted by Te Pariehe, but a settlement brought Te Wera's people into alliance with Ngāti Whatuiāpiti and — eventually — Ngāti Kahungunu, along with other hapū as far distant as Māhia and Te Wairoa.

> "After some weeks, Te Pariehe's people were reduced to eating blue clay, an earth that retained some semblance of its organic origins."

This alliance looked promising. But then — perhaps early in 1824 — rumour came of other forces about to descend on the district, and Te Pariehe decided to take up Te Wera's offer of refuge at Te Māhia. How many moved is unclear, but the population around the Waikokopu whaling station was estimated at around 2000 in the late 1830s.[117] Tareha, whose people were living at Te Pakake on the edge of the Te Whanganui-ā-Orotū lagoon, fortified his pā instead. News that most of Heretaunga had been abandoned prompted Ngāti Raukawa to invade a second time; but Tiakitai, Tareha, Te Moananui and others led forces against them. The intruders had barely been repelled, however, when the feared taua arrived — a composite force of a thousand toa, including Ngāti Maru, Te Arawa, Waikato and others under Te Paewaka. The assailants carried 414 muskets between them and took Te Pakake— whose 300-odd defenders had none.[118] Prisoners included prominent rangatira such as Te Hāpuku, which was a sharp blow to his mana. The pā was later rebuilt by Tiakitai.[119]

Te Pariehe was not left unmolested at Māhia. He and his people settled at Okurarenga pā near Nukutaurua, where they were besieged by a taua under Te Heuheu. After some weeks, Te Pariehe's people were reduced to eating blue clay, an earth that retained some semblance of its organic origins.[120] The besiegers defeated a relief force of Ngāti Porou and Rongowhakaata, but Te Heuheu then withdrew. Te Pariehe subsequently attracted refugees from a wide area and began trading for muskets. With these weapons he had an advantage over non-musket armed opponents — though by this time, such weapons were becoming widespread through New Zealand. Some 6,000 were imported in 1830 alone.[121]

Muskets, in numbers, combined with other British industrial products to give new dimension and endurance to warfare that otherwise remained framed by traditional social values such as reciprocity, systems that had emerged when Māori warfare had sharper resource limits and, partly by virtue of smaller scale, significantly less lethality.

Te Pariehe lost no time using the new resources, leading taua from Te Māhia and, in 1827, driving south as far south as Roto-a-tara. Here he scored a victory that eventually pushed Ngāti Raukawa and Ngai Te Upokoiri out of the district. Kawepo was captured during this battle and taken north with Nga Puhi.[122] Despite this victory, Te Pariehe settled again at Nukutaurua. Enough was enough, it seemed; the east coast remained chaotic, and there was safety in numbers on an easily defensible peninsula. A handful of Ngāti Kahungunu remained at Te Pakake and a few other locales in Heretaunga.

Fighting continued as late as 1836. Hawke's Bay Māori were found working on the whaling station established at Waikokopu in 1837. Christianity arrived about this time, in the form of William Williams of the Church Missionary Society (CMS). He found himself being used as an intermediary for warring Māori,[123] but the primary driver behind the peace that followed was Māori intent, not missionary hope. Ngāti Kahungunu marked one settlement with a carving, placed on the route to Taupō — all this well ahead of any European arrival — which opened the way for an eventual return to Heretaunga. That still took time; as late as October 1840, Williams found only two small communities there.[124] The district was still settling down when William Colenso arrived in 1844 with Renata Kawepo.[125]

The historical question is why peace was sought after a generation of apparently self-perpetuating warfare.[126] Contemporaries and some historians have argued that the missionaries were responsible,[127] but the real agency was Māori themselves. By the late 1830s warfare had been sweeping New Zealand

> "The 'musket wars' guided the immediate response to the arrival of Britain. Some chiefs looked on Britain as a source of longer-term stability... Te Hāpuku told Donald McLean that he wanted Europeans to 'replace my tribes now nearly extinct'."

for a generation. Around 60 percent of the pre-war population, estimated at about 100,000, had been variously killed, enslaved or displaced—deaths are thought to have totalled around 20,000.[128] In percentage terms, relative to the size of population, the annual average death rate implied by these numbers was equal to that of New Zealand's First World War experience.[129] Yet the 'musket wars' went on seven or eight times as long. Such losses and the much larger-scale dislocation that went with them was challenging to everyday social order by any measure, even when spread over 30 years. It did not mean that Māoritanga, of itself, had been broken. However, by the early 1840s Māori had endured this dislocation for a generation, and the rising tide of British settlement could not be ignored.

In this context, missionary teachings offered both a philosophy and a way of resolving disputes that stood outside the parameters of Māori society, which to some extent explains the relative ease with which the Church Missionary Society (CMS) was able to obtain what they imagined to be 'conversions' along the East Coast in particular. However, CMS agents were not the main factor behind the peace-making of the late 1830s; and other pākehā institutions were of little import. In 1995 the Waitangi Tribunal suggested that the Treaty of Waitangi opened the way for Te Pariehe and his people to return to Heretaunga,[130] but such assertion is not credible. Peace was already under negotiation when the document reached the province in May 1840.[131]

The 'musket wars' guided the immediate response to the arrival of Britain. Some chiefs looked on the colonists as a source of longer-term stability, even a source of peoples; Te Hāpuku told Donald McLean that he wanted Europeans to 'replace my tribes now nearly extinct'.[132] Such sentiment withstood the storms of the settler period. When war broke out in Taranaki in 1860, Porangahau chief Morena reassured settlers that 'we deliberately called you here to settle upon our lands as a taonga and to be fathers to us.'[133]

Even when the true nature of British colonialism became apparent — when it became clear that Māori were being marginalised across New Zealand, and when Ngāti Kahungunu were sorely provoked by shoddy land deals, they did not veer from their path of peace.

CHAPTER TWO
Cowboy frontier

Although idle speculation assigns the European discovery of Hawke's Bay to the Portuguese or Spanish, there is no actual evidence of such an event.[2]

The first Europeans we can be certain of were James Cook and his crew who sailed past on board HMS *Endeavour* in October 1769, interrupted only by a collision with Māori off Cape Kidnappers.[3]

With a fine eye for flattery Cook named the bay for Sir Edward Hawke, First Lord of the Admiralty — a point resolving the grammatical questions of apostrophe and indefinite article when referring to the district. As a possessive and personal epithet, the name cannot be either 'Hawkes Bay' or 'the Hawke's Bay'.

A little over 20 years after Cook, Jonathan Trevarthen took his whaler *Mermaid* into the bay and became the second European to visit the district.[4] However, even when enterprising missionaries, whalers and traders from New South Wales and beyond drew New Zealand into the fringes of Empire, opinion in London still stood against formal colonisation. New Zealand was excluded from Acts of 1817, 1823 and 1828 that listed British colonial possessions. However, in the end, private adventurism forced the hand of Colonial Office officials, who reluctantly established Crown government in February 1840. Under the influence of

> "...here, as in too many other places, it is not *right* but *might* which carries off the prizes"
> —William Colenso.[1]

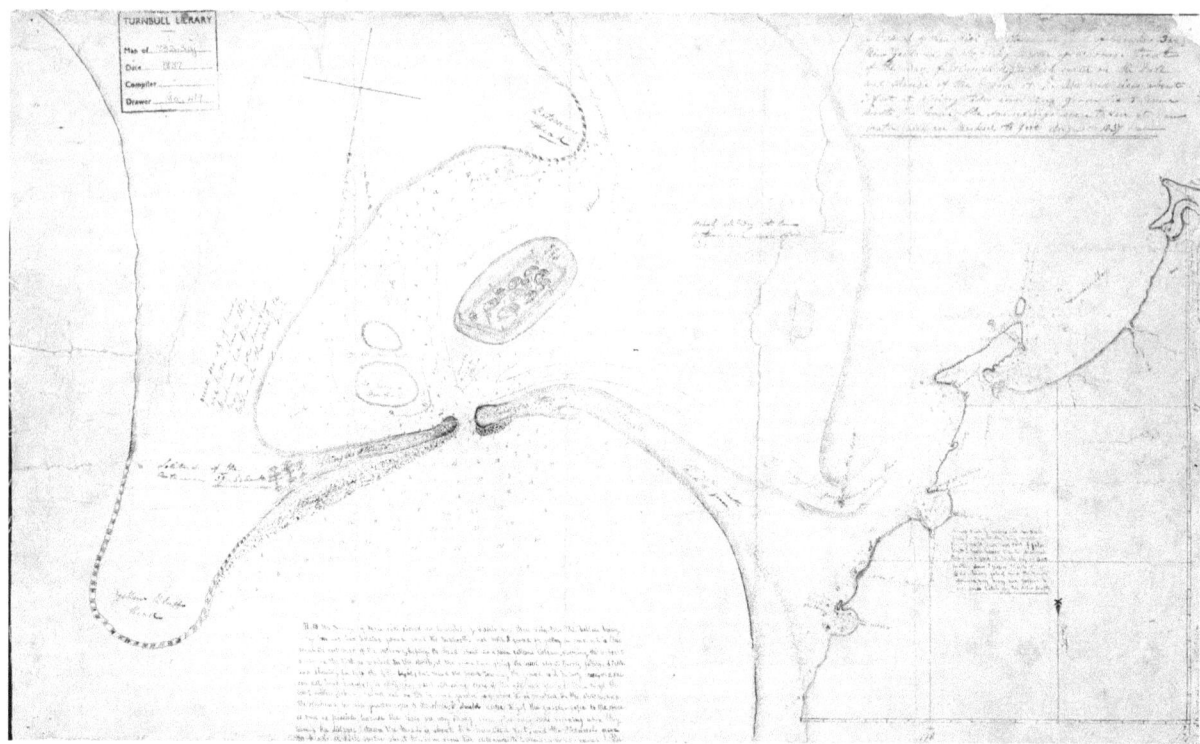

Thomas Wing's sketch of 'Hau Ridi', Ahuriri Harbour, August 1837. A warning that vessels of more than 60 tons should not visit owing to 'bad holding ground about the heads' did not reduce the importance of the harbour to the settlers.

Thomas Wing, Alexander Turnbull Library, MapColl832.3aj/1837/Acc.419

the Church Missionary Society — who argued that colonisation meant destruction for indigenous peoples — this was organised by a hastily written treaty.[5]

Hawke's Bay remained on the fringes of these adventures in accidental imperialism.[6] Cook's map was reprinted with few amendments in an 1817 account of a journey to New Zealand.[7] French explorer Dumont D'Urville swept past the coast in 1827 on the *Astrolabe*. Ashore, Te Pariehe's campaigns were reaching their climax, but D'Urville did not stop. The first European to walk the land was likely Barnet Burns, who was left standing on the Māhia shore surrounded by what he called 'a set of cannibals' in June 1829. He acquired a moko and later found it 'impossible to walk the streets without exciting the curiosity of all who see me'.[8] A map published in London in 1834 identified 'McDonnell's Cove' at Ahuriri, though it has been argued that the district was never visited by its supposed discoverer, Thomas McDonnell.[9]

More reliable accounts of visitors from the era included the trader Joel Polack, who arrived in the early 1830s; and Captain Thomas Wing, who charted Ahuriri Harbour in 1837 with his schooner *Trent*. Jack Duff explored the bush in the south of the region in the late 1830s, and about the same time the Austrian naturalist F. W. C. Sturm settled near Nuhaka.[10]

For the British who began to arrive in numbers in Hawke's Bay from the mid-1840s, this was a time of adventure. Hawke's Bay was the real frontier, isolated from the main settlements, an attraction to ambitious settlers escaping the cloying world of Wakefield-era social engineering in Wellington and its satellites. Collision with Māori was perhaps inevitable. Each people viewed the other through their own cultural lenses — in the case of the settlers, lenses so ubiquitous as to be largely invisible to all but the few who had made themselves intimate with Māori life. Colenso, for one, long felt that local authorities had no actual concept of Māori — remarking later how the pākehā in Hawke's Bay had been 'greatly twitted' by Renata Kawepo in particular.[11] Part of the problem was mind-set. Even those within the settler community who properly perceieved the issues they faced when interacting with New Zealand's indigenous people still interpreted what was happening through their settler-age ideological frameworks.

Land sharks and proselytes

The first and enduring point of collision between Māori and pākehā in Hawke's Bay remained land. Small pieces changed hands during the 1830s, associated with the whaling industry emerging around Māhia and along the Hawke's Bay coast.[12] In late 1839, while Sydney buzzed with talk of annexation, W. B. 'Barney' Rhodes swept into the district on behalf of Sydney land agents Cooper and Holt and concluded a deal to buy an astonishing proportion of Hawke's Bay that was breathtaking on every level— for its scale, for its bewildering shoddiness, and for its dramatic haste. During a lightning sweep across the district he spoke to a variety of chiefs, including Te Moananui, and purchased either 1,228,000 or 1,401,600 acres, depending on who he was talking to.[13] This included a coastal strip between 'Cape Turnagain … around Cape Kidnapper[s] to a white cliff'. The whole lot, again depending on who Rhodes spoke to, changed hands for either 'about £150', or for £323 in goods and cash.[14]

It was out of line even by the standards of the day; but at a stroke, Rhodes and his partners had thumbed their noses at British authority, and colonial officials were not the only ones discomfited. William Williams —

> "In late 1839... W. B. 'Barney' Rhodes swept into the district... and concluded a deal that was breathtaking on every level— for its scale, for its bewildering shoddiness, and for its dramatic haste."

writing from the CMS perspective — found Māori 'altogether opposed' to the deal.[15] But all came to naught in the end. Although Rhodes set up a trading post at Ahuriri and located a potential town site on the banks of the Tutaekuri River,[16] the Treaty of Waitangi put paid to his ambitions. The British arbitrarily cancelled all the pre-treaty land deals on the back of it; and despite a widespread belief that 2,560 acres near the Tukituki River mouth were given to the Rhodes family in compensation,[17] documentary evidence suggests the elder Rhodes actually took a monetary settlement.[18]

> "The Treaty of Waitangi reached Hawke's Bay in May 1840, though the effort to obtain signatures was almost as slipshod as Rhodes' deal."

The Treaty of Waitangi reached Hawke's Bay in mid-1840, though the effort to obtain signatures was almost as slipshod as Rhodes' deal. Williams managed to accumulate about 40 signatures from Poverty Bay during early 1840, including that of a visiting Ahuriri chief.[19] But he never went to Ahuriri, and it was left to Major Thomas Bunbury of the 80th Regiment to get signatures from that district. His main motive was not spreading the Treaty itself, but dealing with the last of the pre-Treaty arrangements. The Treaty superseded the 1835 Declaration of Independence, an earlier effort by British Resident James Busby to secure Māori support.[20] Busby had peddled this document for years, and Bunbury's main mission was finding the chiefs who had signed it and persuading them to put their mark to the new treaty. It was the only systematic effort to find signatories outside the Bay of Islands. It happened that Ngāti Whatuiāpiti chief Te Hāpuku had signed the Declaration while visiting the Bay of Islands in 1839, and Bunbury and Williams turned up off the Hawke's Bay coast looking for him in June 1840.

The chief proved elusive, initially fearing that Bunbury had arrived to arrest him for the 'extortions he had practised upon Europeans'. When the Major and his party reached Te Hāpuku's kāinga, they were told 'the chief had gone into the country'. A messenger was sent, but Te Hāpuku did not arrive, and Bunbury's party were on their way back to the ship when they were overtaken by Te Hāpuku and another 'chief from the Bay of Islands district, named Hara'. However, Te Hāpuku remained reluctant to sign even after Bunbury outlined the treaty, believing that those who did would become slaves. Bunbury had Williams 'ask the chief Hara … how he came not to be made a slave of, and how many slaves he had seen at the Bay of Islands …', to which Te Hāpuku 'endeavoured to explain his meaning' by drawing a 'diagram … placing the Queen by herself over the chiefs'.[21] The Major explained that the arrangement 'was literally as he described it … not for an evil purpose … but to enable her to enforce her execution of justice and good government equally amongst her subjects.' Signature would, Bunbury declared, 'tend to increase his consequence by acknowledging his title'.[22]

Te Hāpuku's concerns partly reflected his 'musket wars' experiences, where he had been enslaved: but he also seems to have had a quite clear understanding of the actual power arrangement the Treaty implied. However, he finally signed. So did the chiefs Waikato and Mahokai, apparently because they were there.[23] Bunbury did not seek anybody else in the district. In the 1990s the Waitangi Tribunal was asked to provide a ruling that Ngāti Kahungunu had signed the Treaty, but could not do so.[24]

The Treaty did not immediately create settler government in the district; Hawke's Bay lay beyond the periphery of British settlement, and the first organised pākehā authority in the district was the Church Missionary Society, an organisation set up by the Church of England. Proselytising to Māori was but one of their goals. Another was saving New Zealand's people from what the CMS considered the evils of British settlement. Prevailing theory declared that British society would by definition bring doom to 'inferior' indigenous peoples. The church took it upon itself to act as a voice of conscience, and missionaries went in to bat for Māori over land purchase. In the small world of early settler New Zealand that inevitably made the arguments personal.

Hawke's Bay drew attention as the CMS spread their wings south during the late 1830s. Bishop George Selwyn and Chief Justice William Martin tramped through the district in late 1842, and the following year William Colenso trudged north along the east coast to the Urewera, laying the groundwork for a mission at Ahuriri.[25] What followed highlighted the dissonance between cultures. For Māori, pākehā were a source of rivalry, part of what has been dubbed a 'currency of mana' built around European goods and people.[26] Every hapū wanted a pākehā, not least because of access to trade, and efforts to find a site for the mission station prompted

William Colenso (1811–1899) — the brilliant yet combatative missionary, explorer, botanist, politician and general settler-age polymath, seen here in April 1868.

Photographer unknown, Alexander Turnbull Library, F-5028-1/2 a spat within Ngāti Kahungunu which — according to J. H. Joll — was resolved by allocating space in a 'wretched, swampy, no-mans land at the mouth of the Waitangi and Ngaruroro Rivers constantly subject to flooding …'[27]

Colenso remains a complex character, a polymath whose interests ranged from botany to linguistics, archaeology, astronomy, ethnography and astronomy. Disingenuously, he once declared that he sought 'neither pelf nor fame … but merely to relate, in plain words, what I believe to be genuine and authentic...'[28] Of course there was more. He had a sharp eye for politics and a fearless disregard for the proprieties of social position. He was present at Waitangi on 6 February 1840, worried enough about the implications of the Treaty to cheekily interrupt the ceremonies and ask Hobson whether Māori understood what they were signing.[29] But genius came at a price. Colenso was intolerant, moody, and as one analyst has argued, habitually settled arguments with his fists,[30] even at risk to himself — as when he punched Kurupo te Moananui in the head.[31]

His attitude to Māori was a recipe for trouble when conversion was nominal. Colenso's Māori teachers and their pupils took up Christianised names — Karaitiana (Christian) Takamoana, Henare (Henry) Tomoana, Renata (Leonard) Kawepo, and so on; but it was a fragile connection, and for Māori, in practise, the teachings of the minihare (minister) were simply laid across traditional values. In 1845, less than 12 months after Colenso arrived, one chief dropped Christianity and took his people with him in the face of the minister's abrasion. Others followed the next year,[32] and these were not the only setbacks. When Tiakitai was drowned in 1847, word spread that Koroneho (Colenso) had killed him by magic.[33] The reality was that Māori did not simply drop their culture: their supposed 'conversion' to Christianity was purely a pākehā conceit, and Colenso knew it. Although by 1850 he was able to trumpet that his congregation totalled some 2,205 out of a local population of around 2,700,[34] he actually despaired of finding an 'avenue into their soul'.[35]

Māori were not the only targets of Colenso's temper. He picked a feud with local Catholic priest Euloge Reignier which descended — with no credit to either party — to muck-raking. And Colenso had an Achilles' heel. Before coming to Hawke's Bay he married Elizabeth Fairburn, a loveless union which he later claimed he had agreed to purely on recommendation of Robert Maunsell, and at Selwyn's urging.[36] In

> "Māori were not the only targets of Colenso's temper. He picked a feud with local Catholic priest Euloge Reignier which descended — with no credit to either party — to muck-raking."

Hawke's Bay he pursued an affair with their maid, Ripeka, a 'merry, laughing soul'.[37] They had a child. Elizabeth found out in mid-1851 and suffered in silence,[38] but whispers soon reached Reigner's ears, and thence the CMS.[39] Colenso formally confessed to his employer in September 1852, but his efforts to defend what he called an 'evil moment' of 'carnal knowledge' came to naught,[40] and Selwyn dismissed him two months later.[41]

So this brilliant, combatative, colourful man passed from missionary service — though not from Hawke's Bay. It is difficult to see Colenso's stormy career with the CMS as anything but a personal disaster. For all that, provincial history would be poorer without him; his intellect was second to none, and his papers — particularly on matters botanical and ethnographic — remain among the more detailed of the period.[42] He was reputedly the first scientist to observe and classify moa, though he always denied that himself.[43] As a member of the CMS, Colenso also played his part in the politics of land purchase — fractious, argumentative and laden with personality. And it is here that we can see his greater influence across the district during those early and vigorous colonial years.

Euloge Reignier (1811–88), called the 'Apostle of Hawke's Bay' by hia flock, but also the man who pursued a vicious personal feud against Anglican missionary William Colenso. Neither were without fault.

Samuel Carnell, S. Carnell Collection, Alexander Turnbull Library, F-146542-1/2

Donald McLean's land purchases

Hawke's Bay quickly attracted interest from traders looking for profit beyond the borders of the Wakefield and government colonies. Hardy explorers such as Charles Kettle, H. S. Harrison and J. Thomas journeyed through the district in the early 1840s. Others settled over the next few years, exemplified by Alexander Alexander (1820–73), a Scot whose parents — with singular lack of imagination — bestowed him with the same first name as his last. He began farming at Wharerangi in early 1847, then joined Thomas Kennedy Newton and opened a store at Onepoto. The venture flourished; Alexander shortly opened other stores around the district,[44] later branching into land ownership. This tiny pākehā community was joined by the McKain, Torr and Villiers families. McKain opened a hotel and general store on the Westshore shingle spit. Villiers

Alexander Alexander's store near Onepoto gully at the south-western end of Mataruahou, the Napier hill, mid-1850s. The building with the chimney is the Survey House, bought by Donald McLean to accomodate his survey team in 1851.

Joseph Rhodes, watercolour sepia wash, Alexander Turnbull Library, A-159-031

owned a schooner, trading with Māori — often for pigs, which he salted — then running his products to Wellington by sea.[45]

The New Zealand Company looked at Hawke's Bay late in the 1840s, envisaging land from Ahuriri to Cape Palliser for their planned Canterbury Settlement. Colenso was asked to negotiate a local sale, but — wearing his CMS hat — insisted on reserving 12.5 percent of any territory for Māori. He also stipulated a two-year time-frame, which torpedoed the deal;[46] and the Association's related Wairarapa effort fell through in 1849 because Ngāti Kahungunu-ki-Wairarapa would not sell to government agent Henry Kemp.[47] The Canterbury Association found a home in the South Island instead,[48] but settlers did not keep their hands off Hawke's Bay for long. The district was too good for sheep.

Pastoralism was New Zealand's growth industry of the late 1840s. There were fortunes to be made from the sheep's back, and by the mid-1840s a few enterprising individuals had leased vast tracts of the Wairarapa. As the district filled, other hardy souls sought more land further north. James Northwood went to Ahuriri in October 1847 to lease land from Te Hāpuku.[49] Colenso's objections as a CMS minister were predictable, as were his personal reasons for stopping Nairn 'on account of a letter he had written to the Government about myself.'[50] Nairn and his business partner Henry Tiffen nevertheless obtained land near Pourere.[51] They hired Tiffen's brother Fred to bring sheep north to graze, and in January 1849 he and Edward Davis headed for Pourere 'with about 3000 merino sheep and a packhorse', arriving after a month-long trek to set up their remote venture. 'Not a run to the south of us nearer than Castle Point (Guthries),' Tiffen declared later, 'and none nearer than Auckland to the north.'[52]

Early isolation swiftly changed as illegal leasing spread like wildfire up the east coast, posing problems for a colonial government that was determined to show strength — but equally reluctant to deter the growth of the colony, even at its fringes where lawlessness prevailed. Hawke's Bay was nicknamed 'Save All' — a haven for 'deserters ... and all minor criminals'.[53] Colonial authorities were well aware of the issue; as Bunbury remarked in 1840, 'Police stations and magistrates will, I fear, be immediately required at the principal whaling establishments'.[54] Local ruffians provided Tiffen with what he called 'white labor'[sic],[55] but while their presence underscored the limited reach of pākehā authority, practical government control depended on a significant settlement. This was a sore issue in the late 1840s. The Treaty of Waitangi aggrandised the sole right to buy land from Māori to government — the intent being to buy cheap and sell at a profit to settlers, funding the colonial administration. The main government target was the Wairarapa, but Māori there were understandably reluctant to sell when they could obtain a steady income from rentals.

A new strategy emerged during 1849 at the urging of Grey's Wellington-based deputy John Eyre. In June that year he received letters from Hawke's Bay chiefs offering land,[56] and shortly hit upon the idea of surrounding the Wairarapa chiefs with Crown land, undercutting their ability to lease. Grey was not convinced,[57] and in September the New Munster Executive Council recommended a further direct effort into the Wairarapa. Government land buyer Walter Mantell was away organising the purchase of South Island land, and the job went to an ambitious young Scot, Donald McLean. Described by more than one biographer as secretive,[58] McLean had made a name for himself sorting out Wanganui and was the rising star of the Land Purchase Department.[59] When the instruction to buy the Wairarapa arrived he was embroiled in a

Donald McLean (1820—1877) seen here probably in the early 1850s.

Photographer unidentified, Alexander Turnbull Library, F-32223-1/2

protracted effort to buy the Manawatu. Amid what appeared to be delays with that purchase, Eyre thought McLean might pick up 'other negotiations to carry on simultaneously'.[60]

McLean saw a way of buying the Wairarapa via Hawke's Bay. When Eyre's summons to buy the Wairarapa reached him, the Scot proposed to go to Ahuriri.[61] Then he received a letter from Te Hāpuku offering land and asking for a 'pākehā to assist me. Make sure he is a good person, do not send an ignoramus, lest I have more problems.'[62] This seemed promising; but while McLean lost no time convincing Domett and Eyre,[63] Grey remained unmoved, instead exhorting McLean to buy the Manawatu 'under any circumstances'.[64] McLean persisted with his personal agenda, writing to Te Hāpuku asking to meet.[65] The ploy was characteristic of this man of secrets: but his boldness paid dividends. In October Eyre asked McLean what steps he intended to take to buy the Manawatu and Wairarapa;[66] but about the time his letter reached McLean in the Manawatu — and before McLean could have been expected to respond — Hawke's Bay Māori offered McLean 'Haretaonga [sic] and Ahuriri from end to end'.[67]

This was the card McLean needed, and he did not hesitate to play it. Three days later he intercepted Eyre on the beach near Otaki, secured a salary for himself,[68] then rushed to Wellington and spoke with Colonial Secretary Alfred Domett and the New Munster Executive Council. Grey turned up from Auckland to take control, was nabbed at breakfast by McLean,[69] and appears to have bowed to the pressure. On 15 November the New Munster Executive Council granted McLean £50 for expenses,[70] and he left for Hawke's Bay three days later.[71] En-route he finished other business on the Kapiti coast, and at the beginning of December alerted Te Hāpuku and the other Hawke's Bay chiefs of his approach 'by special messenger who starts at daylight.'[72]

Talk of sale prompted a sharp dispute between Ngāti Kahungunu and Te Hāpuku's own people of Ngāti Whatuiāpiti, mostly over rights to the land being offered. The argument gained dimension from the fact that chieftainship was in flux; the deaths of Tiakitai and Te Pariehe pushed others forward, notably Takamoana, Te Moananui and Tareha. Te Hāpuku

Waipukurau pā, April 1858. This was where Donald McLean secured the initial agreement to buy land in Hawke's Bay.

Joseph Rhodes, watercolour, Alexander Turnbull Library A-159-027

had his own ambitions, probably including regaining the mana lost by his capture in 1824. Colenso's efforts to oil the troubled waters met with little result.[73] McLean's approach, however, prompted superficial unanimity, and he was met at Waipukurau by a gathering of chiefs and their people from across Hawke's Bay. This opened the way for an offer of blocks around Waipukurau, Ahuriri and at Mohaka. McLean told Domett a few weeks later that he intended to buy 'as great an extent of land' as he could, untill ordered otherwise.[74] A delighted Eyre told Grey that McLean's 'most judicious' efforts had provided the government with a 'considerable tract of good grazing country' as a lever into the Wairarapa.[75]

Māori were eager to maximise their returns. When the time came to settle the price, months later, bids opened at what McLean reported as 'hundreds of millions sterling', finally coalesced around a written request for £20,000,[76] and McLean pushed them down from there. Nonetheless,

Te Hāpuku wanted £4800 for Waipukurau and would not budge.[77] McLean eventually buckled before the 'exceedingly well-informed, clever chief,'[78] and had the deed signed in front of several 'rather disagreeable' pākehā witnesses.[79]

These deals — and many that followed — were subject to claim under the Treaty of Waitangi in the 1990s. The historical work undertaken to support the cases was pioneering,[80] but as more than one commentator observed, there were differences between Tribunal history and the abstraction demanded of general historical enquiry.[81] The problem was that Tribunal work evaluated past events in terms of present legal need, rather than the historical factors that applied at the time.[82] As one historian declared, Tribunal history was post-colonial, politicised and 'overwhelmingly presentist'.[83] The Hawke's Bay experience of the historical aspects of the process highlights the point. A 1994 report commissioned by the Waitangi Tribunal concluded that the Waipukurau, Ahuriri and Mohaka sales were 'calculated to disadvantage' Māori.[84] However, non-Tribunal analysis of the same evidence has made the point that McLean had future sales in mind, offering more concessions in 1850–51 than at other times.[85]

Detail from the only known photograph of McLean negotiating with Māori, full-frame reproduction oppoosite.

Photographer unidentified, Rhodes Album, Alexander Turnbull Library, PA1-q-193-053, F-110517-1/2

This is not to reduce the asymmetry of those deals, but from a purely historical perspective they can only be judged in terms of period values: and to McLean, for all the intensity with which he pursued a bargain, they were also a door-opener. The main issues for Hawke's Bay Māori flowed not from the asymmetry of price, but because the sales exposed the district early to rising settler power. New pastoral regulations flung the doors open: and as the economic power of the settlement grew, McLean was able to short-cut the land purchase process, negotiating directly with chiefs as if they were British-style owners of the land they were selling, all the while deliberately exploiting their need to pay for European goods for their people.[86] A succession of blocks passed into Crown hands across Hawke's Bay in this way, including Tautane, Okawa, Tutaekuri, Waipureku, Maraekakaho and others.[87]

While it has been argued that some of the problems associated with land sales at this time may have flowed from cultural mis-match rather than an intentional attempt to defraud,[88] there can be no doubt about McLean's attempts to use his knowledge of Māori society to exploit the political vulnerability the rangitira had as a result of their peoples engaging with British industrial society and products. He had been gadding about in New Zealand since 1840, and living with Māori, long enough to know broadly what Māoritangi was about. Although Māori efforts to assert and explain their complex skein of rights were often dismissed as 'humbug'

by run-of-the-mill settlers,[89] McLean knew he was intentionally cutting across traditional Māori values, and he also knew that it was likely to cause trouble.[90] Neither issue stopped him. From the historical perspective the question is not whether this was out of line by post-colonial standards — which it was — but whether he was breaking the pākehā values of his own time. And he was, indeed, at fault even by settler-age standards. The CMS, among others, were quick to condemn him at the time. The question is why McLean did it. One is convenience: McLean was under pressure to secure land by any means, fair or foul, and he deliberately chose foul, likely because it was was easier. His habitual secret-keeping — which suffused both his professional and his personal life — obfuscated the fact that much of his actions were below the belt, both for Māori and for the settlers.

However, behind his actions also lurked the general settler-age notion that Māori could be helped by being made to adopt British ways. McLean certainly advocated this approach; and this thinking underpinned many policies of the day, including the way the Treaty of Waitangi was interpreted at the time.[91] The problem for Hawke's Bay Māori was that this exacerbated the 'race for mana' and other pressures caused by the impact of Europe. The eventual outcome was war.

Donald McLean — centre left against the tree — discusses land purchases near Wairoa. This apparent level of community consultation stood in sharp contrast to the system he introduced to the Land Purchase Department in the mid-1850s, which he particularly applied to the Ahuriri district and regions further south across Hawke's Bay, and which arguably provoked war among Māori whose rights were trampled across by the process.

Photographer unidentified, Rhodes Album, Alexander Turnbull Library, PA1-q-193-053, F-110517-1/2

The war at Te Pakiakia

Donald McLean's land system was in full swing across Hawke's Bay by the mid-1850s. Sales in this district made up four-sevenths of all the land that Māori sold nationally to the Crown in 1855–56 alone.[92] The strategy provoked tensions between Ngāti Kahungunu — essentially led and represented by Tareha, Karaitiana Takamoana and Te Moananui — and Te Hāpuku's people, Ngāti Whatuiāpiti. McLean had already observed what he described as 'jealousies' between Ngāti Kahungunu and Ngāti Whatuiāpiti as early as 1851.[93] Arguments flourished under the pressure of sale, and McLean was widely blamed for triggering them. In an attempt to deflect his critics, McLean insisted that these disputes reflected pre-European issues. But this was sophistry; the disputes were actually given force by his land sale process.

> "...by late April Cooper was worried. Both sides seemed 'ripe and ready for a tussle.'"

For Hawke's Bay Māori, the 1840s and 1850s were a period of resettlement after the 'musket wars', but a resettlement that came with a new set of pressures — the British. This cut short the social shifts of the 'musket wars' era and swung Māori society in directions that were instead framed by responses to the growing intrusion and power of the pākehā colony. From the twenty-first century perspective there is a tendency to view pre-European Māori as static, or assume that the pattern of hapū and iwi was 'frozen' by the arrival of Europe.[94] In fact neither is quite correct; Māori political structures were to some extent captured as-is in their 1840s guise, but the normal processes of shift and evolution were not quite paralysed, as the Hawke's Bay experience reveals with the rise and consolidation of Ngāti Kahungunu.

Setting aside the specifics of this iwi, as I have argued elsewhere, the deeper reality is that Europe's arrival pushed Māori socio-political change in new directions.[95] The growth of the settler community added a layer of complication across New Zealand; McLean's land purchase department was under pressure to buy, and chiefs came under pressure from their people to provide European goods — blankets, tools and equipment and consumables such as tobacco and rum. Māori efforts to build the economic base with which to pay for this were initially hampered by indifferent wheat prices. In Hawke's Bay, as early as September 1852, both Ngāti Kahungunu and Ngāti Whatuiāpiti approached McLean and Grey in the hope of fixing value at £2 per bushel.[96]

The main source of cash for Māori across New Zealand became land sale, which was simultaneously part of what has been called a 'race for

mana', because the right to sell translated into rights over land. This was a particular issue for Hawke's Bay, where McLean was quick to exploit any opening he, or his agents, could find. For Te Hāpuku — who had been made prisoner during the 'musket wars' — the eagerness of the Crown to buy local land was of prime importance, because by putting himself forward as seller it helped assert his rights to the land on offer; but it put him at odds with his fellow chiefs.[97] The settlers interpreted this their own way — McLean's agent George Cooper reported that 'their own internal jealousies are leading them to extend the sale of their lands.'[98]

Ultimately it led to war. The *casus belli* was the sale of the Okawa block, to which both Te Hāpuku and Te Moananui felt they had rights. Cooper saw Te Moananui about it in March 1856, warning McLean that the chief 'talked about war — bloodshed — throat cutting etc' over payment for it.[99] This was symptomatic of a wider issue that was polarising, drawing in otherwise disparate hapū, and eventually leading to the general consolidation of all Hawke's Bay's hapū under the umbrella of Ngāti Kahungunu. And while such change was part of how Māori society had always operated, the cause of this particular shift was colonialism, driven in the immediate by Donald McLean's land purchase system.

Joseph Rhodes and family outside Clive Grange during the 1860s. Sheep underscore the fact that Rhodes' wealth derived from the fleece. Rhodes pushed for a provincial capital near his station, but the town of Clive did not flourish in the face of Napier's commercial predominance. Both the township and Rhodes' station were, however, right next door to the war at Te Pakiakia.

Photographer unidentified, Rhodes Album, Alexander Turnbull Library, F-110490-1/2, PA1-q-193-019-1

Tensions rose during Hawke's Bay's first race meeting on Te Moananui's land near Waipureku.[100] Te Hāpuku turned up to this quintessentially British moment with a small party 'armed to the teeth' in an apparent assertion of his rights to Okawa. Cooper reported that the 'guns were not loaded',[101] but the symbolism was clear. Ngāti Kahungunu chiefs responded with threats that they too would carry weapons, and a worried Cooper took Te Hāpuku around his people to 'try the effect of public opinion on him.' This merely provoked an argument,[102] and by April Cooper thought that both sides were 'ripe and ready for a tussle.'[103]

Late in 1857, Te Hāpuku — who was living at Whakatu — decided to further up the ante by asserting his claims over the Te Pakiakia bush, near Clive. He moved to Wakawhiti near the bush and set up a rahui pole.

European officials mediated. Te Hāpuku agreed to withdraw once he had asserted his claim. Te Moananui agreed to let him take dead firewood from the bush. But Te Hāpuku then decided to build a pā at Wakawhiti, and on 17 August sent men to cut timber from the bush for palisades. Te Moananui remonstrated, was defied — and organised a war party. Renata Kawepo and Karaitiana Takamoana hoped to avert catastrophe; but the two forces spent the next few hours firing at each other 'in the neighbourhood of the rahui post',[104] while local settler Joseph Rhodes hastened to Napier to find the doctor, Thomas Hitchings.

Around 3.00 p.m. one of Te Hāpuku's people raised a white flag and proposed a cease-fire. Seven died and 20 were wounded, attended by Hitchings, who saved all but one of the casualties.[105] Te Moananui then called for assistance from outside the district,[106] which was standard protocol, but also much to Cooper's alarm. 'I think that when Moananui's reinforcements come up, nothing short of the retirement of Te Hāpuku to Poukawa will satisfy his enemies.'[107]

> "Matters were not helped when Alfred Domett discovered that many Māori had been illegally sold guns by settlers..."

By this time Te Moananui had the whip hand; Te Hāpuku's support evaporated in the face of what had been a practical defeat, and he had to withdraw to Whakatu, where he was besieged in September. Matters were not helped when Alfred Domett discovered that many Māori had been illegally sold guns by settlers,[108] though Cooper doubted the effectiveness of firearms that had been charged with home-brewed powder.[109] During a second battle on 14 October, despite the range falling to 12 metres, just two men died and three were wounded.[110] Afterwards, however, Te Hāpuku again lost support, and frightened local settlers demanded troops for their own protection. Cooper — though concerned that pākehā were still 'fast disarming themselves'[111] — doubted that Māori would involve the settlers and wrote to the *Hawke's Bay Herald* to say so.[112]

Māori, for their part, were certainly eager not to aggravate the colonists. One battle, fought across the main road to Napier, was interrupted to let John Chambers' wool wagon through. Māori emphasised the point in the local paper 'You have nothing to fear from us,' chiefs assured *Hawke's Bay Herald* readers on 10 October. 'Do you suppose we are so fond of fighting that we are anxious to have two enemies, the pākehā as well as Te Hapuka [sic]. No! Our quarrel is sufficient.'[113] They signed themselves as 'Ngāti Kahungunu, underscoring the fact that this grouping was gaining self-identity. Such sentiment was backed up with action. In the middle of one battle there was a brief pause when John Chambers' wool wagon rumbled up the road between the warring parties.[114]

That did not stop settler alarm,[115] particularly after a third pitched battle on 9 December left five dead, among them Te Hāpuku's relative Puhara Hawaikirangi. There were calls for revenge from other relations outside the district. Settler alarm redoubled,[116] and McLean finally arrived from Auckland to find a settlement. Both sides were prepared to listen — potentially because he made further land sales and payments contingent on a peace settlement; and he shortly organised a two-week armistice to let Te Hāpuku withdraw.[117]

By this time Māori were arriving from Wairoa and the Wairarapa to help keep the peace. Nobody, it seemed, wanted a widespread renewal of fighting across the east coast, and Te Hāpuku began preparing to leave. It took him nearly two months to do so. During the pause a detachment of the 65th Regiment arrived in Napier[118] at the behest of the Governor, Thomas Gore-Browne, who — tipped off by Hawke's Bay settler Joseph Curling[119] — 'thought Moananui might be troublesome.'[120] This was exaggerated, and fears that Te Hāpuku might back out of the deal also proved groundless. He swallowed what the *Herald* called his 'bitter pill'[121] and departed in early March 1858, pausing only to torch his pā with the careful exception of the church.[122] A formal settlement was signed at Taenuiarangi in September.[123]

Ngāti Kahungunu tried to withdraw further land from sale,[124] and there was a scrabble in the pākehā camp to avoid blame. Cooper put the cause 'at the door of Te Hāpuku';[125] and McLean argued that land was but one cause of the war. However, CMS opinion found fault with his land purchase system.[126] The pākehā battle lines seemed set, and McLean found himself on the back foot, certainly in Hawke's Bay. Samuel Williams, in

> "'Do you suppose we are so fond of fighting that we are anxious to have two enemies, the pākehā as well as Te Hapuka [sic]. No! Our quarrel is sufficient'"
> — Ngāti Kahungunu in *The Hawke's Bay Herald*, October 1857[113]

particular, went out of his way to find fault with McLean's subsequent behaviour.[127] The local political mood was not helped by the fact that McLean had a clear conflict of interest. He was hoping to set up a run for himself, at Maraekakaho just west of the Heretaunga Plains. The block in question was implicit in the dispute between Māori, but that did not stop McLean from urging Cooper to buy it for the government even as tensions rose in 1856. Then, once it was in Crown hands, McLean focussed his own time and attentions on freeholding as much of it as he could, so as to avoid having his leasehold poached from him by rival settlers. That took up much of 1858, a period when he was supposed to be on hand in New Plymouth to sort out problems there for his employers. Arguably, McLean's dereliction of his official New Plymouth duty was one of several factors that led to war breaking out there between pākehā and Māori in 1860.

Meanwhile, McLean allowed Crown land purchase to continue in Hawke's Bay as far as was possible, and it was 1861 before he called a halt to government purchase efforts in the district.

CHAPTER THREE

The land of the shepherd kings

Settler Hawke's Bay exploded into life during the 1850s, a microcosm of the hopes of nineteenth-century Britain, filtered through the sieve of social idealism and the practical realities of frontier life.

Contemporaries sold the district to prospective colonists for its sheep rather than its climate.[2] Like Marlborough and Wairarapa, the district was settled by young entrepreneurs spreading from settlements elsewhere in New Zealand.[3] Many of the earliest arrivals turned up in the hope of escaping Edward Gibbon Wakefield's disastrous efforts at social engineering,[4] among them Daniel Riddiford, who dubbed his 13,000-acre central Hawke's Bay holding Woburn after his property in the Hutt Valley. Others arrived after trying their luck elsewhere in New Zealand.

The ruin of Wakefield's ambitions did not dampen spirits across the colony. Although few other settlers were as idealistic as the New Zealand Company founder, all hoped to escape the turmoil of industrialising Britain, shedding their origins and building a new and better life. They sought a bigger Britain, a better Britain[5] — and in isolated districts such as Hawke's Bay, those who came in first had virtually free reign. They were helped by a political system that focussed power in the periphery;

and what emerged on this fringe of the New Zealand colony was an oligarchy — one powerful enough, within a few years, to dominate the political centre. This mind-set eventually fell prey to the forces of failed general ambition and the demolition of the provinces as a politican entity, replaced in the twentieth century with visions of provincial life as staid and somehow less sophisticated. However, none of this was anticipated by the settlers who came to Hawke's Bay in the 1850s — ambitious, eager men who seized opportunity and sought to shape their futures.

Much flowed around the export outlet. Settler authorities were well aware of the value of Ahuriri Harbour, the only significant all-weather haven along the east coast between Turanganūi (Gisborne) and Wellington. Rhodes reported the potential of "Howready" or "Aoiriri" in the *New Zealand Gazette* of April 1841, adding that as there was no suitable land nearby for a town, a site 'ten miles inland' might suit, 'near the centre of a fine alluvial valley'.[6] Others talked of a town around the harbour, though George Rich dismissed the locale as a 'barren bleak place'.[7]

The earliest traders and merchants were swiftly overtaken in the race for power and status by pastoral land-holders. Hawke's Bay was, as McLean put it, 'the country for the fleece'.[8] Wool offered an easy road to riches in the 1850s — not least because, for a few heady years, pastoralists had merely to let their flocks roam, burning regrowth and letting the sheep trample the debris back into the soil.[9] Few employees were needed outside shearing time; it was the classic low-cost, high-return venture beloved of nineteenth-century capitalism. Hawke's Bay became a major pastoral district, and — like the Wairarapa and the pastoral regions of the South Island — low-density industry drove provincial development down a particular line, shaping Hawke's Bay during the colonial period and into the twentieth century as the legacy of this initial asymmetry played out.

The race for wealth began early. McLean was followed about the district by would-be pastoralists in 1850-51, all hoping to gain favourable leases on the back of his government land purchases. Rich was among them, dismissed by McLean as 'extravagant in his speculative ideas on sheep grazing etc. He thinks of making a fortune at once.'[10] But this was exactly what it was about. Government offered 14-year depasturing licenses at £5 per annum, plus £1 for every thousand sheep over 5000.[11] Rich got the lease on the Ruataniwha plains — part of the Waipukurau purchase — a region which, surveyor Robert Park declared, 'stands unrivalled in New

"… we should be up and stirring … to rescue and preserve our own adopted land from being wrested from us by a band of selfish monopolists …"

— 'A Mechanic' in *The Wellington Spectator*, March 1853[1]

Out-station on Purvis Russell's property, Hatuma, probably in the 1860s. Tussock is noteworthy; in these pioneering days of pastoralism, even down-country operations often relied on existing grasses and residual soil fertility. Danthonia prevailed, and stock was frequently merino — a hardy breed able to handle the rough fodder.

Photographer unidentified, C. R. St. Clair Inglis Collection, Alexander Turnbull Library, F-31211-1/2

Zealand' for its 'beauty of position, fertility of soil, mildness of climate and abundance of wood and water'.[12] As McLean suspected, ambition outstripped reality; 'Somerset House', as Rich called his property, did not last.[13]

There were howls of protest when these initial leasing arrangements were cancelled in 1852, but new regulations the following year opened up the prospect of outright purchase, and run-holders scrabbled to buy; among them Henry Russell, T. Purvis Russell, Alexander Alexander, Thomas Guthrie, Curling, Northwood, John Harding, F. S. Abbott, J. D. Canning, John Ormond, E. S. Curling and John Chambers.[14] All were notable for their enthusiasm, their ambition, and their youth. Ormond was just 20 when he arrived in 1851, former secretary to Eyre and a man of 'bumptious manner'.[15] Fred Tiffen departed for the Australian goldfields, but was back by 1852 and set up station on the banks of the Tukituki River.[16] By the middle of the decade there were more than 30 significant holders running about 55,000 sheep across the district, a third of the total in the vast Wellington province.[17]

Settlers did not hesitate to bend the rules when there was so much at stake. Ambitions collided, tempers often ran hot. Domett's classification of T. H. Fitzgerald as a 'desperate sneak' over a land issue was mild.[18] The

T. Purvis Russell's Hatuma station on the Ruataniwha plains, probably during the 1860s.

Photographer unidentified, Rhodes Album, Alexander Turnbull Library, F-110506-1/2

fractious politics of the later colonial period were founded here in the initial scrabble for land and profit. Some settlers leased directly — and illegally — from Māori. Edmund Tuke obtained 25,600 acres around Matipiro that way, and John Ormond did the same around Porangahau. Eyebrows were raised, though these deals were eventually regularised.[19] Yet the stakes were high. Those who got in on the ground floor stood a good chance of catapulting themselves to the top of the ladder, financially and politically, and of then staying there. Later, there was suggestion that a hopeful run-holder might need £3000 or more to get in the door — roughly around $295,000 in early twenty-first century sums[20] — but most needed more. Hector Smith arrived in Hawke's Bay in 1858 with £8000 in his pocket.[21] Some, such as Walter Lorne Campbell and his business partner F. H. Meinertzhagen, or Ongaonga founder H. H. Bridge, were helped with family money.[22]

All had aspirations. Campbell was told to make a 'New Zealand plan' and take up farming. 'Mr Findlay thinks I will get on much better as a sheep farmer than in business as, he says, I would have to be a clerk for 10 years.'[23] Campbell eventually settled near Waimarama, though he 'could not see how we are to make money out of the place'.[24] He worked hard in pursuit of the dream, battled an indifferent labour force — and, tragically, died aged 29 while working his station.[25]

Perhaps the most ambitious of these early settlers was Thomas Tanner, who came to New Zealand in 1849 on the *Larkins*, discovered 'some of the most magnificent scenery that it would be possible to describe', and decided to settle in Hawke's Bay.[26] Back in England he chartered a ship to take out his gold and silver plate, furniture, servants, pedigree farm animals — even a race horse, the 'Bishop of Osnaburgh'.[27] Once ensconced in Hawke's Bay he spared no expense on an extravagant lifestyle,[28] ultimately settling on the edge of the Heretaunga plains where he built a magnificent homestead and entertained on a colossal scale. One event in April 1874 was attended by more than 400 guests.[29]

Donald McLean, who thought Hawke's Bay was 'not surpassed in beauty by any I have seen',[30] joined them. He initially ran sheep in Tiffen's holding, then acquired 30,000 acres near Maraekakaho — this, as we have seen, despite accusations of a conflict of interest.[31]

> "Ambitions collided, tempers often ran hot. Domett's classification of T. H. Fitzgerald as a 'desperate sneak' over a land issue was mild."

Others arrived in Hawke's Bay with cash to invest, among them James Watt, Matthew Miller and Algernon Tollemache. The latter reached Hawke's Bay in 1853 and offered loans at extortionate rates to McLean, C. J. Nairn, J. N. Williams and Alexander McHardy, among others. Ursury was a way to succeed quickly in this colonial world, and when he died in 1892, Tollemache was estimated to be worth £1,267,000, just over $212 million in early twenty-first century money.[32] Here too there were winners and losers; Cartwright Brown ploughed £12,500 of his father's money into Hawke's Bay properties, then became a run-holder himself, but went bankrupt in 1869 when wool prices fell.[33] Few knew much about farming, nor did they need to; skilled hands could be hired. Some, such as George Carlyon — a veteran of Crimea and the archetypal officer and gentleman — insisted on directing his staff anyway.[34]

By the 1860s the district was effectively run by a clique of perhaps 50 pastoralists and businessmen — Donald McLean, John Ormond, Henry Russell, J. N. Williams, J. G. Kinross and John Chambers among others. Only a handful had actual or proclaimed descent from Britain's upper classes, and even then the connection was tenuous; Walter Ogilvy drew origin from a Jacobite earl. Thomas Tanner was descended from Wiltshire landowners.[35] But while professed descent added a veneer of authenticity to a lifestyle that aped the British aristocracy, what counted in the colony was opportunity — and the profit and power that flowed from it.

Rural urbanity

Hawke's Bay's oligarchs were not country folk in the traditional British sense. As in Australia and on the American frontier, Hawke's Bay's pastoral society was indomitably urban in outlook.[36] A rural locale and pretensions to feudal grandeur did not mask ideals and aspired lifestyles that descended from the rising middle class of Liverpool, Birmingham and other grim industrial towns.[37] In a practical sense, all New Zealand's settlers aspired to town living — and large-town living at that. By 1881, 20 percent of the populace lived in towns of 25,000 or more.[38] In any case, urban lifestyle was a state of mind rather than location, and the ethos was visible across Hawke's Bay in everyday behaviour, such as the way many country-dwellers created a fenced quarter-acre for their homes, aping the town garden in style and design.

The real focus of Hawke's Bay settler life was nonetheless in its urban areas. Here the pastoral elite vied for status through local councils and boards. John Chambers, for instance, took a lead role in the Havelock Roads Board, set up the Havelock Mechanics Institute and became a trustee of the Havelock school.[39] A key venue for expressing this province-wide rivalry remained the Hawke's Bay Club, set up as a deliberate effort to emulate middle-class British urban lifestyle. But while such clubs attracted captains of industry in Birmingham or Manchester, some 53 of the 76 founding members in Hawke's Bay were sheep farmers.[40] Most of the elite had town houses in Napier; John Ormond — urged by his wife Hannah — even built 'Tintagel' as their family home on Mataruahou, the Napier hill.[41] Although she confided to her diary that Napier was a 'dull place', she apparently enjoyed a vigorous social life.[42] Fred Tiffen, owner of Elmshill station, maintained a house in what became Napier's Tiffen Park. Other station owners preferred to stay at the Masonic Hotel or the Hawke's Bay Club.

For a roll-call of the upper echelons of this elite we need look no further than those who founded the Hawke's Bay Agricultural and Pastoral Society in 1863 — Donald McLean, George Whitmore, J. D. Canning, John Ormond, Henry Tiffen, John Chambers, Henry Russell, Thomas Tanner, Charles Lambert, Thomas Lowry and Joseph Rhodes among them.[43] Many gained nicknames to suit their roles; Ormond — abstemious, intolerant and dictatorial — became variously 'the Master' and 'the Hon. J. D.' to family and friends.[44] The kindly yet determined John Chambers was 'The Governor'.[45] Henry Russell was so imperious that

> "By the 1860s the district was effectively run by a clique of perhaps 50 pastoralists and businessmen..."

Archetypal settler house; this is Samuel Williams' home at Te Aute, during the 1870s.

Photographer unidentified, Alexander Turnbull Library, F-26766-1/2

his employees and enemies called him 'Lord Henry' or 'Lord H.', though never to his face.[46] Thomas Tanner, a 'little man of marvellous aplomb' to J. C. Richmond, became variously 'Tommy Tiddles' and 'Tizzy the Tanner' to his peers.[47] Few accumulated as many monikers, however, as the acerbic and diminutive Colonel George Whitmore — 'the little brute', 'the beast'[48] and 'the disgusting little pig' among them,[49] all of which fell in the shadow of 'The Gravedigger', which he earned during his first campaign against Te Kooti.[50]

They were joined by an urban-based commercial elite, led by woolbrokers such as J. G. Kinross. By the early 1870s there were five brokers in Napier. Financiers, too, were near the top of the Hawke's Bay heap, notably James Watt, whose 40-room mansion on Napier's hill was reputedly worth £7000[51] — a fortune in settler-age values. Beneath them came traders such as Geordie Richardson, who reached Napier in 1858 and set himself up with a Captain Charlton as 'general and commission merchants' on the Meeanee Spit. Another was J. J. Kelly, whose Carlyle Street store in Napier offered everything from ironmongery to rum. Others set up services, among them Thomas Taylor, who opened a bakery on Shakespeare Road.[52] Most lived off their wits, epitomised by William

'The Master': John Ormond

John Davies Ormond (1831–1917)

Photographer unidentified, General Assembly Library Collection, Alexander Turnbull Library, F-156-35mm-E

John Davies Ormond (1831–1917) — usually nicknamed 'The Master' — was one of Hawke's Bay's key local figures during the settler period; hard-working, dedicated and endlessly devoted to his district. He started young, appointed clerk to Deputy Governor Edward Eyre in 1848, aged just 17. Like many in the early 1850s, Ormond crossed the Tasman in the hope of making money off the goldfields, but he had better prospects back in Hawke's Bay where he leased land in Porangahau, subsequently purchasing just over 19,000 acres which he dubbed Wallingford. He married Hannah Richardson and settled down for the duration.

Over the next decades Ormond acquired other properties across Hawke's Bay, including a town house in Napier, where Hannah insisted on living; land near Wairoa; and another property on the Māhia Peninsula to which he sent his son George as manager. He also leased — and subsequently purchased — land at Karamu on the Heretaunga Plains, where he developed a top-class horse stud. Oak Avenue, near Hastings, began its long existence as his driveway.

Ormond's political career went from strength to strength; he was a leading light in the separation movement of 1858 and took a major role in Hawke's Bay politics, spreading his interests to encompass national politics from 1861, when he was elected to the Clive seat, eventually becoming the Minister of Public Works. He and his close friend Donald McLean were the effective rulers of Hawke's Bay through the 1860s and 1870s. Controversy inevitably followed; both men endured attacks from Henry Russell. Ormond survived both these scandals and the later axing of the provinces, remaining a key figure in Hawke's Bay politics and a much respected elder settler into the first years of the twentieth century.

Morris, the iron-legged storekeeper operating from the Napier Spit, who had fingers in every pie from ship-building to store-keeping, and business interests stretching from Māhia to Napier.[53] Some women joined the ranks of the entrepreneurs; a Mrs Yates, for example, ran a small millinery business at Onepoto.[54]

Hawke's Bay towns — like those around New Zealand — embodied the essence of period *laissez faire* capitalism — exalted and thought able to achieve perfect form in the rugged colonial frontier unfolding around the Pacific rim. And yet, in defiance of purist catechisms, these urban centres also drove the expansion of government.[55]

This tension emerged early in Hawke's Bay, initially because of its isolation at the northern end of Isaac Featherston's vast Wellington province. Everybody wanted towns, but the problem was paying for them. Māori were also eager for urban centres, seeing them as concentrations of trade. Colenso reported that Ngāti Kahungunu planned a town at the mouth of the Tukituki, and McLean received other proposals during his first land-buying tour, including visions of a town 'fully formed with streets … in the centre of the Heretaonga [sic] inland plains'[56] Another chief declared that 'a town shall be formed here, and there is no-one to oppose it.'[57] In January 1851, Hemi Tahau and others asked McLean to 'take a part of our land for a township.'[58] A few months later Te Hāpuku considered that a town should be part of the payment for sale of the Waipukurau block, on top of the cash settlement. 'Let it be a large, large, large, very large town for me'.[59] Later still, Ngāti Kahungunu floated plans for a town called Korauru, near Pakowhai, with 'new pākehā houses'.[60]

> "McLean urged Domett to start the [urban] ball rolling as early as September 1851, largely to make good on his promise to Māori that they would get a town as part of the sale of the Ahuriri block."

In practice none of these hopes came to pass. Prospects for Korauru were apparently killed by the 1857 war,[61] but McLean urged Domett to start the urban ball rolling as early as September 1851, largely to make good on his promise to Māori that they would get a town as part of the sale of the Ahuriri block. This was the origin of Napier. But he did not just see it as deal-fulfilment with Māori: to him the greater benefit was to the colony. 'I feel confident,' he declared, 'that a considerable extent of town and suburban lands judiciously laid out would meet with ready purchasers from among the Wairarapa stockholders, traders, and others, who intend settling at Hawke's Bay.'[62] The Executive Council endorsed the proposal for a port-town at Ahuriri,[63] asking Robert Park to survey a site south of Mataruahou.[64] Nothing came of the effort, however, and

Emerson Street, Napier, in 1862, looking south-west. Clap-board buildings amid a barren landscape share a look with the American mid-western frontier on the other side of the Pacific, underscoring the commonalities of a shared nineteenth century 'Pacific rim' settler culture, which flourished in defiance of pākehā New Zealand's British origins. Donald McLean even looked to US practise towards their own indigenous people for inspiration in his land dealings with Māori.

Photographer unidentified, Rhodes Album, Alexander Turnbull Library F-110520-1/2, PA1-q-193-056

nearly 18 months passed before Domett, some-time poet and government factotum, got the job of preparing a street plan.

The site was dismal, a pocket-handkerchief of shingle in the shade of the hill, but colonial authorities envisaged a town only large enough to serve the port. Domett certainly thought it was unsuitable for a provincal capital; and because settlers wanted the intended capital to be Clive, he sought a name 'subordinate' to that great hero of the age, but one still redolent of an Indian theme. He had in mind 'one of our greatest and best Indian Captains just dead',[65] General Sir Charles James Napier (1782–1853).[66] This 'hard-swearing, religious, ambitious, quarrelsome man'[67] was the hero of the Punjab; but as Domett was doubtless aware, the name resonated on many levels in that high noon of the Victorian age. There had been three prominent Napiers during the Peninsular War, along with General Mark Napier, Sir William Napier the historian, General Edward Napier, General Thomas Napier, Admiral Henry Napier, Admiral Charles Napier and finally General Sir Robert 'Bob the Bughunter' Napier, who eventually made his name at Magdala in 1868.[68]

Domett, rejecting what he called the 'low and disgusting' Māori names of the area,[69] extended the Indian theme across town and district; Simla, Corunna, Hyderabad, Scinde (Sind) and Meanee (Meeanee).[70] Some of these names fell out of British favour after the Indian Mutiny of 1857–58; but they stuck in Hawke's Bay. He found further inspiration in the names of his literary friends; Robert Browning joined Emerson, Carlyle, Dickens and Tennyson. Domett further leavened the mix with scientists such as Dalton and Faraday, adding that he did not want to be 'constantly reminded' of the 'ruffians... ... and runaway convicts' who would otherwise 'render the places distasteful.'[71]

There Napier remained for months, a prospect on paper only. The region was administered as an outlying part of Wellington province, which the diminutive and volatile Superintendent, Dr Isaac Featherston, ran as his personal fief. Fearful of diluting Wellington's growth, he refused to allow land sales around Napier until early 1855. Some 108 sections were auctioned that April, and more followed early in 1856.[72] In this age of private enterprise the place remained the only government-founded town, 'subordinate'[73] to the intended main centre which — reflecting an 1853 request from Joseph Rhodes, Curling and other settlers — was dubbed Clive.[74]

> "...as late as September 1857 the *New Zealand Spectator* highlighted the costs incurred in getting the wool clip out 'for want of a few bridges over swamps'..."

Rhodes had the intended local capital laid out in 1856, near his land at the mouth of the Ngaruroro. The first sections went on sale in 1857,[75] but the land was prone to flooding and most settlers and businessmen wanted to be near the port. Napier flourished. Clive did not.

Other towns were notable by their absence. Agriculture lagged, and there were fears that the working classes had been shut out. An outspoken editorial in the *New Zealand Spectator* during March 1853 bemoaned the 'apparently exclusive right of occupation...exercised by a mere fraction of the population' across the southern North Island, warning that British ideals would shortly be 'crushed and trodden underfoot by the iron despotism of a grasping and selfish oligarchy'.[76] Readers agreed; 'A Mechanic' bemoaned the way land was 'being wrested from us by a band of selfish monopolists'. There was, he suggested, 'no point paying the last instalment on Ahuriri when the whole of that fertile district is bespoke if not already occupied by a few wealthy flockmasters and storekeepers'.[77]

This debate reflected more than just the gripes of the have-nots. In 1855, some 63,069 acres were under cultivation in Auckland province, contrasting with just 10,531 in the huge Wellington district — then stretching from Wellington to Hawke's Bay.[78] The asymmetry extended even to such basic issues as roads and bridges; as late as September 1857 the *New Zealand Spectator* highlighted the costs incurred in getting the wool clip out 'for want of a few bridges over swamps'.[79] Part of the issue was practical. Provincial governments around New Zealand did not have the funds to meet vaulting demand for public works. The only way out was by raising loans, a move that did not go down well in Hawke's Bay, where pastoralists felt they were footing the bill for development elsewhere. And there was a political sequel. News that land sales had netted £20,000 for Wellington province — of which less than five percent was spent in Hawke's Bay — joined a feeling that more could have been done over the Te Pakiakia war.[80] There were calls for separation during 1858, and a petition began doing the rounds. Thanks to property-based suffrage, just 158 of Hawke's Bay's 1,185 pākehā inhabitants were required to endorse the split. A riotous public meeting at the Golden Fleece Hotel sealed the deed, and in November that year Hawke's Bay became New Zealand's seventh province.[81]

> **"Thanks to property-based suffrage, just 158 of Hawke's Bay's 1,185 pākehā inhabitants were required to endorse the split [from Wellington]."**

Members elected to the local council — all on less than thirty votes each — included Thomas Fitzgerald, Colenso, Thomas Hitchings, Tiffen and John Carter. Rhodes was elected to represent Clive, and a three-day party with racing, a 'Separation dinner', and a 'Separation ball' heralded the arrival of the new province.[82]

By the time the council met, small blocks had been put up for sale around Otatara, some of them taken up by Henry and George Alley, who later developed Taradale on their property. But the uptake was not enough, and early in 1859 Fitzgerald, wearing his hat as Provincial Superintendent, urged that Karanema's Reserve — the site of Havelock North — should be divided for agricultural settlement, telling the council that 'I trust that at no distant date a further portion of the Ahuriri plains may be acquired'.[83] Such strategy promised to relieve Hawke's Bay's reliance on imported grain and agricultural products. Ormond, heading a select committee on land regulation, was determined to 'encourage the location of the working classes',[84] looking to a block purchased in the Ruataniwha Plains.

Fitzgerald was still thumping the tub at the end of the year, when he revealed plans to survey and divide blocks every three months, 'so that no great intervals shall elapse between the arrival of persons in the Province and land sales at which they can acquire suitable farms for settling down upon....'[85] This was the spur the pastoralists needed. John Chambers led the way in 1859 with Havelock North, a combination of urban and 'suburban' small-holder sections on Karanema's Reserve.[86] Town sections were sold the same year at Blackhead, Porangahau, Wanstead, Wallingford, Tautane and Hampden (Tikokino).[87] Despite competition with Frederick Abbott's self-styled Abbotsford (Waipawa),[88] the first sales around

Shakespeare Road, Napier, in 1862 Long exposure times obscure human activity, captured only by a ghostly image standing near the ladder mid-frame and other hints of movement in front of the building on the right.

Photographer unidentified, Rhodes album, Alexander Turnbull Library F-110523-1/2, PA1-q-193-072

Havelock in January 1860 were received with 'spirited bidding'.[89] Buyers included military men such as Colonel Alfred Wyatt of the 65th Regiment and his Colour Sergeant, Henry Morton Blandford.[90] Another early player was William Colenso, who — after being thrown out of the mission — was trying his hand at being a cowboy capitalist.[91]

A few pastoralists were opposed, among them 'Justus' of Porangahau, who felt that while New Zealand was not 'specially suited for agriculture, it is eminently qualified for wool growing.'[92] But for most at the middle and lower ends of the socio-economic pile, a town on or near their land was another way of bolstering incomes and levering themselves up the social ladder. This did not reduce the risks. Havelock's 30 acres were surveyed for £136 9s 9d, but the cost of laying out Porangahau topped £349.[93] This had to be made back from sales.

Part of the problem was a glut of town lands across the district as everybody tried to cash in. There was an explosion of new towns across the district in 1860, their sales mostly administered by surveyor Thomas Triphook.[94] Opportunities ran well ahead of demand. Abbotsford (Waipawa) did well on the main road south. Fitzgerald — wearing his hat as a businessman — opened a general store there with L. N. du Noyer.[95] But even speculators shied away from some areas. The Hampden (Tikokino) sale of July 1860 was particularly dismal; just 19 of 86 town sections were sold, and most of the surrounding agricultural land was purchased by the government.[96]

> "Although the wealth was generated in the hinterland, towns remained the true social and economic focus of the district."

Towns often faced an uphill battle once founded. Pastoralism cast a skein of settlement across the land; there were no vigorous markets around the new towns for small-holders to key into. Havelock flourished by proximity to the main settlements and export harbour. Abbotsford (Waipawa) was on the main road south. Wairoa staggered into life, its first land sales in 1865 disrupted by war.[97] But as one historian has remarked, a fair percentage of Hawke's Bay's urban enclaves and surrounding small-holdings were 'dud'.[98] Within a few years only the ghosts of these colonial hopes remained.

The towns that did flourish embodied a good deal of settler idealism, albeit toned down from Wakefield's extremes. When Henry Russell bought 207 acres known as 'pā flat' adjacent to his Waipukurau station in 1867 he used it to set up a model village,[99] personally interviewing settlers and allowing the place to have just one example of every trade. Nor did he sell the settlers their land: instead, it was leased for 99 years. Aside from underscoring how towns were being used to validate the status of Hawke's Bay's new landed gentry, Russell's idealistic framework smacked of an attempt to establish an urban utopia within the pastoral arcadia he was building on his station. And, like similar efforts elsewhere in New Zealand, it did not actually work in practise. But that did not prevent the attempt: and while few Hawke's Bay towns were subject to all the strictures that Russell initially placed upon Waipukurau, most of the urban areas across the district embodied the latest ideals of town design, which styled themselves practical applications of period social idealism. All featured the classic gridwork streets with defined urban sections, open recreation areas, and division of function across space of the period.[100]

The fact that geography often prevented the perfect grid being applied did not reduce the intent; although occasionally it was leavened with patriotic fervour. Havelock North — whose street plan, despite local mythology, was apparently a design of surveyor August Koch[101] — played on Imperial sentiment with a Union Jack built into the grid.[102] Such designs gave physical shape to colonial hopes, and what followed was a direct reaction to the cluttered slums of industrial cities such as Birmingham, Sheffield and even London. Straight streets could not be used by the poor as living spaces, and to a middle class who associated physical cleanliness with moral purity, offered the inestimable advantage of allowing the dirt and foul air to blow away.[103] New Zealand's Municipal Corporations Act 1876 actually required roads to be 66 feet wide.[104]

House and garden on the Napier hill, mid-1870s. Picket fences emphasise the domestic 'quarter-acre' with its ideal of insular, private living — and, in the New Zealand context, offering security of accommodation and, to some extent, survival. Not all urban sections were an actual quarter-acre; but the domestic vegetable garden, chicken coop and occasional livestock such as goats at times made all the difference for hungry families.

Photographer unidentified, Hawke's Bay Museum, 5527

Another function of the grid, crucial to people escaping the turmoil of industrial Britain and the threat of revolution, was establishing social barriers — to German economic thinker Frederick Engels, 'separate territories, assigned to poverty.'[105]

The nineteenth-century urban environment was, in short, a place for the insularity thought ideal for middle-class urban life,[106] a venue for flourishing suburban mansions and properties. And the colonial frontier offered a blank canvas on which those ideals could be laid out in the form of towns that, to the settlers, encapsulated the essence of progress.[107] And Hawke's Bay's town planners thrust these grids across hill and dale alike, often irrespective of local geography,[108] and frequently in defiance of the practicalities of establishing a town at a time when migration did not often match the anticipated influx.

This was the real problem for Hawke's Bay's ambitious would-be gentry, who saw status and money from having a town on or near their properties. Many of the would-be towns set up across Hawke's Bay in the early 1860s, particularly — often existing only as paper entities — guttered and died in the face of indifferent settlement, their town sections snapped up by speculators but otherwise ignored by anybody with a

The history of Hawke's Bay

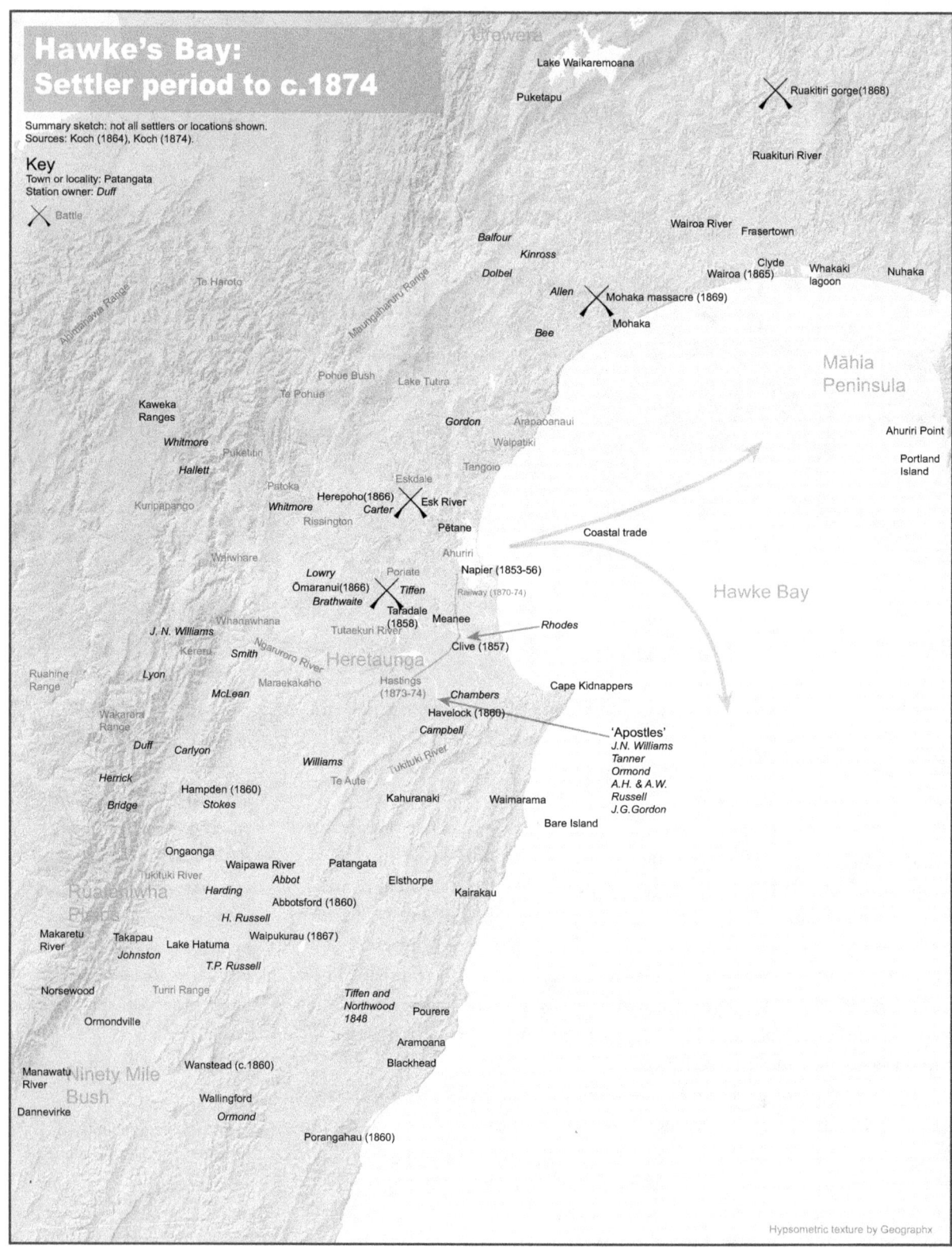

Fringe of Empire: European settlements on The Spit, Napier, June 1860. A steamship waits in the roadstead; other vessels, including a dredge, sit in the harbour.
Charles Decimus Barraud, pencil, watercolour and Chinese white, Alexander Turnbull Library, B-004-009

practical bent to live there. Some 163 urban sections dubbed Wanstead were put on sale in the early 1860s, arranged around streets with names echoing the nobility — Queen, Duke, Lord and Regent among them. Nobody was much interested. Town sections near Blackhead and Porangahau stations drew little interest when first put up to market in 1860, even less when attempts were made to promote them in 1862. One of the biggest of these attempts was Hampden — Tikokino — nestling in the foot of the Ruahine Ranges southwest of the Heretaunga Plains, which hit the market on a large scale but met little interest, despite having everything by period values: the streets were laid out in the ideal grid pattern, by the mid-1860s there was even a school, and the place was considered sufficiently important to have its own blockhouse. Yet, like so many hopeful Hawke's Bay towns, it never grew.

There were reasons why this was so. One of them was simple lack of people: pastoralism was not a labour-intensive activity, and the hinterland had few settlers by comparison with transport and access points such as Napier or Wairoa. Nor, given the likely employment prospects, was there much chance of a hopeful pastoral squire obtaining settlers for a town laid out on his property. Back-country roading was minimal, and there was little chance of towns there developing much of a life. There were reasons

The Grange, Napier, July 1874. Fencing highlights the insular urban ideals of the time.

Photographer unidentified, Rhodes Album, Alexander Turnbull Library, F-110489-1/2, PA1-q-193-017

why most of the successful inland towns were along the transport routes — Abbotsford (Waipawa) and Waipukurau among them. Even then, none really flourished until the advent of railway in the mid-late 1870s, which revolutionised provincial transport and, with it, the economy.

Location on transport and access locii meant that Napier and the handful of other successful provincial towns such as Wairoa (1865), Havelock (1860), Abbotsford (Waipawa) (1860), Waipukurau (1867) and others were economically viable and attracted a cross-section of settler society; stevedores, labourers, brokers, shed-hands, storekeepers, blacksmiths, bankers, doctors, teachers and ministers, though few servants. Towns were also places where the poor could live and work, home to blacksmiths, labourers, tanners, butchers, carpenters, tradesmen, shopkeepers, publicans and ne'er-do-wells of the settler world. Although the wealth was generated in the hinterland, towns remained the true social and economic focus of the district.

This world found its voice through local papers, at once political mouthpieces, vehicles for gossip and community notice-boards. In Hawke's Bay the charge was led by Auckland newspaperman James Wood. Like any shrewd businessman he canvassed his market, breezing through the district in May 1856 to gauge opinion. In October 1857, 'despite many difficulties', he launched a four-page weekly broadsheet,[109] one of the earliest regular newspapers in New Zealand.[110] Like most settler-age papers his *Hawke's Bay Herald* was opinionated — as one historian put it, a medium for local pastoralists to 'ventilate their views'.[111] But it was more than that. Napier's pākehā population stood at around 340 in 1857,[112] the wider district around 1185. At a time when everybody knew each other, often very well, the newspaper carried a personal intimacy that became impossible to achieve even a generation later. It was, in many ways, the 'social media' of its time — just as opinionated, just as closely followed, and just as emotionally owned by its participants. And it was not hard for anybody to rag Wood for his opinions.

Pastoral living — urban ideals

Settler Hawke's Bay encapsulated all the social tensions of New Zealand's settler world; a celebration of middle-class British social values, framed by the conceit that British class structures had been shucked off. In fact they had not. In the colony, money rather than birth became the arbiter of status, and like many of Britain's rising middle class, those at the top adopted what they imagined to be the lifestyle of the nobility. The coveted Hawke's Bay Club was a case in point. Merely to join cost ten guineas — always the currency of the elite — plus an annual subscription that started at six guineas, but finally rose to fifteen.[113] This was significant when shepherds were earning around £70 and even a farm manager might only earn no more than £100 per annum.[114] Sometimes the distinction was overt, as in 1868 when Donald McLean barred mechanics from attending a ball. The fact that it was a private function did not prevent 'A Napier Tradesman' complaining to the local paper that 'snobbishness' had become 'rampant'.[115] Claims that there were no social barriers to advance did not prevent a practical glass ceiling. Some-time gold miner and swagger David Balfour 'landed in Napier for the second (and last) time' in 1866,[116] and eventually dragged himself up the ladder — but got no further than manager at Mangawhare.[117]

Power was as much motivator as wealth and land; when the split came from Wellington province in 1857–58, Domett offered to stand for the Provincial Council if asked. T. H. Fitzgerald privately dismissed him as a "lazy, indolent fellow, clever though he may be as a literary man'; but to Alexander, Fitzgerald was a 'scheming Jesuit' — and Joseph Rhodes a 'donkey'.[118] A minimal franchise explains the depth to which local politics plunged; Fitzgerald was elected with a grand total of 25 votes, just beating Colenso. He did not seem to relish the job. He had power, but as he complained to McLean, no salary. Ultimately the elite broke into two

Another side of frontier life. The Chambers family homestead at Te Mata. John Chambers (1819–1893) had been on the property about 15 years by the time this picture was taken around 1870. Unlike some of his neighbours, Chambers — hard working, abstemious and capable — did not display his wealth through ostentatious housing. When he eventually splashed out, he rebuilt his original house rather than looking to a wholly new structure.

Photographer unidentified, Alexander Turnbull Library, F-31208-1/2

broad factions; Donald McLean and his friends Ormond, George Cooper, J. G. Kinross and others, stood against another group led, *de facto*, by Henry Russell, with supporters that included George Whitmore, E. A. Carlyon and other central Hawke's Bay station owners.

Although founding their world in an idealised exaltation of nineteenth-century middle-class British social ambitions, Hawke's Bay's pastoralists and businessmen looked to the free-wheeling United States frontier for colour, in Napier to the point where Vinsen and Forster opened an 'American Carriage Factory'.[119] Even spelling was Americanised — honor instead of honour, clamor instead of clamour, and there were druggists as well as chemists.[120] While Hawke's Bay had shrugged off much of its early sense of lawlessnes by this time — particularly in Hastings, where the first policeman was a Constable Lawless[121] — there was the same sense of pioneering spirit that suffused the American frontier. Business veered to the rough-and-ready, matching the rugged newness of town, road, bridge and farm. It was a relationship of ideas; America provided inspiration rather than mould, its concepts adding a dimension to the principally British world of the settlement.

Efforts by Hawke's Bay's 'landed elite'[122] to ape the British aristocracy extended to the hunting ritual, albeit clothed in a practical colonial spin. Pigs stood in for foxes, and nobody could deny the practical need to keep this back-country pest down. But the way they were hunted was socially symbolic, as when the 'genial sheep farmer' Joseph Rhodes led several military men on a hunt one day in 1860 'with a revolver in his belt, slouch hat, knee boots and nonchalant air' which left him looking 'more like a Spanish hidalgo than a sheep farmer as he led the way at a rattling pace'.[123] His parties were large-scale, the woolshed 'draped and decorated', featuring an 'immense table groaning beneath its abundance of liquids and solid refreshments'.[124]

The debate over whether New Zealand's pastoral elite enjoyed a personal work ethic or sought the easy life has considerably exercised historians.[125] The practical lives of Hawke's Bay's oligarchs ran across the spectrum, from the hands-on adventures of John Chambers, whose soap-making exploits got him 'laughed at a good deal at home',[126] to the more management-oriented approach of Ormond and McLean. Much reflected upbringing. Chambers, a Quaker, had no fear of soiling his hands; and although not every pastoralist 'mucked in', a puritanical attitude to personal hard work was itself often a device for gaining social status among many of the elite.

> "Although founding their world in an idealised exaltation of nineteenth-century middle-class British social ambitions, Hawke's Bay's pastoralists and businessmen looked to the free-wheeling United States frontier for colour".

Much relied on distinguishing roles. It was acceptable for a pastoralist to work with the employees through the day, swapping jokes and associating on a first-name basis. But of an evening the pastoral squire often returned to his fine home, shed his dirty clothes, put on a suit or smoking jacket, and sat down at a table covered with white linen and set with silverware, where the family meal was brought to the side-board by a servant, if any were available. Either way the roast joint was presented to the master of the house for ritual carving and serving. The whole meal was usually washed down with a glass or two of claret, the dessert perhaps followed by a brandy chaser — both of them the period drink of choice for the social elite.

Even Hawke's Bay's less well-to-do station holders sought to make such role distinctions. Walter Campbell, struggling to make ends meet as he established his Waimarama station and spending long hours labouring over his own property, nonetheless appeared at Christmas dinner 1868 with Fritz Meintzerhagen in 'full dress, white neckties and all' and they all 'sat down …like respectable people'.[127]

Those at the bottom of the social scale adopted aspects of the ritual but lacked the context of wealth. Mothers in Napier's Thackeray and Carlyle streets swept and scrubbed their houses out, pinned up home-made lace across the windows, spent hours starching their linen, and made sure their children were clean, but money remained a barrier. Beer or cheap spirits stood in for cognac; meat was a lesser cut, stewed for tenderness; clothing was patched rather than renewed. Despite a professed lack of barriers, real opportunities came knocking only for a minority. A shepherd such as John Fleming — hired by Sir William Russell to work on Tunanui at £1 a week in 1864[128] — could not get far enough ahead. Sometime gold miner David Balfour managed to save £80 towards bettering himself. He left Otago, leased land in northern Hawke's Bay, ran it for a while, then found work as a station manager.[129] But he could get no further.

> "Despite a professed lack of barriers, real opportunities came knocking only for a minority."

Money became the true arbiter of class,[130] often expressed in the homes the pastoralists built for themselves. Colonial mission and colonial military were the styles of the moment, with surrounding verandahs and floor-to-ceiling French doors opening into drawing rooms, servants' quarters, at times ball rooms. Most homes were set amid wide gardens and lawns, often with a tennis court. Even R. P. Williams' 'very elegant and chaste' home at Mangateretere featured ornamental gardens and a croquet lawn.[131] All were topped by Thomas Tanner's Riverslea, a magnificent two-storey mansion near Havelock with twelve bedrooms and five bathrooms. No expense was spared. He even had a landscape gardener brought out from England to manicure the surrounds, and when Sir William Jervois came to visit in 1883, Tanner had the taps gilded in silver.[132] More abstemious settlers merely rebuilt. Bernard Chambers came home one day in early 1876 to find 'carpenters pulling down the right wing of the house, where Johnny and Willy had their rooms', and the family home was still 'a great mess' in May, 'all the old middle part of the house was taken away and the framework of the new was up.'[133]

How this society of rich and poor interacted has been subject to a good deal of historical attention. In the early 1980s one historian took a statistical approach to suggest that the data showing convictions for drunkenness, assault and defamation cases revealed a New Zealand colonial society that was a world of maladjusted loners, isolated human 'atoms' with no social structures who took out their frustrations at their lonely lives by getting drunk, picking fights, and suing each other. The idea seemed particularly applicable to New Zealand's thinly populated, demographically unbalanced provinces such as Hawke's Bay. But why

Frontier refinement; : a group on the Clive Grange croquet ground, 1875.

Photographer unidentified, Fulton Collection, Alexander Turnbull Library, F-94363-1/2

settlers could be bothered with suing and hitting strangers they felt so totally disconnected from was never fully explained. Nor did the theory explain why frustrated and apparently uneducated settlers chose the academic-intellectual technique of legal recourse to settle their differences, and did not simply blow each other away with the shotguns, rifles, pistols, revolvers, carbines and other small-arms with which the colony was awash. The whole argument ultimately presented as little more than a technical artefact of academic methodology, with little practical relevance to what was actually happening in the settler period. While the hypothesis initially gained ground with the academy on the back of its intellectualised clothing, the notion of an 'atomised' society was swiftly discredited,[134] not least through a study of colonial-age Taradale that portrayed a complex, multi-level society in a clearly urbanised environment.[135]

The reality was that New Zealand settler society, including in its back-country blokish expressions, had vigorous social links. Hawke's Bay was no exception. At a time when few travelled far outside their region, people looked first to immediate family, then to local friends and business connections. Communities emerged — characterised in Hawke's Bay particularly by Havelock North, where a special local spirit emerged and flourished from the end of the nineteenth century.[136] These settler-age communities were often linked closely to each other by family or business ties which sometimes extended across the country.

Family was particularly important in this settler-age world of complex and tight social connections; the marriage rate peaked at over 10 percent per annum during the mid-1860s and remained at 7–8 percent until the depression of the 1880s.[137] Settlers at both ends of Hawke's Bay society favoured early marriage and large families, and it has been argued that these trends were little different from the English, Welsh and Scots societies from which most of the settlers hailed.[138]

The main problem in Hawke's Bay was demographic. Like other pastoral provinces, the initial pākehā population — particularly in the back-country — was skewed towards men. Station hands often found it difficult to meet women, and those they did meet were often within their direct social group. David Balfour, for instance, met and married Elizabeth Roberts, the niece of his employer Philip Dolbel.[139] There was more opportunity in the towns, where the demographic balance appears to have been better. However, money again created potential opportunities for the hopeful colonial bachelor. Although some pastoralists such as John Ormond married in the district — in his case, Hannah Richardson, sister of the Napier mechant Geordie Richardson — others found brides in Britain. Pastoralists who married while on a visit 'home' included Thomas Tanner, George Whitmore and Hector Duff.[140]

Race, wars and politics

Māori hoped for much from the arrival of settlers in Hawke's Bay, but the cultural frameworks of the two peoples were poles apart.[141] Settlers perceived the mis-match in the terms of the day. This was a problem. Amid the notion that civilisation developed in linear fashion from 'primitive indigenous' to 'sophisticated British',[142] most settler officials assumed that Māori should adopt 'superior' British ways. As McLean confided to his diary, 'it would be an excellent thing if the natives would join with the Europeans in purchasing sheep, or shares. It would ... lead to their eventual wealth and improvement.'[143]

In the 1850s, George Grey tried to provide Māori with the skills and equipment to become farmers, funding a significant agricultural school at Te Aute.[144] Samuel Williams opened this institution at Grey's urging in 1854, starting with a dozen pupils.[145] It was a bold move. Williams was sure the school would 'confer a benefit' on Māori by 'teaching

Pā Whakairo, mid-1860s. The European structure on the right is apparently Tareha's house.

Photographer unidentified, Rhodes Album, Alexander Turnbull Library, PA1-q-193-054-2

them to cultivate their land in a proper manner, also to look after their stock, milking &c.'[146] In fact the school failed to attract many pupils, and Williams had to close it in 1859. He put the issue down to poor accommodation, the hard work demanded of the pupils, temptations of high wages in adjacent stations — and what he called the 'excited state of the native mind on the Land question.'[147] Williams was no fool, but his observations were sieved through a period mind-set and proximate events. The wider historical issue was that this British-style institution failed to socially connect with Māori of the 1850s. When the school reopened in 1872,[148] it did so for a later generation of Māori, more familiar with settler culture and seeking new ways of engagement.

In the 1850s, common ground eluded both peoples at many levels. Yet Māori had an urgent need to engage. Demand for European consumables spiralled, and all of it had to be paid for.[149] Small-scale agriculture helped, but the crunch came in 1856 when wheat prices fell 75 percent, hitting the Māori agricultural economy hard.[150] Settlers whose mind set revolved around puritanical rectitude and a patronising attitude to indigenous peoples inevitably found fault. Māori had 'got into dissipated habits and squandered the money in debauchery at Auckland and Wellington, and in the purchase of useless, and extravagant articles'.[151] The fact that European goods had become part of a 'currency of rivalry'[152] and that there was a failure of minds to meet did not occur to most observers. Some Māori deliberately obfuscated the point. 'I continue to strive to uphold your

Hau te Ananui meeting house at Waiohiki, 1870s.

A. Walker, A. Walker Collection, albumen print, Alexander Turnbull Library F-103654-1/2, PA2-1816

beliefs,' Karaitiana Takamoana wrote to McLean in September 1851, as part of a plea for payment and more medical aid, 'and those of of the Queen and our God'.[153] Astute and cynical observers such as McLean likely saw through the sophistry; but these remarks also carried a face-value meaning to settlers trapped in a liberal-progressive mind-set.

Aspects of this experience were shared across New Zealand, and in combination with settler land-buying pressure helped prompt the Kingitanga movement, which emerged under Te Wherowhero of Waikato, elected King Potatau I in 1858.[154] The Hawke's Bay response was guided by local imperatives. Te Hāpuku, who had suffered at the hands of Waikato and their allies during the 'musket wars', did not join. Ngāti Kahungunu prevaricated, but the injunction to halt land sales struck a chord after the Te Pakiake war. Even European officials appreciated the point. Cooper thought a ban might prevent 'lands from being sold by claimants with doubtful titles; or... by rightful and acknowledged claimants, against the wishes of the majority of those interested.'[155]

Paheka pressure arguably led to Ngāti Kahungunu becoming one of the largest iwi in New Zealand. During the settler period, many pākehā loosely called any Māori from Hawke's Bay 'Ngāti Kahungunu', although at the time the district was populated by related but separate kin-groups, such as Ngāti Hawea and Ngāti Whatuiāpiti. The confusion was not helped by McLean. Tamati Waka explained the relationships to him in 1850,[156] and the Scot apparently understood them. However, for his own purposes he then dealt with this diverse group as if they were factions of a single iwi, promoting Te Hāpuku — who was Ngāti Whatuiāpiti — as his principal agent.[157] And yet over the next few years, Ngāti Kahungunu became, in practise, just such a unified bloc. It has been argued that the underlying forces reflected, in part, issues flowing from the eighteenth century.[158] We also cannot ignore the effects of the 'musket wars' as a unifying force across the district. However, as we have seen, the more compelling factor remains the politics of land purchase and the war at Te Pakiaka. McLean's promotion of Te Hāpuku drove Ngāti Hawea, Ngāti te Upokoiri and others in the Heretaunga area together against Ngāti Whatuiāpiti. By April 1856, as Cooper observed, the Heretaunga chiefs were calling themselves 'Ngāti Kahungunu'.[159] Te Hāpuku's military defeat at the hands of this group in 1858 cemented the process.[160] Chiefs such as Karaitiana Takamoana — who drew descent from Rangitāne as well as Kahungunu[161] — gained ascendancy. This again suited pākehā authorities — and, as has been argued, the emergence of Ngāti Kahungunu was further cemented as Hawke's Bay Māori moved towards political solutions to the problems of British settlement.[162]

> "Hawke's Bay's race relations came under tension during the 1860s in the face of new land laws."

Hawke's Bay's race relations came under tension during the 1860s in the face of new land laws. The Native Land Act 1862 was meant to 'greatly promote the peaceful settlement of the Colony and the advancement and civilization of the Natives' by making sure their 'rights to land were ascertained defined and declared.'[163] Three years later another Act consolidated previous legislation, introducing a key change. Under Section 23, Māori 'interested in a piece of Native land'[164] could be granted titles of ownership. They were, as Judge Monro put it, 'trustees for the benefit of themselves and of their co-proprietors.'[165] It was an attempt to adapt English-style ownership to Māori customary tradition, intended to protect Māori — but although couched in terms of meeting the Crown's obligations under the Treaty of Waitangi,[166] in practise this was simply the trigger for a new cascade of injustices.

Hawke's Bay accounted for nearly a third of the total Māori land certificated nationally in 1866, some 68 blocks, of which 54 were granted to more than one person.[167] However, the push by Māori to legitimise their titles in pākehā terms backfired because, as Justice C. W. Richmond observed in 1873, land granted to an individual was 'liable at once to be taken in execution for his private debts.'[168] This was unintended, but Hawke's Bay storekeepers swiftly took advantage of the loophole, much to the disgust of settler authorities. It did not take long for alarm bells to ring. T. H. Haultain alerted the House of Representatives that 'unscrupulous and dishonest' people had been encouraging Māori debt, then 'taken advantage of their ignorance or intemperance to receive mortgage over the lands … a sure preliminary to transfer on their own terms.'[169]

An amendment to the Act, passed in 1867, failed to halt the rising tide. The interpreter F. E. Hamlin finally blew the whistle in 1869, telling the Attorney General that the system had been created by Napier wholesaler and general merchant Frederick Sutton, who had been 'assisted in doing so by [interpreter] Mr G. B. Worgan, every-one else having set their faces against it.'[170] Hamlin persisted:

> the barefaced manner in which the trade is carried on is beyond credence. Several Natives have come into the town without the slightest idea of treating with their lands; they have been watched in the street by Mr Sutton (who, I need not say had Mr Worgan within call), the Natives decoyed away — introduced as a rule first to a glass or two of spirits, then into his shop where he or she is invited to take an unlimited quantity of goods … at the same time, the Deed is introduced and requested to be signed which, considering the state they are in, is not generally refused.[171]

Sutton responded by implicating Hamlin.[172] But the flood gates had been opened. Stories circulated, among them the claim that Sutton pressed Paora Kaiwhata with a gig that the chief then drove through Napier, its lamps blazing in full daylight, 'much in the spirit of a seaman who has just been paid off'.[173] While such imagery played on prevailing stereotypes of Māori, the fact that Sutton had lit the lamps was also pointed out by colonial media at the time — and shortly seen as less an issue than the fact that he had pushed Paora into debt and, later, foreclosed on the mortgage, enabling bank manager J. B. Brathwaite to buy land he had been leasing from the chief.[174] Other storekeepers, notably the Meanee-based merchant Richard Maney, were also alleged to be forcing sales through Māori debt.[175]

Such behaviour stood outside the accepted values of the day, and had significant implications for race relations at a time when peace had not been made with Kingitanga, when renewed war flared in south Taranaki, and when Te Kooti remained at large.[176] This helps explain the sense of outrage that news of Hawke's Bay's dodgy storekeepers generated across the colony. The scandal was disproportionate; as John Sheehan remarked, most sales derived from the 'machinations of a few designing Europeans known as "The Ring"', which he estimated was no more than 'some twenty five [sic] or thirty' people.[177] Henry Russell put the number at twenty;[178]

and when the whole affair was finally investigated in 1873, 97 complaints out of 301 were directed against Maney and Sutton.[179] The number of participants did not reduce the fact that something had to be done to stop it: but the problem was that government had only a technical lever available. The law required a licensed interpreter to be present at any negotiation, and their registration could be cancelled if they were found to have misrepresented the deal. Therein lay the rub. When the Premier, William Fox, wrote to Ormond in 1869 to ask whether Worgan's license should 'be withdrawn',[180] the problem was finding enough evidence.

The New Zealand Wars in Hawke's Bay

Dodgy land deals provided a backdrop for the wider tumult that swept Hawke's Bay in the mid-1860s. The district had avoided war largely because Ngāti Kahungunu were determined to keep the peace. However, the rise of Pai Mārire in Taranaki during the early 1860s added a dimension. This response to culture-contact was radicalised in 1864,[181] and over the next 18 months Pai Mārire proselytes roamed the North Island, offering a syncretic amalgam of traditional and Christian teachings that stood at odds with Victorian-age evangelism, striking fearful chords among the settler community. The murder of Opotiki minister Carl Volkner at the beginning of 1865 cinched the settler image of Pai Mārire as murderous and godless savages,[182] provoking a climate of irrational fear.

Pai Mārire first came into Hawke's Bay in early 1863, before the movement was fully radicalised. Then in February 1865 another group arrived, paused briefly to meet Ngāti Kahungunu, and pushed south to Te Aute — apparently at Te Hāpuku's invitation. McLean, now Provincial Superintendent, suspected Te Hāpuku wanted to use them as external allies against Ngāti Kahungunu.[183] The *Hawke's Bay Herald* echoed his

Donald McLean as Hawke's Bay's elder statesman. By the mid-1860s, as Provincial Superintendent and General Government Agent, he was the effective dictator of the province.

Photographer unidentified, Alexander Turnbull Library, G-5166-1/2 sentiments.[184] But Te Hāpuku admitted nothing, giving what Cooper called a 'very lame excuse for his conduct'.[185] The *Herald* then speculated that 'Te Hāpuku and four other hapus' had thrown in their lot with Pai Mārire, and others were 'said to be wavering'.[186] In the end nothing came of the visit; but after Pai Mārire priest Paora Toki visited Pētane (Bay View) in March,[187] McLean was appointed Agent General for Hawke's Bay. When combined with his position as Provincial Superintendent and with his mana with Māori, the result was a substantial concentration of personal power.[188]

In April 1865, around 400 Pai Mārire arrived at Te Uhi, not far from Wairoa.[189] McLean oiled the local waters but was unable to prevent a war between northern hapū of Ngāti Kahungunu.[190] Around the middle of the year Pai Mārire came to Heretaunga, in direct consequence of a dispute between Ngāti Kahungunu and Ngāti Hineuru of Te Haroto, over the division of payment after McLean's 1851 purchase of Ahuriri.[191] Once again the old 'musket wars' mechanisms of external allies emerged; Te Rangihiroa of Ngāti Hineuru sought help from Pai Mārire of Waikato, alarming Ngāti Kahungunu who urged an immediate assault on Te Haroto. McLean demurred,[192] but the issue simmered on through the winter. Rumours flowed of impending attack.[193]

McLean prepared for the worst, securing Te Hāpuku's support of Ngāti Kahungunu in the face of the new threat, but the crisis did not come until October, when a party from Te Haroto under the Pai Mārire prophet Panapa marched for Napier and took the village of Ōmaranui, on the Tutaekuri river River near Tareha's village of Pā Whakairo. Another group appeared to be threatening Napier from the north. Ngāti Kahungunu were in no doubt that Panapa intended to fight and warned McLean. Rumours flowed of a co-ordinated plan to sack Napier,[194] so McLean issued instructions to Whitmore — New Zealand's national militia commander and a local Hawke's Bay landowner. Politics simmered; Whitmore hated McLean and had already tried to undercut the Scot's local power, but as fellow McLean opponent J.E. Fitzgerald pointed out, 'The authority is infuriatingly … his'.[195]

Ngāti Kahungunu — Tareha, Karatiana Takamoana and other leading chiefs — were eager to join in,[196] partly because Pai Mārire forces were only about 30 minutes walk from Tareha's main kāinga . As a result nearly 180 settler militia were joined by a taua of 200 from Pā Whakairo. They expected to face 140 Pai Mārire, but McLean had been told that another

'The Gravedigger': George Whitmore

The diminutive Major-General Sir George S. Whitmore, KCMG (1829–1903) came to New Zealand as Military Secretary to Lieutenant-General Sir Duncan Cameron in the early 1860s, decided to settle, and purchased land not far inland from Napier, which he named Rissington.

A military background and ongoing ambition propelled him to prominence in the militia, and he finally rose to command national field forces against Te Kooti and Titokowaru in 1868–69. He proved himself a highly capable military commander, brave, resolute, leading from the front by example; and able to inspire the few he did not alienate.

The problem was that alienation was too common a fate; he suffered from an execrable temper that often let him down. His bitter arguments with his own forces were legendary. After an incident in 1868 when he threatened to have one unit courtmartialled and executed — and got them to start digging their own graves — he gained the nickname 'The Gravedigger'. It stuck.

More to the point, he never got along with McLean, and was effectively sacked when McLean became Defence Minister in mid-1869. But his star rose again in the 1870s, when he took a lead role in organising New Zealand's nation-wide defence forces. He continued to live in Hawke's Bay, moving to Clive where he took a close interest in Hawke's Bay local politics.

He finally retired to a house on Napier's Marine Parade. Never one to forget or forgive, he was still railing about his political enemies of the colonial era when he came to write his memoirs, a quarter-century or more after some of them had gone to the grave.

Major-General Sir George S. Whitmore, KCMG (1829–1903)

Photographer unidentified, war history collection, Alexander Turnbull Library F-117757-1/2

Captain Charles Westrupp's camp, Poverty Bay, mid-1860s. Most of the campaigns across northern Hawke's Bay and the East Coast during the last years of the New Zealand wars were run from Napier, the political and economic power-house of the eastern North Island at the time.

William Leonard Williams, Rhodes Album, Alexander Turnbull Library, PA1-q-193-092-1

150 were at Te Pohue. This was not actually true, but McLean felt he had to prepare. The battles that followed, at Ōmaranui and Herepoho on 11 October 1866, have thoroughly exercised historians. Both were short and decisive[197] — giving rise to the persistent but misleading idea that the Hawke's Bay war was a 'one day' affair,[198] and that Ōmaranui was a massacre. McLean — who appears to have been credited with Whitmore's battle plan,[199] and hailed as Napier's saviour[200] — lost no time taking political advantage, trumpeting that they had smashed a 'deep and cleverly planned scheme of attacking the Town of Napier'.[201] Actually, the idea of such an attack was true: but it was more likely hope than genuine strategy, though details, including an attack on the Napier barracks, were outlined afterwards by Pai Mārire prisoners.[202] Talk of a massacre at Ōmaranui finally reached the Colonial Secretary back in London, triggering a vigorous spat with the Premier, Edward Stafford.[203]

Some historians have since portrayed the battle of Ōmaranui as a settler effort to crush peaceful Pai Mārire.[204] And, indeed, as Ormond observed at the time, 'there cannot be said there was anything heroic in the fight'.[205] However, setting aside the months of tensions and the provocative march into a Ngāti Kahungunu village, we have to take into account both the context of irrational fear among the pākehā community— and the documentation. McLean ordered forces in only when weeks of diplomacy had failed.[206] Whitmore, under strict instructions to avoid bloodshed, waited well beyond the expiry of an ultimatum and again sent interpreter Ned Hamlin towards the kāinga under a white flag. He returned with the news that 'they meant to fight'.[207] At the time this was seen as decisive by the settlers, although it is also likely that Pai Mārire felt they had been pushed into a corner; and may also have genuinely believed that with divine intervention proofing them to bullets, they could win. However, McLean's efforts to avoid bloodshed seem clear, and to the settlers any decision to fight lay with Pai Mārire.

The last 'hot' phases of the New Zealand wars intimately involved Hawke's Bay. Napier was the largest town on the east coast between Auckland and Wellington, and most of the East Coast campaigns were run or supported from there. That was how the former Napier harbour dredge ended up aground in Whakatane harbour in 1866, the militia on board potting away at Māori on shore.[208] Napier's role did not change when further warfare broke out on both sides of the North Island in 1868–69. Fighting flared in south Taranaki mid-year at the hands of Ngāti Ruanui chief Riwha Titokowaru. At the same time, Te Kooti Te Tūruki a Rikirangi escaped from the Chathams and landed near Turanganūi (Gisborne). He had been imprisoned in 1866, without trial, despite writing to McLean. It appears that McLean, who was not in Napier at the time, never received the letter, and Te Kooti was despatched to prison and exile in the Chathams, where he joined many of the Pai Mārire survivors of the Ōmaranui battle. Te Kooti remains an extraordinary figure; complex, literate, a religious leader — yet, despite the sympathetic picture portrayed in his primary biography[209] — also ruthless and able to kill in cold blood if needed. 'If the government will let me alone,' he once told Josiah Firth, 'I will never fight again, but if they jump on me from all sides, I will rise up and fight'.[210]

The main problem for Hawke's Bay in 1868 was that central government took Te Kooti's protestations at face value and saw a greater threat in Taranaki, where Ngāti Ruanui chief Titokowaru was fighting a small but significant war. Neither had any chance of defeating government forces in the long run; and for Te Kooti, the Urewera provided a haven into which he shortly vanished.[211] That did not alleviate settler fears in Hawke's Bay, where government focus on Taranaki created a sense that their own district had been abandoned. McLean, wearing his combined hat as Provincial Superintendent and Agent General, swiftly exploited the point. The resulting politicisation worked against the efforts of Defence

> "Whitmore was blamed for the 'wretched collapse' of the expedition at the hands of his 'system of vituperation, insult, and menace'…"

Thomas Tanner (1830–1918) cut a swathe through Hawke's Bay's frontier society. To Christopher Richmond he was a 'self-confident little man — some might say conceited, but I don't give it that name'. Others were more charitable.

Photographer unidentified, General Assembly Library Collection, Alexander Turnbull Library, F-125-35mm-C, PAColl-0838

Minister Theodore Haultain to end the conflict and deepened rifts within the Hawke's Bay settler community.[212] The only positive outcome for McLean was that, despite the provocation of the debt-for-land deals, Ngāti Kahungunu remained eager to assist the settlers, and as Agent General he was able to order kupapa ('collaborator') forces from Wairoa and Heretaunga to assist Ngāti Porou and local militia against Te Kooti.

Whitmore's personality added complexity. He upset the Turanganūi militia after the battle of Paparatu.[213] At the end of July, as a combined force of settler militia and kupapa marched for the Ruakituri River, the Napier troop took took the edge of his tongue. The upshot was a kangaroo court in which the 'condemned' men were made to dig their own graves. The incident has usually been confused with Whitmore's dismissal of the Turanganūi force a few days later.[214] It gave him a new nickname — 'The Gravedigger' — and as a result, he set out to catch Te Kooti in freezing weather with only a fraction of his initial force: 52 men of Fraser's No. 1 Division of the Armed Constabulary and 42 kupapa — including a contingent from Heretaunga, technically under command of Captain J. L. Herrick, but in practice led by Henare Tomoana. And it was Tomoana who pulled Whitmore's irons from the fire in the battle that followed a few days later, bringing his forces in with a charge up a bullet-swept riverbed.

Whitmore was blamed for the 'wretched collapse' of the expedition at the hands of his 'system of vituperation, insult, and menace',[215] and feelings ran so high he was even accused of abandoning his friends Davis Canning and Carr 'to the mercy of the enemy'.[216] Thomas Tanner was so moved by the 'melancholy intelligence' he offered to raise a troop. McLean accepted, and the Hawke's Bay Yeoman Cavalry was ready for action by early 1869.[217] The political issues came to a head in Taranaki, where the chief Titokowaru defeated settler forces outside Te Ngutu o te Manu. Despite post-colonial claims,[218] government hold over the colony was not threatened.[219] But settler morale took a dive. 'What are we to do with these bloodthirsty rebels?' one editorial declared.[220] Then Defence Minister T. H. Haultain had to disband one division of the Armed Constabulary to avert a threatened mutiny in wake of the defeat.[221] At Whitmore's urging, the government transferred Fraser's 58 men from Napier across to south Taranaki to make good the loss. This triggered a crisis. The *Hawke's Bay Herald* had already complained that there were '725 men and 34 commissioned officers … in Patea' against a 'probable strength' of 150 Māori, while 'Government provides us with an enemy 160 strong, well found with every munition of war'.[222] While Napier was safe, there were fears for Wairoa, Clyde and Turanganūi (Gisborne).[223]

McLean responded with a resolution to the House, expressing 'alarm at the position the colony has been brought to by the conduct of the Government in native and defence matters'.[224] As a capper he asked for £56,000 — around $5 million in early twenty-first century money — with which he proposed to personally organise the defences of Hawke's Bay,[225] clearing up Te Kooti and the East Coast in 12 months.[226] When Stafford refused, McLean took fellow MPs John Ormond and Tareha Te Moananui — his 'pocket Māori vote' — and joined the faction of his 'implacable enemy', William Fox.[227]

It was a public scandal. The *Advertiser* condemnned the move as 'one of the most unconscionable instances of ratting ever known in the Colony',[228] but to McLean his dramatic *volte-face* was entirely justified: and just to drive the lesson home, he then proposed his third motion of no-confidence that year, which the government survived by just one vote.[229] Stafford hastened to oil the waters, even allowing McLean to retain his agency, within limits.[230]

Meanwhile, Haultain authorised Whitmore to open negotiations with Te Kooti — but the latter sought pardon, which was not on offer.[231] At the end of the year Te Kooti raided the district around Turanganūi, then melted back to his hilltop fortress of Ngatapa.[232] Whitmore blamed McLean for the debacle.[233] McLean, who looked on the situation not just as a threat to northern Hawke's Bay but also another round in his struggle with the government, turned to kupapa under Rapata Wahawaha and others. They attacked Ngatapa in early December, without taking it.[234] The government, against McLean's opposition, then ordered Whitmore across from Taranaki with a force of Armed Constabulary. Although the settlers took the hilltop fortress, Te Kooti escaped at the eleventh hour.[235] And on the night of 9–10 April he entered northern Hawke's Bay. His target was Ngāti Pahauwera, a hapū living near Mohaka. Most of their toa were away, with the result that Te Kooti's raiders scored a swift victory at Te Arakanihi, then went on to besiege two pā and attack the Lavin family on Mohaka station.

> "…if we went one way we might run on to the Hauhaus [sic], and if we went another way we might do the same…"
> — D. P. Balfour

The alarm spread quickly. David Balfour was at nearby Springhill station when:

a man brought the news, and the thing was — how to get out from where we were; if we went one way we might run on to the Hauhaus [sic], and if we went another way we might do the same.[236]

Settlers sent to look for the Lavins on 14 April found only tragedy,[237] and the fact that Te Kooti's primary targets were Māori did not halt a ripple of panic across the whole district. One reporter ran into 'twenty carts bound for Napier from Meeanee and Puketapu, laden with timid women and tender children'.[238] It was worse further north. Balfour's business partner George Farrow fled, leaving Balfour with debt and a flock to shear. He survived with help from his friend and neighbour Philip Dolbel. 'From today I became a *desperate man*,' he wrote on 30 April.[239] Craig Newton walked off Tutira station, leaving his sheep to run wild. Morale took a hit across the whole province. John Northe was despondent: 'it would appear no one can stop them … Col. Whitmoor [sic] can't do anything.'[240] The *Hawke's Bay Herald* blamed Henry Russell, then commanding the Napier military district, for trying to 'pooh pooh every indication of danger'.[241] Then the editor laid into the general government

John Lavin's homestead, Mohaka. The childen seen here were shortly murdered by Te Kooti's forces, tomahawked in cold blood, from behind, while fleeing for their lives.

Alfred John Cooper, pencil, ink and watercolour, Alexander Turnbull Library, A-235-012

for 'mismanagement'.²⁴² Actually, the government response — led in the field by Whitmore — was decisive: a full-scale invasion of the Urewera designed to flush out Te Kooti and simultaneously punish Tūhoe for sheltering him. It worked. By June Te Kooti was heading for the central plateau, where he hoped to establish his long-promised Babylon at Tauranga-a-Taupō.²⁴³

The Stafford ministry collapsed as these events unfolded. William Fox became Premier, bringing McLean in as combined Defence and Native Minister. John Ormond took up McLean's former role of Hawke's Bay Provincial Superintendent and Agent General for the government — and his district suddenly became the lynch-pin of national politics. It was on Ormond's shoulders that responsibility fell for the final campaign against Te Kooti. Money was short, and he also lacked a commander; Whitmore fell ill after the Urewera campaign,²⁴⁴ giving McLean the pretext to sack him,²⁴⁵ and Ormond found himself having to persuade a reluctant Thomas McDonnell to come on board.

Ngāti Kahungunu were supportive; Henare Tomoana offered to raise a force, buying the gear he needed on credit from Sutton. As he was about to leave, Sutton presented him with a writ for £900 — about $91,000 in early twenty-first century values — and when Ormond sent Frederick Hamlin to argue the point, Sutton gave a 'rather saucy' answer. 'If he goes into battle and gets shot, where would my money be?'²⁴⁶ In the event, Tomoana played a decisive role in the campaign. His force was besieged near Tauranga-a-Taupō in September, but he held on for two days, denying Te Kooti victory. In wake of the battle, Rewi Maniapoto — who had been considering alliance with Te Kooti — abandoned the idea.²⁴⁷ Settler forces and kupapa converged on the central plateau, led by McDonnell who came up from Napier across the 'Gentle Annie', meeting a Ngāti Kahungunu force under Renata Kawepo at Moawhango. Foul weather, a stygian overcast and Mount Ngaruhoe's rumblings lent an

Henare Tomoana (?–1904); Ngāti Kahungunu chief. Although dismissed by Thomas McDonnell as a 'fat Leicester wether', he was a capable leader in the field, and his defence of a position during the campaign against Te Kooti in late 1869 helped convince Kingitanga not to pursue an alliance with the Ringatū leader.

Samuel Carnell, E. G. Spraggan Collection, Alexander Turnbull Library, G-22168-1/4

Karaitiana Takamoana (?–1879), leading chief of Ngāti Kahungunu ki Heretaunga. Although sorely provoked by the Heretaunga sale, he was determined to make his point through legal and parliamentary means, driving the politicisation of Māori in the 1870s.

Photographer unidentified, Alexander Turnbull Library, F-94408-1/2

apocalyptic air to the campaign. Te Kooti was defeated at Te Porere and, although he made good an escape, lost a significant part of his support and never fully regained his poise.

Ngāti Tūwharetoa chief Horonuku Te Heuheu capitulated to the settler and kupapa forces and was escorted back to Napier by Tomoana. 'Friend, I am very much pleased with you,' McLean told Tomoana a few weeks later.[248] Settler authorities thought Te Heuheu might become an ally,[249] and Ormond decided to 'deal leniently with him',[250] handing the chief to Karaitiana Takamoana. Meanwhile, Tomoana returned to find that Sutton had pursued the writ in his absence. The result was that Te Heuheu had a front-row seat for the debt crisis into which Ngāti Kahungunu fell through the summer of 1869–70 — triggering the sale of Heretaunga.

Repudiation and land rings

The Heretaunga sale was the largest of Hawke's Bay's debt-for-land deals, the trigger for Ngāti Kahungunu strategy into the 1870s and beyond — and the signal for fresh battle within Hawke's Bay's elite. The sale epitomised Hawke's Bay's pākehā business culture of the period. Farce abounded, from the precipitate flight of a 20-stone (127 kg) Manaena Tini up a tree to escape buyer Thomas Tanner with proffered deeds, to Henare Tomoana hiding in his minister's loft to avoid the same fate. One negotiating session in a hotel bar resulted in 'both parties' getting 'so drunk as to be unable to transact any business'.[251] The final purchase price at £21,314 10s was nearly half as much again as negotiated, partly because two chiefs arranged secret annuities for themselves, but also because during the divvy-up Tanner ended up paying £1,632 10s 6d more than agreed. He was 'unable to explain' the accounting error,[252] which amounted to about $184,500 in early twenty-first century values.[253]

J. N. Williams' homestead at Frimley, on the Heretaunga block, during the 1870s.

Photographer unidentified, Alexander Turnbull Library, F-26744-1/2

The plains were broadly under the mana of Ngāti Kahungunu ki Heretaunga, led by Karaitiana Takamoana. In the early 1860s, Tanner arranged to lease the block — illegally, and opposed by Henry Tiffen, then Chair of the Hawke's Bay Provincial Council, who thought the plains were better suited for agriculture. Tanner ignored him, bringing Ormond in as business partner and a political ally in 1865. The seven partners divided the block into 12 sections, attracting the nickname 'apostles', and Tanner regularised the lease in 1866 under the new land laws — though, as Tanner pointed out, 'no one understood what the position of grantees was.'[254] His 21-year lease deducted improvements from rent, making it virtually cost free to the partners. And like other blocks granted under the land court, Heretaunga became vulnerable to foreclosure on loans held by chiefs on security of their grant.

It did not take long for parts of the block to change hands. Napier merchant Henry Parker tried to buy the portion granted to Waka Kawatini of Ngāti Hinemoa in December 1868. Tanner, who had 'great objection to Heretaunga getting into Parker's hands', decided to buy the grant himself.[255] He put the notion to Waka, and then offered him £1000 during a chance meeting. The deal immediately fell foul of Parker, whose lawyer argued that Waka was 'not fit to transact business'.[256] Tanner persisted. The net balance, once Waka's debts to Parker, Sutton and Maney had been paid off, was £15.

While this went on, J.M. Stuart turned up from Wellington looking to buy Apera Pahoro's grant. That failed, so Stuart then tried to buy the grant of Tareha Te Moananui, the Māori member of Parliament for the East Coast. When the chief refused, Stuart sent Meeanee storekeeper Richard Maney to corner him in Wellington's Empire Hotel. Tanner wanted Tareha's grant himself and pursued Maney to the capital, where he ran into Ormond and Samuel Williams, who — seeing scandal — advised 'against dealing with Tareha'.[257] So Tanner dutifully stood aside while Maney did the work for him. It was, as Christopher Richmond later put it, one of those 'pieces of finesse which so often throw a shade upon transactions with natives.'[258] Tareha, caught off his own land, without his runanga, was at a disadvantage. 'Where is my strength here?'[259]

> "The resulting cash balance of £2,387 7s 3d — inflated by over £1600 due to Tanner's error — was taken by Karaitiana."

Tomoana's war debt added another wedge for unscrupulous settlers to exploit, but though Stuart offered the young chief £6000 for his share of Heretaunga, Tomoana turned him down on the basis that he had offered to sell to Tanner.[260] He eventually did. As 1869 drew to a close, Karaitiana decided to see McLean over the crisis. Te Heuheu had been let free on good-behaviour promises and the two chiefs decided to head to Auckland. They were about to board a boat in Napier when Sutton handed Karaitiana a writ for £100.[261] Karaitiana then decided he could not leave and was on his way back to Pakowhai when Tanner — conveniently — intercepted him 'at the water trough at Mr Maney's', talking sale. On 6 December Karaitiana and Tomoana signed a contract to sell Heretaunga to Tanner and his associates for £13,500 — about $1.35 million in early twenty-first century terms[262] — less what had already been paid to the grantees. The deal was coloured by a secret arrangement between Tomoana and Tanner for a ten-year annuity.[263] Exactly what followed is difficult to reconstruct; accounts differ, but Tanner ended up paying Karaitiana an annuity as well.[264]

This did not close the deal. Solicitor James Wilson told Karaitiana not to sell, whereupon James Watt — who had agreed to lend Tanner £29,000 to buy the land — apparently tried to bribe Karaitiana to sign. The chief 'very properly' refused,[265] and Tanner decided he had no option but to buy the grants individually. This took the rest of the summer, including a trip to Waipukurau to get the signature of Te Hāpuku's niece Airihi te Nahu, one of the grantees. Her inclusion introduced further complication. She was a minor and her share had been placed in trust, administered by J.N. Wilson and Henry Russell. Tanner met them in the Tavistock Hotel, where they talked Tanner up to £2500.[266] Karaitiana still held out, and Tanner finally took out a writ to force him to comply with the original sale agreement. The land changed hands in March 1870, in solicitor Joshua Cuff's office, where the total was netted against the grantees' debts. The cash balance of £2,387 7s 3d — inflated by over £1600 due to Tanner's error — was taken by Karaitiana.[267]

With that, just on 17,000 acres of the 19,385 acre block granted in 1865[268] — the most fertile district in Hawke's Bay — passed into settler hands. The Native Land Frauds Prevention Act 1870 — in which Hanson Turton was appointed Trusts Commissioner,[269] came too late. Karaitiana realised a new strategy was needed, and the growing strength of central government offered opportunity. He began petitioning the House — delivering 11 between 20 September and 11 November 1871 alone.[270] Meanwhile, Porangahau chief Henare Matua, an assessor with the Land Court, began an effort to legally invalidate sale deeds by locating flaws in the arrangements. This was not too hard in that colonial age of rough-and-ready business, and the tactic finally drew in the settler community. Henry Russell purchased Airihi's section when Tanner defaulted on payment, found a problem with the deed — and promptly invited Māori to lay complaints over any purchase.

Ormond thought Russell had gone mad.[271] In fact, Russell knew what he was up to. It has been argued that he had genuine concern for Māori.[272] However, he was not above his own manoeuvres, including obtaining Te Hāpuku's 'whole estate and interest' on trust, raising eyebrows with provincial authorities.[273] His real motive in asking Māori to raise anything they felt unjust was political; he saw a golden opportunity to exploit their grievances to bring down the McLean-Ormond faction. He had been off-side with this group for years, partly because he disagreed with McLean's conduct of the war, but more particularly because McLean, Ormond and his associates favoured stronger central government, whereas Russell, Whitmore and others had more provincial interests. Personal rivalry spiced the mix. McLean fell from grace in 1869 with the Stafford government, whereupon Russell was appointed General Government Agent for Hawke's Bay — until the Stafford administration fell.[274]

Henry Robert Russell (1817–1891) — central Hawke's Bay settler, 'Lord H' to his enemies, and a prime mover behind the Repudiation movement of the early 1870s.

Photographer unidentified, Alexander Turnbull Library, F-43057-1/2

Christopher W. Richmond (1821–1895), solicitor and judge presiding over the 1873 Native Lands Alienation Commission in Hawke's Bay.

Photographer unidentified, detail, Alexander Turnbull Library, F-12439-1/2

McLean then took up Russell's role with the incoming Fox government. Such gyrations of power rankled. It is possible that Russell also had in mind repayment of the money he had advanced to local Māori — by 1871, more than £5448, a figure that rose to £11,821 by 1875,[275] some $1.35 million in early twenty-first century sums.[276]

Inevitably Russell found little support around Hawke's Bay. Local solicitors sided with what he called the 'land stealers',[277] but he was able to hire the Auckland barrister John Sheehan and Wairarapa-based interpreter Edward Maunsell.[278] Māori flocked to his side, leading Russell to trumpet to J. C. Richmond that 'the *whole* native population are with me — a great change since 1869.'[279] In July 1872 Russell even managed to facilitate a public meeting between the repudiationists and Karaitiana's parliamentary party.[280] More than 400 Māori attended.[281]

Another petition followed, drawing national attention to the less than exemplary behaviour of Hawke's Bay's gentry.[282] It was a scandal. The dust had not settled from the New Zealand wars; and amid a potentially volatile situation, government listened. The upshot was the Hawke's Bay Native Lands Alienation Commission Act, establishing a commission of two judges and two chiefs under C. W. Richmond.

By the time the commission sat in April 1873, some 599,220 acres had been granted to 558 individual Māori in Hawke's Bay, out of a population of 3,773, though as Richmond observed, some names appeared 'over and over again on many grants'.[283] Māori hoped for much, providing 301 complaints covering blocks from Heretaunga to Raukawa west, Maharahara, Umutaoroa, Pētane, Tunanui, Tahoraiti, Wharerangi, Ngatarawa, Waipureku and many others. pākehā named in complaints included Ormond, Maney, Sutton, Kinross, Worgan, McLean, Brathwaite, J. H. Coleman and others. Māori were also named, usually in conjunction with claims of unfair distribution of purchase money.[284]

Hearings began amid a barrage of claim, counter-claim and intense public interest. The *Hawke's Bay Herald*, reputedly prompted by Ormond, declared that the commissioners were working through a 'chaos of irrelevant gossip and falsehood, which the Native evidence to so large an extent consists.'[285] Sloppy book-keeping was exposed to the hard light of accounting, although the errors were often in Māori favour. But pākehā fraud seemed lacking. Even the Heretaunga case, examined in detail during February 1873, did not produce 'anything that can be called a rat'.[286] Nor could Richmond uphold most of the complaints, arguing that Māori had discredited themselves by exaggeration.[287] The dissonance between

Māori and settler culture was never more apparent, though Richmond was in no doubt that Māori had been disadvantaged by the settlers. Ngāti Kahungunu had 'real grievances in the matter of their landed rights' — the 'evils of the existing state of the law' had been 'fully exemplified' in Hawke's Bay.[288] But to him that was a separate issue. Claims of fraud, inadequate sale prices, debts for alcohol purchases built into the deals, secret gratuities, improper translation, non-payment of agreed sums and unfair division of the money[289] were all considered, but 'nothing was proved which ought, in good conscience, to invalidate any purchases investigated by us.'[290] While it 'cannot be satisfactory to anybody to part with property when he has already dissipated the price',[291] Richmond declared, this was simply the way the law worked, and 'the sooner the natives learn to recognise their liabilities in this respect, the better it will be for them.'[292]

For Māori, in short, the answer was tough cheese, and Richmond was backed by the other European judge, 'pākehā Māori' Frederick Maning, who had lived with Māori during the immediate pre-colonial period, and thought the affair a 'natural and unavoidable' consequence of culture contact.[293] These voices over-rode those of the Māori commissioners, who seemed more ready to accept cultural issues.[294]

This was not what Ngāti Kahungunu had hoped for, and the news spread like wild-fire across the North Island, alarming settlers. Discontent was 'deeper seated than was supposed', Henare Potae declared from Poverty Bay, urging government to 'keep the Court open'.[295] Afterwards there were what Samuel Locke called 'secret meetings for the purpose [of] keeping up the excitement, and getting up fresh petitions for parliament.'[296] He feared war. McLean met Ngāti Kahungunu in the Napier court house, reminding them of the losses suffered by other iwi who had persisted in 'their evil course'.[297] McLean went on to trumpet the message around the North Island,[298] while Sheehan counselled legal action.[299] Ngāti Kahungunu agreed to petition government,[300] though Sheehan's advice was promptly lampooned in the *Hawke's Bay Herald* with a call to 'collect large funds for your loving friend Johnny Sheehan.'[301] Ormond, who regarded Sheehan as a 'little blackguard',[302] asked McLean to republish the article in the *Southern Cross*, and had another version circulated among Māori.[303] Confusion reigned,[304] but the petition was still presented in August.[305]

What eventually emerged was the Komiti (Committee),[306] an effort to re-examine past land deals, publicised through a newspaper edited by Henare Tomoana and former Wanganui magistrate John White. Russell

> "For Māori, in short, the answer was tough cheese, and Richmond was backed by the other European judge, 'pākehā Māori' Frederick Maning,"

bankrolled the movement,[307] even holding 'repudiation parties' for leading Māori and factional supporters such as Whitmore.

The dirt of Hawke's Bay's elite was dragged through the national spotlight again in 1875, when Sheehan was elected to the House of Representatives and began trumpeting the issues from the government stage. National media went into another feeding frenzy. The *Otago Daily Times* alleged that Hawke's Bay's wealthy had 'prostituted official administration to personal aggrandisement', and that this 'robber gang' controlled the local media.[308] This was not actually true. Wood's *Hawke's Bay Herald* had long been a voice of the pastoralists out of choice and inclination, as was the new *Daily Telegraph* — though in 1872 Ormond apparently tried to curry favour with the editor by backing his effort to get a militia commission on the basis that it might 'assist in keeping him quiet'.[309] The *Evening Star* went further. Hawke's Bay was 'synonymous with land robbery', a 'land of the shepherd kings' whose 'wealth has been acquired by simply robbing the Natives of their land … and to such an extent has the moral contagion spread that the very fountains of justice are poisoned'.[310]

Karaitiana was elected MP for Eastern Māori in December, and that month Māori from across the North Island visited Pakowhai for a hui.[311] There were more meetings in 1876,[312] and McLean came under attack, decried as a 'monstrous sham and imposture' in the pages of *Te Wananga*.[313] Russell was behind much of the activity; between 1872 and 1876 he spent £10,668 on the movement, with a further £13,500 in legal fees to Sheehan.[314] His opponents responded by trying to undermine his finances, and by mid-1876 — as Ormond revealed to McLean — Russell's 'home agents will not honor [sic] his drafts nor wd [would] any bank here advance'. This was apparently Ormond's doing. 'I can't tell you in a letter the trouble I have taken over this business — repeatedly just when he thought he had arranged funds I have stopped it.'[315] It did not dent Russell's pace; his spending between February 1876 and January 1877, at just over £2,781, was higher than in any other year.[316]

For a few years Russell seemed to be making headway. In August 1876 he turned down an olive branch proffered by Ormond.[317] Then in late 1876 McLean fell ill. He resigned as Native Minister at the end of the year and died in early 1877.[318] Henare Matua told Ormond it was a 'day for establishing a truce',[319] but Russell remained unrepentant, seeing McLean's death merely as removing an obstacle to an 'ultimate triumph'.[320] He got

Repudiation party at Henry Russell's Mt. Herbert station, near Waipukurau, in February 1876. Russell sits centre; Henare Tomoana on his left.

Photographer unidentified, Alexander Turnbull Library, F-38687-1/2

on to his lawyer, H. D. Bell, calling for a 'vigorous bombardment'.[321] And he had need for speed; the repudiation movement had 'cost a great deal of money first and last.'[322] He forced the pro-settler newspaper *Te Waka Māori o Ahuriri* to close after suing it for libel,[323] a victory Renata Kawepo and Te Hāpuku celebrated by hosting a lunch in the Napier Oddfellows hall for 'members of both Houses of Parliament, professional gentlemen, leading merchants, and others, together with a large number of native chiefs'.[324]

By this time much of the steam had gone out of the effort. Julius Vogel's decision to abolish the provinces, fuelled in part by Hawke's Bay's misbehaving gentry, cut the power of local elites at a stroke. In November 1876, the Counties Act replaced the semi-autonomous provinces with 63 local counties.[325] Foot-dragging by the old guard achieved nothing — in Hawke's Bay, as the *Hawke's Bay Herald* opined, three counties were formed from the old district 'in spite of Mr Ormond'.[326] Amid this radical shift of focus, Russell's pro-provincial sentiments were old hat, and by 1877 there was little benefit other than personal satisfaction to be gained from sinking Ormond. So the movement faded; and in 1883 Russell returned to Britain.

Ngāti Kahungunu swung into the national political arena. Ormond, who was considerably more scrupulous than the Russell faction were prepared to admit, went on to a long and successful career in local politics. So did many of the other leading elite, including Sutton who — if the *Hawke's Bay Herald* is to be believed — did so to escape the taint of his land deals.[327] But New Zealand was also changing around them. A new generation of settlers, many born in New Zealand, others newly arrived from Britain, were gaining power. By the 1880s the rugged, individualistic, cowboy days of the early colony were passing, supplanted by a world of boards, national issues and new infrastructure: a world in which new arrivals from Britain, turning up in some numbers on the back of government-subsidised emigration policies, further reinforced the older colonial notion of 'home' being half a world away. The mix underpinned a renewed lurch towards the mother country that emerged with fuller force in the 1890s and beyond — a sentiment shared even by those settlers who had been born in New Zealand never left the country.

It was a significant sea-change, and Hawke's Bay was no exception. Amidst this new world with its more centralised national government, better communications around the country, and the growing power of bureaucracies, the often bitter feuds of the some-time provincial aristocracy seemed somehow out of place.

CHAPTER FOUR
Iron horse towns

In 1852, Fred Tiffen picked a 'convenient spot for a woolshed and residence' on the banks of the Tukituki. He had to. The only way to get anything heavy to Ahuriri was upriver.

'Four bales of wool were generally taken by each canoe,' he wrote, 'and it required steady balancing … On one occasion I had to go to Port Ahuriri to dry and repack wool which had so become wet.'[1] Roads — like most public works — remained elusive for years. Despite paying lip-service to philanthropy, settler-age businessmen and pastoralists did not display much enthusiasm for costs that did not benefit either their bank balances or their social status. General stores flourished. Public water supply, sewers, hospital and schools did not, although the practical need for them gradually won out over small-government voices.

These forces for intervention were further stoked by the New Zealand wars, which drove the growth of central government through the 1860s and transformed the country from a collection of often disparate provinces into a more cohesive whole. The pressure reached hurricane force the following decade, and was particularly prominent in Hawke's Bay, drawing the personalised, wild frontier world of the district into the wider embrace of the rising power of central government.

The catalyst for this centralisation was a period of economic stagnation that began in the late 1860s.[2] The downturn was driven from the south by the end of the gold boom, from the north by the cost and disruptions of the New Zealand wars. Trade dropped from its dizzying gold-rush peaks of just over £72 per capita in 1863 to a dismal £39 by 1870.[3] Hawke's Bay shared the effects. Falls in the price of wool spurred fears of 'prompt ruin',[4] and there was a mood of gloom. 'Everything is at present adverse to the colony,' an 1868 editorial in the *Hawke's Bay Herald* declared, seeing a 'very black' cloud ahead and — perhaps predictably — calling for 'more personal and household economy', more 'economy in government, and new industries.'[5] Some thought gold was an answer. The provincial government offered a £1000 prize, spurring an effort by John Ormond, Joseph Rhodes, Henry Russell, John Chambers and J. G. Kinross, but there were no useful quantities in the province.[6]

Hawke's Bay's key problem remained a lop-sided production base. By 1869, after several pushes to create small-holder settlements, the local wheat crop was still only 1.07 percent of the national total. Potatoes stood at 3.14 percent and oats a dismal 0.64 percent. While Hawke's Bay lacked Canterbury's vast plains — where the national lion's share of these crops were grown — the Hawke's Bay rate still ran at less than half the level of comparable districts such as Marlborough. Sheep, by contrast, had disproportionate place. An 1867 count showed 841,814 head, behind Otago and Canterbury, but just over 45.5 percent of the North Island total. Most of the rest were in the Wairarapa.[7] Such numbers reflected both local pastoral dominance and the fact that Hawke's Bay had escaped the worst ravages of the New Zealand wars. But development was still slow, and it was at this moment that Julius Vogel appeared on the scene.

Vogel rail, Vogel settlers

Colonial Treasurer Julius Vogel came to power alongside Donald McLean in the Fox government of 1869; and while McLean devoted his energies to improving race-relations and ending the wars, Vogel looked to longer-term answers. They made an effective double team. Vogel envisaged loans of up to £10 million — around $1.18 billion in early twenty-first century sums[8] to build communications, kick-start the economy, and insert pākehā into the bush-clad 'triangle' of the central North Island, a region that stretched from southern Hawke's Bay into the northern Wairarapa, across

Lack of roading forced early pastoralists to use waterways and beaches. In some places, such as Pourere, the practice continued for years.

Photographer unidentified, Alexander Turnbull Library, F-31505-1/2)

to Taranaki and north into the Waikato. 'I have an absorbing affection for New Zealand,' he told a friend, 'and it is intolerable for me to see its prosperity marred and retarded'.[9] Although from a mid-twentieth century perspective this looked like state intervention,[10] in reality it was a pragmatic effort to meet the issues of the 1860s, and he did not envisage government taking more than a starting role. He was shifting the focus of Victorian-age capitalist adventurism, not the structure.[11] And there was good argument for it, certainly in Hawke's Bay, where public works — such as they were — flowed around the commercial centres. Locales outside the commercial hub were often left out — in one year, Wairoa received enough money to build just one mile of roading.[12] Vogel's policy also consolidated the role of central government, a move accelerated by his abolition of provincial governments in 1876.

The immediate excitement flowed around rail. Steam was the icon of nineteenth century greatness, a status symbol — and a way to grease the wheels of the economy.[13] By the mid-1860s envious eyes in Hawke's Bay were looking south to Canterbury, which was building a provincial line at local expense.[14] The vast bushlands in the south of Hawke's Bay — which Fred Tiffen thought could be easily roaded[15] — were a more substantial barrier for rail, but J. M. Stuart called for a line through the bush in March 1866.[16] McLean liked the idea,[17] but the problem was paying for it. Debate fell foul of national arguments, including the issue of gauge. A government committee of 1867 came down in favour of unified lines — and strongly against 3'6".[18] But that gauge was what the country got in the 1870 Railways Act, largely to keep costs down. Vogel also planned to offset the expense by giving land to the contractors, John Brodgen & Sons. Even so, national public works spending hit stratospheric levels, rising from £284,000 in 1871 to £2,332,000 in 1874.[19]

Locating the line provoked other disputes. Most of Hawke's Bay's elite wanted rail near their properties — though not too close. The Provincial Council backed it,[20] and Ormond sent Charles Weber to investigate the 'most practical lines' for a railway between Napier and the 'Manawatu bush' as early as October 1870. He came up with two routes to Karamu — one from Ahuriri Harbour, the other from Napier. The latter included a station at Farndon 'to accommodate the Clive, Waitangi and Pakowhai' districts,' and he thought that at £1000 a mile this would be the 'cheapest line to be constructed in New Zealand'.[21] Ormond reported a few months later to the Minister for Public Works that Weber had found a 'really good' line from Waipukurau to the Manawatu gorge.[22] Ormond negotiated the state purchase of the 'Seventy Mile Bush' block that year, pushing it through the Waipawa land court.[23] The Heretaunga dispute was at its height; Karaitiana stepped in to ramp the price up, delaying the sale.[24] An exasperated Ormond confessed to Minister of Works William Gisborne that he would 'be very glad when the final deed is signed'.[25]

Taradale landowners were dismayed at the discovery that their district would miss out, but even representations to the Provincial Council did not alter the plan. John Brodgen and Sons got the contract to build the first 18 miles (28.9 km) of track in August 1872.[26] The line from Napier, with its puffing Dubs 0-4-0 construction locomotives, was complete as far as Waitangi by October that year. But it was October 1874 before the line reached Karamu. As far as Ormond was concerned Brogdens had 'completely failed in carrying out their contract', and the tender for the next 8½ miles of line went to public tender.[27] Ormond refused to pay for a public celebration to mark the arrival of the line at Karamu junction, but Brogdens put on a train anyway. The event had elements of farce: as Bernard Chambers observed, they only killed one sheep on the way to Hastings, 'on … the north side of Pakowhai.'[28] Gales tore down a marquee, then demolished the half-built Karamu station roof, 'carrying along the corrugated iron like bits of paper for hundreds of yards.'[29] The settlers jammed into William Goodwin's railway hotel, where Joseph Rhodes led the toasts. Hampden settler G. G. Carlyon's daughter

A 2-6-0 J-class locomotive at Te Aute during a trial run from Napier to Waipukurau, 1887. The type of locomotive — not to be confused with the later J-class 4-8-2 of 1939 — was introduced in the South Island in 1874 and this example was later brought to Hawke's Bay. The motley collection of carriages is typical of the era.

William Williams, E. R. Williams Collection, Alexander Turnbull Library, G-25481-1/1

christened the locomotive 'Miss Hastings', and the four-car train chugged back to Napier.[30]

Progress further south was problematic, partly owing to 'an error of judgement on the part of the engineer who surveyed the line',[31] but also because the track crossed Te Hāpuku's stockyard at Poukawa. The old chief wrote to Ormond to complain about the plan in late 1874:

> this is the same way you acted about the road. You both strove to bring the road over my graves and it was only through my perserverance that Mr Cooper and Henry [Tiffen] consented to take the road below and now with this you must hearken to my wish to leave the line for the Railway on the swamp side of the stockyards.[32]

Ormond recommended a deviation at 'trifling' cost, telling McLean 'you are aware of the difficulty of dealing with a case like this …'[33] There were more problems the following year when the line occupied Māori land,[34] but the commercial side of the venture was more successful. Traps, carts and wagons fed passengers and cargo into the stations from the outlying districts. The early Dubs were joined by Blair and Blackett

A 2-6-0 J-class locomotive with another carriage collection on the Matamau viaduct north of Dannevirke, probably 1887. The train appears to be posed for the camera; passengers cluster at the windows and on the carriage platforms.

William Williams, glass negative, E. R. Williams Collection, Alexander Turnbull Library, G-25505-1/1

0-6-0T F-type tanks, bellowing back and forth between Napier and Hastings with ever-heavier loads of goods and people. Although, as Harriett Russell observed, the speed was 'not terrifying',[35] rail transport was cheaper than ox-cart as early as 1874.[36] Business re-oriented to suit the timetables and carters sprang into action — Grant's Mail Coaches even advertised their connection with their train as a selling point.[37] In 1876, estimated revenues from the short stretch were thought likely to top £20,574 — around $2.5 million in early twenty-first century values.[38] The scale of rail traffic was unprecedented, and as Napier's local railway manager reported in 1879, the low-cost rails of the permanent way were 'too light'.[39]

By July 1874 some 40.25 miles (64.77 km) of line had been authorised between Napier and Waipukurau, for an estimated cost of £220,000, around $24.2 million in early twenty-first century values.[40] A branch to Ahuriri was completed in November 1874. Pakipaki was reached in early 1875, and progress after that was faster; the rail-head reached Waipukurau late in 1876 and Takapau in March 1877.[41] Just over 58 miles

(93.3 km) of line were operating that year, second only to the Wanganui district around the North Island.[42] Borne over the rugged terrain south of the plains on trestle-viaducts, the line bypassed Norsewood, took in Ormondville and got to Kopua — a tiny locale amidst the bush — in 1878, though Ormondville passengers had to flag the train down until a station was built in 1883.[43] The line even had a name, the 'Wellington-Napier railway', in anticipation of an actual link.[44] There were hopes that the rail-head might connect to the line being built to the Manawatu, and calls for an extension to Woodville and beyond were endorsed at an energetic meeting of the Napier Chamber of Commerce. Other sentiment called for inclusion in a main trunk,[45] but all such hopes were premature. The Wellington and Manawatu Railway company reached Longburn in 1886,[46] but the Hawke's Bay line did not make the connection to Palmerston North until 1891. And it was 1897 before the government rail-head from the Wairarapa finally reached Woodville.[47]

"By July 1874 some 40.25 miles of line had been authorised between Napier and Waipukurau."

Vogel matched his rail venture with a determined effort to populate the bushlands of Taranaki, Manawatu, Hawke's Bay and the Wairarapa. A great swathe of forest — variously the Forty, Seventy or Ninety Mile Bush, depending on where it was measured from[48] — stretched from the southern end of the Ruataniwha Plains into the northern reaches of the Wairarapa. With the exception of the wide Oringi clearing, which Ormond partly leased, this was impenetrable territory. Vogel intended to settle this area with migrants who would convert these regions to farmland. Some at the time saw it as eco-vandalism; in the mid-1880s, gazing on a desolate landscape of blackened stumps, James Inglis condemned Hawke's Bay's 'wholesale denudation' which, he claimed, would 'exact its retribution in widespread ruin and desolation.'[49] Vogel himself had conservationist leanings, revealed by his forest legislation; but as G. H. Scholefield remarked in 1904, the 'doctrine of progress declared that the bush must be destroyed under the guise of improvements.'[50] Others lamented the loss of commercial milling opportunity. Beneath it all was the political issue of denying Māori a refuge.

Who might settle these rugged lands was another issue. Vogel was inspired by stories of Scandinavians working bush successfully in the Manawatu,[51] and sent Isaac Featherston and Francis Dillon Bell to scout Denmark and Norway for prospective settlers. They were helped by Bror Erik Friberg, who emigrated to New Zealand in 1866;[52] and by early 1872 the first two shiploads were on the way to Ahuriri. This was the origin of southern Hawke's Bay's Scandinavian community. How willing some of the new migrants were to travel half way around the world is unclear;

Stumps and bush; clearing at Matamau, 1880s. Nineteenth nineteenth-century pioneers usually saw the transformation as a demonstration of the power of Victorian-age science and industry.

William Williams, E. R. Williams Collection, Alexander Turnbull Library, G-25788-1/1

and the 57 single women reported to be on board the first ship — all with 'blue eyes and flaxen hair', as far as the *Hawke's Bay Herald* was concerned, were greedily welcomed as potential servants.[53]

Hawke's Bay was an eye-opener for the new settlers. Vogel was determined to reduce the mortality rates common on the voyage out; but the first migrant ship to Hawke's Bay under the new scheme, the *Hovding*, arrived in Napier at the beginning of December 1873 after a difficult 110-day passage during which several children died.[54] An effort to indict *Hovding*'s captain, Carl Nordby, failed because it turned out he did not come under the jurisdiction of the Emigration Act 1855. Ormond could not take the matter further. However, he thought the migrants a 'good useful class of people' despite their lack of English.[55]

What the Scandinavians thought is another matter; their passage out was a mere aperitif for the hardships of southern Hawke's Bay. When they arrived, the women were put up in barracks in Napier, and the men went south where they found they had to clear bush for the railway to work off £6 for their passage and journey south through Hawke's Bay.[56] Then they had to fell their own properties, allocated by ballot.[57] Rough split-timber huts made poor houses. 'Some poor women cried when they saw their home,' one settler wrote, 'while others with a weaker sense of humour perhaps, laughed.'[58] Many eked out an income, splitting railway sleepers at a shilling and threepence a shot,[59] supplemented with sales of 'Jew's ear' fungus. Their new land was prone to fire, deliberate and otherwise — an 'untidy story', as one historian put it.[60] The landscape became a dismal waste of stumps, wood debris and regrowth. Fire remained an ever-present hazard, underscored by disastrous blazes in 1888.[61] Timber was sent north to Napier and out, making up 58 percent of all railed goods in 1885–86.[62]

Towns followed. Some were named in Scandinavian fashion. Dannevirke — 'Danevirk' to some originals[63] — was joined by Mellemskov (Eketahuna) in the northern Wairarapa. Other town names were English-style, such as Norsewood and Mauriceville. Around 4000 Scandinavians settled in New Zealand, many of them across southern Hawke's Bay and the northern Wairarapa, in the ten years from 1872. They brought much of their culture with them, including the Lutheran church and such culinary delights as pancake balls.[64] By the 1880s, as the forests melted under axe, saw and fire, many were turning to dairying.

In one of history's ironies, although Scandinavia gave lasting character to Hawke's Bay's southern settlement — one that still featured in town promotions 140 years later — the majority of new arrivals under the Vogel system were British, many from Scotland, others from Milton-on-Wychwood and its nearby villages. Why so many of those from this small Oxfordshire area sought new lives in New Zealand has puzzled historians. Social tensions culminating in the general 1872 'revolt of the fields' and the imprisonment of the 'Ascott Martyrs' in Milton-on-Wychwood seem to have played a part.[65] Certainly this was the case for Philip Pratley, who emigrated to Hawke's Bay on the *Mongol* after his wife became one of the 'martyrs'. In a classic expression of chain migration, he drew other relatives with them.[66]

> "...the 57 single women reported to be on board the first ship — all with 'blue eyes and flaxen hair', as far as the *Hawke's Bay Herald* was concerned, were greedily welcomed as potential servants."

Town boosters

Rail did much to offset the fact that Hawke's Bay remained a pastoral province with skewed economy and demographics. As Ernest Weston

A ssettler family stand around a stump for William Williams' camera at Matamau, northeast of Dannevirke, 1880s.

William Williams, E. R. Williams Collection, Alexander Turnbull Library, G-25773-1/1

observed as late as 1888, Napier would 'be a town of great importance if she had more small settlers around her instead of run-holders. Some have as much as 75,000 acres and do not employ a hundred men'.[67] The power of railway was never more evident than in the way towns flourished or died at its hands. Wairoa was too far north; as late as 1878, the rateable value of the whole Wairoa Riding was just £15,950,[68] and rail did not reach the district until the twentieth century. Hampden (Tikokino) dwindled forever when the rail took the eastern route. Dannevirke, founded in 1872, was essentially created by rail and flourished. Further south, Woodville at first attracted only speculators, among them John Ormond and C. H. Weber;[69] but more substantial settlement grew when Ormond set aside 20,000 acres for the Woodville Small Farms Association, attracting a group of Methodists who arrived as railway workers.[70]

The largest of Hawke's Bay's railway towns was Hastings, founded in 1873–74 as a consequence of the decision to route the line through Karamu. Legend names former gold-miner, labourer and small-holder Francis Hicks as founder.[71] In fact he was but one of several small landowners who saw opportunity in plans to run the line through

Another Hawke's Bay bush town, Weber, early 1890s. Limed roads, five-rail fences and grass betray efforts to settle; but even years after first clearing the district remains a wasteland of stumps and debris.

Photographer unidentified, Hawke's Bay Museum 5550

Karamu. Hicks, James Boyle, Gilbert Norris and Guy Hamilton, among others, obtained an initial foothold when a cash-strapped Tanner offered land in exchange for ploughing.[72] Later he sold small blocks varying from 22 to 100 acres. There was talk of founding a town around the Karamu rail-head as early as May 1873,[73] a year or more before the line reached the station. Tanner joined the band-wagon, apparently suggesting Hastings in commemoration of Sir Warren Hastings of India.[74] This was public knowledge by June,[75] and was the only name ever considered — it is on the original town plan. Although 'Hicksville' appeared on the deed conveying land for the railway station, it was never applied to the town.[76]

Repudiation was at its height, but Karaitiana's opposition did not dampen land sales.[77] Hicks' sale in July 1873 raised £3500, around $391,500 in early twenty-first century money.[78] He threw a champagne party and levered himself up the ladder, buying property near Cambridge. Boyle — John Chambers' nephew-in-law[79] — followed with 'South Hastings'. This became 'the city of the plains' in the puff-talk of the day.[80] Within the month Tanner had 80 urban sections for sale, and the *Hawke's Bay Almanac* of 1875 trumpeted that Hastings, though 'as yet only in its infancy' was, thanks to the railway, a 'township of great promise'.[81]

> "Town fathers sought to promote their own towns as desirable social and economic centres."

Although some cynics dismissed such pitches as 'wild ideas of the future importance of the place,'[82] there was little question about the power of railway to open up districts. Perhaps more crucial from the historical point of view was the language that framed such talk, which encapsulated the reality of Hawke's Bay's frontier-age urban world. Town fathers sought to promote their own towns as desirable social and economic centres. Their amalgam of social hope, religious and economic zeal — in a word, boosterism — embodied what one historian has called an 'exaltation of municipal government'.[83] It was a shared urban phenomenon around the Victorian-age world and on the Pacific Rim frontier, first revealed to historians in a mid-twentieth century study of what was called 'marvellous Melbourne'.[84]

Settler-age Hawke's Bay towns had the period ethos in spades. There was competition for industry, population, commerce, wealth, grandeur of civic buildings,[85] town amenities, scale of the town district, and rivalry even over what James Buckingham called 'social balance'.[86] At the time this was often equated with physical structure; Tanner summed up the ethos in his call for a 'symmetrical township' that could grow while 'preserving regularity of plan',[87] with roads 'a chain wide',[88] and space for the essentials of the civic world in this age of urban idealism — 'school, athenaeum and town hall,'[89] along with wide parklands.[90]

Boosterism was competitive at every level. When Hastings gained a town board in January 1884, local pastoralists vied to be seen as town father or, at best, its 'eldest son'.[91] Town amenities were a particular hot-point of competition, especially if they involved technology. When Waipukurau got a telegraph relay station in 1868, Waipawa folk promptly demanded one of their own.[92] News that Napier might be investigating electricity in 1885 prompted the Hastings Town Board to introduce the telephone.[93] Status also flowed from comparison with other towns — as one land agent told buyers in 1885, Hastings would not become the 'Christchurch of the North' — Christchurch would become Hastings of the south'.[94] Later the place was called the 'garden of our district', likely to become the envied spot of the North Island'.[95]

Everything was underpinned by a race for scale — mostly of population, wealth, borough administrative areas and public buildings. Size counted, and amid this race for status, rail-fed towns in open areas — notably Hastings and Waipukurau — had advantages over places such as Dannevirke, where urban areas had first to be hacked out of the bush. Hastings won, largely in consequence of Thomas Tanner's financial woes. Three colossal sales carved an ambitious urban area from his Riverslea station between 1879 and 1889, driven partly by his self-appointed role

Waipawa, mid-1880s, Edward Bibby's store on the left, Daniel Moroney's Settlers' Hotel to the right.

Burton Brothers, Burton Brothers Collection, Alexander Turnbull Library, F-45058-1/2

as colonial squire, but more particularly because he needed the cash. Karaitiana was right; Heretaunga had been too much for Tanner to afford, even with business partners. The 1200-acre sale of 1879, coming on the cusp of economic downturn, had an air of desperation in its easy terms,[96] and even a late-repudiationist effort to disrupt the sale did not disturb buyers.[97]

Agriculture — the very antithesis of pastoralism because of its labour-intensive land use — was a key part of the Hastings mix, driven to a large extent by the fertility of the alluvial plains. In 1885, when Tanner shed nearly a third of his remaining Heretaunga holdings for town and agricultural sections, land agents Hoadley & Sons trumpeted the suitability of the land for 'hops, tobacco, European flax, beetroot and grain' while industries for 'tobacco, oilcake, linen and woollen goods' were 'proposed to be immediately established.'[98] They were not: and in line with Hoadley's promises that Hastings' land was an 'improving investment of undoubted character and value,' most of the sections went to speculators — among them some of the 'apostles'. By 1882, 90 of the 195 landowners in town were absentee landlords.[99]

Waipukurau, mid-1880s. By this time Henry Russell's 'model village' had developed significantly since he set it up, a rural service town of significant import — a point underscored by the arrival of the railway.

Burton Brothers, Burton Brothers Collection, Alexander Turnbull Library, F- 79289-1/2

Another pivot of urban competition was the status accorded by scale. Every town styled itself a potential 'city' irrespective of actual population or room to grow, and there was hot competition for status. When Napier became a borough, Hastings had to follow. Other areas lagged. Dannevirke did not become a borough until 1897,[100] while Havelock — stunted by the growth of Hastings — remained a Road Board district until 1912.[101] Municipal rivalries also flourished in other ways, often reflected in ever-grander town halls, business premises and civic amenities. In 1880, before Hastings even had a town board, C. A. FitzRoy set up a Town Hall Company and raised £900, around $128,000 in early twenty-first century money, by subscription.[102] He had the structure raised on Omahu Road. But although featuring such acts as 'Washington Norton's Famous Merrymakers',[103] the hall was not well patronised and in 1889 reporter H. H. Murdoch declared that its prospects were 'as cheerful as ever … the ventilators are going round and chirping merrily, and the echo is in good working order.'[104]

Such experience underscored one of the realities of boosterism; ambition outstripped reality. Hastings seemed to have fallen into the trap. In 1889 the town administrative district encompassed 5000 acres, putting the town well on the way to city status;[105] but most of it was empty fields. As Robert Dobson put it, the town was 'too large for the population.'[106] Part of the cause was an abortive effort by the town board to expand their rating district and fund a sewer system. But the whole was suffused by idealism, and in this age of town boosters and status envy, size counted.

Hastings' lack of a sewer underscored an issue shared by all Hawke's Bay towns of the era. In theory private enterprise should have provided amenities ranging from sewers to water piping. In practice these lagged. As early as 1882, Robert Wellwood petitioned the Heretaunga Road Board to do something about Hastings' deep and noisome drains.[107] But it took a typhoid scare before any action was taken,[108] and even when a town board was formed, they were warned not to 'rush blindly into expense'.[109] Amid a mind-set that associated physical dirt with moral decay, by-laws prohibited 'filth, refuse and rubbish of any kind'.[110] That did not prevent it accumulating: and although it was clear that period ideology had no answer to human effluent, still there were protests from free-marketeers that the town was subject to 'grandmotherly government'.[111]

Competitive-minded Hastings fathers doubtless drew satisfaction from the fact that contemporary Napier was worse off — in 1873 a town

The nineteenth century urban social phenomenon known as 'boosterism' catapulted Hastings into the forefront of the district, but civic works lagged; and when this picture was taken towards the end of the century., both road and footpath remain to be sealed.

Photographer unidentified, Alexander Turnbull Library, PICT-000038

of 'undisturbed drowsiness, without street lamps, without gas, without water, and without a municipal corporation'.[112] Henry Tiffen thought it a shame that a town the size of Napier should be reliant on cart and barrel for its domestic water. There was pure water aplenty in the aquifer beneath the town, some of it already tapped.[113] But it was not reticulated, and nobody was prepared to stump up the estimated £1800, about $208,000 in early 21st century money, required to build a reservoir.[114] Water carters, some of them dipping from the limpid Tutaekuri, did not make up the difference,[115] but the main problem was lack of fire-fighting capacity. Townsfolk also had to endure the local swamp — a 'pestiferous nuisance' that defied even the Swamp Nuisance Act of July 1873, intended to force locals to fill it in.[116] Just to add spice, a 'disagreeable lake' filled Clive Square.[117] Pundits declared the town 'not a healthy place' in summer.[118]

> "Competitive-minded Hastings fathers doubtless drew satisfaction from the fact that contemporary Napier was worse off…"

The issue came to a head when Vogel-subsidised immigration overwhelmed local services. Ormond called a public meeting, and a town board elected in January 1875 set about organising a water supply, ultimately sinking six wells producing 420,000 gallons a day.[119] By 1877 Napier even had a steam fire-engine,[120] causing hilarity in 1885 when a 'well known glazier' managed to shatter windows with the water jet during brigade practise. His day job did not, the paper declared, 'account for the windows being broken, no matter what the censorious may say.'[121] More to the point, in 1878 new mayor J. H. Vautier sought to raise loans of £70,000 — around $8.85 million in early 21st century terms — to handle pressing sewerage, reclamation and drainage issues.[122]

Napier was not alone in overdue works. Waipawa even lacked a fire bell. When a blaze threatened to destroy the town centre in 1886 the best that could be done was to put the Napier engine on the train and whisk it south.[123] Dannevirke did not get a borough water supply until the mid-1890s, and lacked its own civic fire-fighting equipment until 1906.[124] A fair number of these works foundered at the hands of ratepayers. Bottom-up reluctance to support council loans put paid to efforts to give Dannevirke a sewer system in 1895, among other works around the district.[125] Rural districts were often worse off.

One of the biggest issues was provincial roading, which followed the major export routes and had never been properly developed. Even provincial feeder roads often fell behind, despite the advent of local Roads Boards: the first coach did not reach Taihape until 1893.[126]

Practical disdain towards public spending stood in sharp contrast to settler business life. The 'invisible hand' of the unfettered market did not

provide for public safety, health, welfare, or education, but it made a handy job of turning a profit for some businessmen. Pastoral demands topped the Hawke's Bay list. In 1880, ironmongers Ruddock and Fryer offered pastoralists and farmers a remarkable range of mowers, reapers, chaff cutters, ploughs, — 'single and double furrow'— winnowing machines, 'for hand and power', rollers, harrows, even 'Turnip and Marigold pulpers'.[127] H. Williams' ironmongery sold blasting powder and dynamite — the latter at 'greatly reduced rates' — with 'instructions given to those unaccustomed to the use of it'.[128] R. W. Jensen offered 'jewellery, watches, clocks, etc' at sale prices, disingenuously declaring 'this is no trade puff'.[129] Even tropical fruit such as oranges, bananas, peanuts, pawpaw and 'dessicated cocoanuts' [sic], imported via Auckland by P. A. Herman, could be bought in Napier's green-groceries.[130] J. S. Welsman's 'The Pharmacy' opened in both Napier and Hastings, offering 'Pratt's Cough Linctus, Tonic Worm Powder, Irish Moss Balsam, Quinine Tonic Wine and Odontalgic Elixir for toothache'.[131] This commercial world generated its own social life — as As Alec Rainbow recalled, the Hastings

Coach on the Tarawera saddle, Napier-Taupō road, probably during the 1890s, with the driver apparently calling the horses to greater effort,. Spare horse at the rear is noteworthy. This road had one advantage over others: it had begun as a Māori route and was adopted for military purposes in the 1860s, ensuring an initial road was built and paid for. The journey to Taupō by coach was nonetheless arduous.

Photographer unidentified, Post & Telegraph Collection, Alexander Turnbull Library, F-19629-1/2

blacksmith — for all the fascination of 'the smell of the horses and the phizz of the hot steel in the water', was also a 'gossip shop'.[132]

Although harking to British urban ideals, Hawke's Bay's settler-age towns looked distinctly frontier American, in part a function of available building materials. Where stone was available — such as Oamaru — New Zealand's settlers emulated Britain. Where it was not, meaning virtually every other frontier town in New Zealand, the style of the age was usually Wild West. Common building materials lent force to common social values; Napier, Hastings, Wairoa, Waipukurau or Waipawa could have done double duty as Dodge City. All shared the same rows of clap-board buildings, limed, dusty roads, the sense of newness with untamed verges and a landscape where trees had yet to grow, and the piles of detritus dumped higgledy-piggledy in empty sections. Even the hitching-posts outside the saloons were much the same; and inside them, men on both sides of the Pacific did 'full justice' — as the period term usually put it — to whiskey, cards and billiards.

Provincial life swirled around these towns, a complex, sophisticated whirl of events suffused with the values of the time, particularly self-betterment — financially, socially and intellectually. This was pushed along in Napier with the help of the Athenaeum and Mechanics Institute, a library opened in 1863. As McLean remarked, the 'want of such a place' had been felt for 'a very long time'.[133] By 1877 the Athenaeum, solidly housed in its Browning Street premises, owned some 1500 books.[134] Education sometimes doubled as entertainment; one Napier visitor in the 1880s attended a 'free lecture on spiritualism in the Hoadley salerooms' and thought the 'larrikins were so noisy that I almost thought there would be ructions'.[135]

Much revolved around local hotels. Despite the hopes for town halls and athenaeums, social life in New Zealand's rugged colonial frontier inevitably focussed on hotels and their public bars. These were the public centres of their towns in practise, offering not just accommodation but spaces for townsfolk to gather and socialise. Business deals were often made in them — and in Havelock North, hotels even provided a public space for inquests[136] They were, in short, gathering places for their communities, the 'hub of the countryside', as one settler put it.[137] Dozens flourished across Hawke's Bay. In Napier, there were four in Shakespeare Road alone. Others around the district included Wairoa's Clyde Hotel, the Duke of Edinburgh in Porangahau, Waipawa's Empire Hotel, the London Hotel on Napier's spit, the Tavistock in Waipukurau, the Sawyer's Arms in Hampden (Tikokino), and the Patangata Hotel.[138]

> "As Alec Rainbow recalled, the Hastings blacksmith — for all the fascination of 'the smell of the horses and the phizz of the hot steel in the water', was also a 'gossip shop'."

Many were put up on a shoestring. Harriet Russell, arriving in Napier one day in 1874, confessed to a friend that Napier's Criterion hotel Hotel was a 'vast improvement on the Masonic', but still 'very slightly built [,] one can hear every noise'.[139]

Competition was intense and pivoted, it seemed, largely on the quality of liquor and billiards tables. The Farndon Hotel, 'opposite the railway station, West Clive', featured Alcock's Billiard Tables, 'every comfort … large bath rooms … good stabling and paddocks' — and, of course, 'wines, spirits and malt liquors, of the best qualities'. Arthur McCartney's Greenmeadows Hotel advertised its Alcock's Prize Tables 'just … imported from Melbourne', a place where 'a good glass of ale is always to be had'. The Takapau Hotel was 'replete with every comfort and accommodation for travellers and visitors', including 'wines, spirits and malt liquors of the best brands'. James Johnstone marketed his Ferry Hotel, on Napier's Northern Spit, as launch-point for the three-day Taupō coach journey. 'Travellers crossing the Ferry the night before can always depend on being comfortably breakfasted before commencing their journey.'[140] H. R. Clist promoted his Pacific Hotel in Havelock North with what one resident

Napier's Masonic Hotel, 1870s, complete with self-promotional street signs and an audience for the photographer. The fact that they are virtually all male, with the exception of a woman on the left and a child mid-frame, speaks much about period society. Hotels were the life and soul of provincial social life through the colonial period. Stones to separate footpath from road underscore the state of Napier's public works of the day.

Photographer unidentified, Alexander Turnbull Library, F-8574-1/2

> "Times changed for Hawke's Bay in the 1880s as New Zealand entered a period of significant ...upheaval."

called an 'outstanding' sign, a 'mural of a ship in full sail on a rippling sea ... painted by a huge man familiarly known as Billy Swanson'.[141]

Theatres offered other amusements. Venues included Napier's Theatre Royal, the Gaiety and the Oddfellows Hall. The English Opera Company swept through Napier in 1863, offering 'perhaps the best musical treat ever heard in this Province'. Later there were such contemporary touring spectacles as 'Thompson's Diorama of the War in Zululand', which did the rounds in 1882, and locally-developed song-and-dance spectacles. In 1885, St Leon's Circus opened in Napier's Clive Square, 'sure to be largely patronised'.[142] Exotic beasts continued to entertain Hawke's Bay folk for years, and in 1909, elephants from a passing circus were pressed into service to haul a traction engine out of the Waipawa River.[143]

Sporting life was quintessentially British, with a colonial twist, horse racing appeared appeared early and became well established; most towns and locales included a racing or jockey club. A Tradesman's Cricket Club was founded in Napier in 1874, and two years later a Napier Cricket Club, Chess Club, gymnasium, a bowling alley and even a roller-skating rink opened. There were regattas on local rivers, and the wide Ahuriri lagoon prompted citizens to form a sailing club.[144] Often the clubs acted as social centres — as in 1885 when the Napier Rowing Club provided a 'surprise for the public in the shape of a first-class minstrel and burlesque entertainment'.[145]

Highs and lows

Times changed for Hawke's Bay in the 1880s as New Zealand generallly entered a period of significant social upheaval and economic downturn. Historians have often called it the 'long depression',[146] and times were indeed hard: but the economic problems seem to have been partly driven by the consequences of dislocation as the economy matured. This is not to deny the difficulties. The 1878 collapse of the City of Glasgow Bank, usually given as arbiter of the downturn, led to a period that economically and socially stretched the colony, but which did not break it. Land and agricultural prices fell, there was net emigration, and some elite fell on hard times; however, economic data suggests that at the same time the economy was switching from a collection of regional economies into a national entity. Public works such as the Main Trunk Line, begun that decade, made a significant contribution to prosperity, and a variety of small industries emerged — including dairying in southern Hawke's Bay. Vogel, in short, had done much to lay a solid foundation.[147]

Looking north along Napier's Hastings Street during the 1880s. Most of those in the picture, including a woman pushing a pram, are looking at the camera, although it is otherwise apparently unstaged. This was typical of an age when photography involved custom-prepared glass plates and prominent equipment — in this case set up in the road. The fact of the photographer being obviously there made such instances a public moment.

Burton Brothers, Burton Brothers Collection, Alexander Turnbull Library, F-654-1/2

Against this background, the rise in unemployment, arguably, was also a reflection of seasonal shifts,[148] and a function of deeper dislocation as the economy re-balanced. Of course, this did not reduce the plight of those who found themselves without work in the welfare-less colony.[149] This had always been an issue. 'I do not know what I shall do next,' George Maunder declared to his sister as early as 1869.[150] It was worse in the 1880s. Both the issues of seasonal shift and wider economic dislocation were true in Hawke's Bay, where Ernest and Harold Weston trudged north in the early autumn of 1888, looking for work. It was the off-season — but Ernest's diary reveals little that smacked of general depression. Dannevirke was 'quite a new town' with clean buildings and 'plenty doing'. Waipukurau was 'tidy and clean', while he was struck by the 'immense hotels' of Waipawa. They pushed through to Gwavas, found no accommodation at Maraekakaho, and reached Hastings one evening at dusk, alerted by a gasometer that loomed 'up against the sky with the moon showing behind it'. However, it seemed that while general prosperity was one thing, finding casual work off-season in a

James J. Niven's Napier works during the 1890s. Some economists have argued that the depression of the 1880s was also a period of re-adjustment from a colonial economy to a more complex socio-economic environment with balanced demographics. Small industries such as Niven's played a role in the economic transformation.

Photographer unidentified, Mr MacRae Collection, Alexander Turnbull Library, F-146138-1/2

pastoral province quite another. They gravitated to Napier, where there was 'nothing, nothing to do, unless you push yourself to the fore among a lot of roughs at card playing etc.' The brothers found sanctuary in the Athenaeum. 'if it weren't for these in many townships, goodness only knows how idle people are to amuse themselves whilst waiting for something to turn up.'[151]

Most of Hawke's Bay's elite survived these years, not least because sale prices for greasy merino wool hovered around 8–10 shillings a pound for much of the decade.[152] Financial problems did not always flow from a poor general economy. M. R. Miller put all his properties up for sale in October 1884 because he had 'by far too many irons in the fire' and reportedly found that his own interests were a 'secondary consideration' to those of his managers.[153] Kinross was one of several hammered when the City of Glasgow Bank collapsed.[154] Others fell altogether, among them Thomas Tanner; but his collapse seems to have been independent of the wider economy. His problem was that his aspired lifestyle — that of a rich country squire — had never matched his income. An 1872 sheep return revealed 8,051 sheep on Tanner's Riverslea station, but his more abstemious neighbour J. N. Williams had 9,504 and another 7,257 at Kereru.[155] A disastrous flirtation with hops cost Tanner around £43,000, and by late 1888 he was in debt to the tune of £80,000 to the Northern

Investment Company and £60,000 to the Bank of New South Wales,[156] all up about $24.1 million in early twenty-first century values.[157]

The Northern Investment Company belonged to John Ormond, J. H. Coleman, J. N. Williams and John Chambers — and money won out over both friendship and even business association. They foreclosed in March 1889 when Tanner defaulted on interest payments. Riverslea fell prey to mortgagee sale, fuelling the major growth of Hastings. An embittered Tanner saw conspiracy, but despite the support of Robert Stout, lost a court case in 1890.[158] Just to top things off, his magnificent house — purchased for him by his nephew F. L. Gordon — burned down a few years later.[159] Tanner never forgave his friends, sought political revenge, and almost upset Opposition leader William Russell's safe Heretaunga seat in the 1893 elections.[160] But Tanner's experiences were relatively rare. For most of the pastoral elite the 1880s were years of opportunity as export markets opened up for a whole new product — meat.

Hawke's Bay's wealthy had made fortunes from the fleece, mostly Merino, which was better for wool than for meat. Other breeds offered

Napier, looking north along the Tutaekuri River bank, late 1880s. The town stretches to the right, the 'pestiferous nuisance' of a swamp to the left, with the railway line snaking through, partly behind the line of houses, its course betrayed by the signal mid-frame above the punt. Tree growth underscores the fact that it is a generation since the town was founded; but the sparsity of houses on the hill is noteworthy.
William Williams, E. R. Williams Collection, Alexander Turnbull Library, G-25613-1/1

Onepoto gully, Napier, during the 1880s. Mataruahou — 'the hill' remains grassed, but telegraph lines running around Corunna Bay underscore the pace of development.
William Williams, Alexander Turnbull Library, F-15735-1/2

better eating potential, but the problem was finding a market. John Chambers sent carcases to Auckland for sale as early as 1859, though without much success — Kinross put his failure down to 'prejudice' and 'butcher combinations.'[161] The more crucial issue was getting that meat to market and then to domestic tables before it spoiled. As early as 1868 the *Hawke's Bay Herald* opined that prosperity would not come until 'the processes of boiling down and meat preserving are in full operation, and until fresh industries are ready to take the place of wool growing.'[162] It was an apt point, and the 'great question of meat preservation' exercised local minds for years.[163] There was 'somewhat wild' talk of live sheep exports to Britain, despite an expectation that they would not arrive in saleable condition.[164] Chambers got involved in a boiling-down works and experimented with other techniques, including packing the meat in straw, soaking it in brine, or potting it in tallow. When refrigeration technology emerged in the 1870s he invented a blast-freezer which he tried to patent in 1881.[165] The system was efficient,[166] but he was turned down for lack of specification. He persisted, building a working model in 1885.[167]

In the event, Chambers was pipped at the post by Otago businessmen, who began frozen meat exports in 1882; but that October, Chambers, Tanner, C. J. Nairn, Henry Russell, H. H. Bridge and G. M. Waterhouse stumped up £30,000 between them — about $4.42 million in early 21st century money — to build Hawke's Bay's first freezing works on the Ahuriri spit.[168] Competition was tight. Henare Tomoana donated land for William Nelson's works, opened near Hastings at the same time. Nelson 'was subjected to a good deal of quiet chaff' for his audacity, but the venture paid off.[169] The freezer ship *Turakina* reached Napier in March 1884 to take carcases to Britain at 2½d a pound. Visitors amused themselves playing with snowballs on the deck.[170]

Steamships became common during the decade, slashing transit times and offering economies of scale.[171] These innovations, along with a growing dairy industry — made possible by the invention of mechanical separators — added strings to New Zealand's export bow, though it was the early 1890s before the refrigeration-driven export boom really began.[172] And it took the First World War 'commandeer' to make New Zealand meat and dairy products both acceptable in Britain and socially decisive for New Zealand.[173]

Sydney Johnston (1841–1917), owner of Orua Wharo station.

Alexander St. Clair Inglis, F-26746-1/2

Growing fortunes and imminent retirement prompted fresh spending among Hawke's Bay's elite. Some of Hawke's Bay's self-made gentry — including Henry and Purvis Russell — returned to Britain, where colonial wealth purchased status.[174] Others, among them Henry Tiffen, Ormond, Walter Shrimpton and Chambers, preferred the high life in Hawke's Bay; and the late 1880s brought new expressions of opulence. William Russell thought it all far too pretentious,[175] but his sentiments were in a minority. Grand homes remained a key to social status across the district, and architect C. T. Natusch obliged with a succession of magnificent designs, including the new Carlyon station house at Gwavas.[176] Sydney Johnson had a magnificent ballroom added to his Orua Wharo home.[177] All were outdone in the end by Mason Chambers, who hired Auckland architect W. H. Gummer to build a fabulous mansion in the latest modernist stylings on his Tauroa property in 1915–16.[178]

Any excuse sufficed to hold a dance or display status in these last days of the old settler world. When Sydney Johnson completed a new woolshed

Muritai, Havelock North — moved to this site and enlarged by J. N. Williams.

Photographer unidentified, Alexander Turnbull Library, F-79488-1/2

at Orua Wharo in 1889 he invited 150 guests to a bash in special rooms constructed for the event, decorated with laurel leaves.[179] In 1894, the Johnsons chartered a train to bring guests to Takapau for an event at Orua Wharo.[180] Staff and residents of John Harding's station 'assembled in full force' at his house on Boxing day 1892 to 'partake of that gentleman's hospitality and receive the Christmas gifts he so liberally provides for them …'[181] The same year the McHardy family hired coaches to take a hundred guests from the Waipawa railway station to a ball on their remote Blackhead station;[182] and in 1897, not to be out-done, G. P. Donnelly hired Napier's Gaiety theatre to celebrate his daughter's birthday.[183]

This late-century display of wealth and status was framed around new technology — telephone, gramophone, electric lights, and finally motor cars. The younger John Chambers led the way, installing Hawke's Bay's first hydro-electric plant on his Mokopeka property at the back of Havelock North. He even devised pop-up toasters and other conveniences. For others, gas was an easier option; acetylene was put on at Orua Wharo in 1901.[184] Bernard Chambers imported one of the first cars in the district.[185] Others hastened to join him, many driving Wolseleys imported by a Hastings garage — including Donnelly, whose 24 hp 'whare on wheels' was the largest car in the district for some time.[186] Other settlers took up similarly expensive hobbies, including travel to exotic destinations of the period, such as Japan or, in the case of Bernard Chambers and one or two others, wine-making.

Superficially, this eruption of late-colonial hedonism reflected the interests of a society of self-made settler-era entrepreneurs — and deservedly so. Most had worked hard for their wealth. Now, in their old age, it was time to enjoy it. Yet this last flourish of the settler elites was not solely an exercise in conspicuous consumption. In many ways these expressions of wealth pioneered Hawke's Bay's twentieth century. Expensive, high-risk ventures such as grape growing broke the ground for others to follow; personal power plants opened the eyes of a populace to the potentials of electricity.

Inevitably, somebody had to crash the party. John Ballance, Premier from 1890, was the first of a new breed. He led the Liberals, New Zealand's first real political party — distinct from the shifting settler-age alliances of self-interested elites — and had a different agenda. In many respects the Liberals were of their time, representing the emerging society of native-born pākehā, introducing welfare and universal suffrage and reforming the labour laws. Much flowed from Ballance's graduated taxes, cancellation of leaseholds and — *in extremis* — forcible sale of large estates.[187] This was as much an effort to break the political power of the elites as to make room for the rising small-and-medium-holders who dominated the twentieth century pastoral landscape.

Hawke's Bay was a key target, and second Liberal Prime Minister Richard Seddon — a man huge of both girth and will — made the terms clear to Walter Shrimpton of Matipiro station. If Shrimpton did not reduce his holdings, Seddon would do it for him.[188] In practice, the Liberals did not have to do much pushing. William Russell was 'sad at parting with a property I have worked for nearly forty five [sic] years,'[189] and there was a good deal of grumbling among many of the Hawke's Bay elite at what they saw as a litigious attack on their property. But others saw opportunity in the change. There was money to be made from subdivision, and a fair number of Hawke's Bay elite did not need much incentive to sell their properties into a rising land market. A. H. Russell apparently eliminated his mortgage that way.[190] J. R. B. A'Deane's Ashcott station had been valued at just over £2 an acre in 1902, but by 1906 he was able to sell parts at between £5 and £15 — around $700 to $2100 in early twenty-first century money.[191] E. J. Watt sold Tukituki and Longlands stations, Douglas MacLean divided 38,000 acres of Maraekakaho.[192]

The eagerness with which some of the local gentry put their properties on the market, though, did not stop the nay-sayers, for whom the issue

> "Prime Minister Richard Seddon — a man huge of both girth and will — made the terms clear to Walter Shrimpton of Matipiro station. If Shrimpton did not reduce his holdings, Seddon would do it for him."

Guests shelter from the Hawke's Bay sun under a tree outside the Frimley homestead.

Hawke's Bay Museum 7553 (a)

was one of principle and property rights. Purvis Russell — now retired in Scotland — found his Hatuma property was vulnerable to legislation that targeted absentee landlords. He fought the sale through the courts, lost in 1900, then offered £60,000 'ransom' to retain the property. Government refused. A few years later, T. E. Crosse's 3,774 acre Kumeroa was sold for £24,300, around $3.4 million in early twenty-first century sums.[193] Other stations and farms were sold as the twentieth century dawned, among them Duart, Frimley, Flaxmere, Matipiro, Kereru, Gwavas and Mangawhare.[194] But as Guthrie-Smith declared, the 'general denunciation' of 'wealthy squatters' ignored the fact that many were 'struggling against bankers, bad climate, bad land and bad titles.'[195]

Elite protestations over the way they were being made to shed their holdings underscored a curious historical point. To the casual observers of the day — and many historians since — estate-busting was a howling success. But a look at the numbers reveals that in reality New Zealand's pastoral gentry, in general, held on to both their wealth and, by and large, their scale of land holding.[196] The figures are clear; in 1891 there were 584 land-holders nationally with more than 5000 acres in New Zealand,

Jessie Riddiford, Sophia Johnston and Miss T. St. Clair Inglis at Orua Wharo, around 1905.

Photographer unidentified, Alexander Turnbull Library, F-37834-1/2, PAColl-4433

of whom 24 had more than 50,000 acres. Twenty years of Liberal 'elite-busting' produced an increase to 926 holdings of more than 5000 acres by 1911, of which 90 were more than 50,000 acres.[197] The process reflected a re-allocation; some estates were broken — 28 in Hawke's Bay by 1912[198] — and small settlements were created. But new leaseholds opened up to replace the old. The notion, then, that the etsates themselves were being dismantled was an illusion: it was as much re-allocation as loss. So what was happening? Much of this was former Māori land, sold into Crown hands — as one historian has observed, the 'greatest estate of all'.[199] In short, Māori were the real losers in the Liberal-driven land reform.[200]

This is not to deny the wider decline of Hawke's Bay's gentry as a social and political force, even as they generally held on to land and money. But there was more to their influence and power than their cash balances. Times were changing. The settler era and its small, stratified society was

119

passing in the face of the more complex, multi-generational and balanced population that emerged from the 1880s. Overseas movements fed into the mix, particularly the radical left, albeit given a New Zealand twist. New groupings — the 'Red Feds' and others — highlighted the changing world. Money alone did not buy power in an emerging country of small business interests, medium holders, a changing balance of power between capital and labour, and growing government function.

The elite protested in various ways. G. P. Donnelly's public protest, *Looking Backward*, was as much a lament for the old days as an effort to protest government policies.[201] Others took a harder line, and national opposition was led from in Hawke's Bay. It was perhaps predictable; the district remained the North Island's key pastoral province, home of William Russell, leader of the Opposition grouping in parliament.

The younger John Chambers led the charge, ostensibly on the basis of the injustice of Liberal land policies. As he put it, the 'compulsory taking of land from one owner, and handing it over to several others cannot be excused on the plea of public requirements … and what security has a landowner, or for that matter any property-owner?'[202] But his real target was what he saw as the evils of socialism and government spending — including free education. He was determined to act, floated a company and gathered the support of local Hawke's Bay pastoralists. Their 'special duties', he declared, 'included the guiding of public opinions'.[203] He purchased the local Liberal voice, the *Hastings Standard*, shut it down, and created a new conservative paper, the *Herald Tribune*.

It was a bold effort, and Chambers knew what he wanted. But he could not fight society. The Liberals were responding as much as leading, the details of their policies perhaps less crucial than the ground-swell of social change they were addressing. It was an age of re-balancing, an age of new socio-economic groupings, and Hawke's Bay was changing with the rest of the colony. By 1914, as one historian has suggested, the gentry had become 'but one form of rural society'.[204] Still, their old money endured. In a twentieth-century New Zealand that took pride in the myth of financial equality, some Kiwis were more equal than others.

CHAPTER FIVE
Farmer backbone's engine

Fresh winds of change blew through Hawke's Bay as the twentieth century unfolded. The first decade brought the rise of New Zealand's second major political party, led by William 'Farmer Bill' Massey, champion of the medium-scale farmer.

The wealth of the new medium-farmers derived from the frozen meat industry, and they dominated New Zealand's twentieth-century life and economy for years. Hawke's Bay was one of the strongholds of this new class — 'farmer backbone' — and, by extension, a stronghold of Massey-style conservatism. Labour, the third political force in the young Dominion, stood less chance in the district — though that, too, changed.

External forces bore down across the region. War became an arbiter of life, and remained so for two generations. Historians took years to first realise and then properly explore how thoroughly the two world wars moulded New Zealand's mind-set and social character.[1] Hawke's Bay was no exception, and equally, did not miss out on the growth of government, a late nineteenth-century phenomenon given particular impetus in the early twentieth century by the demands of world-engulfing war. This new

Bringing the wool clip down from the back-country; a classic picture of Edward Jones' carters outside the Kuripapango Hotel, near the base of the 'Gentle Annie' climb on the Napier-Taihape road, around 1910. This road had legendary repute and was an essential connection to Napier for major inland stations such as Moawhango.

Photographer unidentified, John Moore Collection, Alexander Turnbull Library, F-110938-1/2, PAColl-4520-02

twentieth century world was characterised by the emergence of command economies and conscription. Bureaucracy flourished, a world of boards, committees, towns and tentacular government control. At everyday level in the suburbs, towns and country districts there was a homogeneity of life.

Hawke's Bay became a part of the larger wheel, a twentieth century world of dual patriotism and emergent nationality where egalitarian ideals were expressed in first-name familiarities and professed equality of income; a pākehā male-dominated world of rugby, racing and beer.[2] This society had its roots in the 1880s with its social militarism and pro-British mindset, an overwhelming rush to the 'good old mother flag' that was arguably a product of failed colonial dreams.[3] New Zealand had not become a bigger or better Britain, but by the 1890s there were hopes of being the best of Britain's children. This thinking was bolstered during the early twentieth century by the war-driven dominance of Britain as an export destination, and then by Britain's deliberate inter-war policy of trading with its Dominions. To some extent the New Zealand attitude stood against Britain's own aim of confederating its empire, but that did not diminish the Kiwi determination to be more British than the British. The

Dannevirke's High Street early in the twentieth century. Like all central Hawke's Bay towns the main street was also the main highway — both a blessing and a curse as traffic volumes grew.

Photographer unidentified, C. S. James Collection, Alexander Turnbull Library, F-44185-1/2

ideal was upheld to the point where success by individual New Zealanders was not even recognised unless it had been earned in Britain.[4]

The mind-set of the 'cultural cringe' had its 'try hard' flip-side — the expectation that New Zealanders nonetheless punched above their weight.[5] It was a curious duality, symptomatic of a social inferiority complex; and both ideas were reflected in microcosm in the provinces. Hawke's Bay's self-view for the period epitomised the mind-set; a feeling that, just as New Zealand as a whole was backward, a province by comparison with metropolitan Mother Britain, so provincial districts within New Zealand such as Hawke's Bay were unsophisticated by comparison with New Zealand's own metropolitan areas such as Auckland. Yet while this was cause for self-deprecation, it also provoked fierce provincial assertion, a sense that Hawke's Bay's slower world was also by nature better. Provincial loyalties were tight, the individuality of the long-obsolete provinces remembered through sports contests such as the Ranfurly Shield and through individual public holidays. Hawke's Bay's own celebration was associated with an annual Agricultural and Pastoral show held after 1925 in the Tomoana Showgrounds.[6] The spring show, a keystone of the Hawke's Bay popular calendar, highlighted ongoing regional focus on pastoral and agricultural matters.

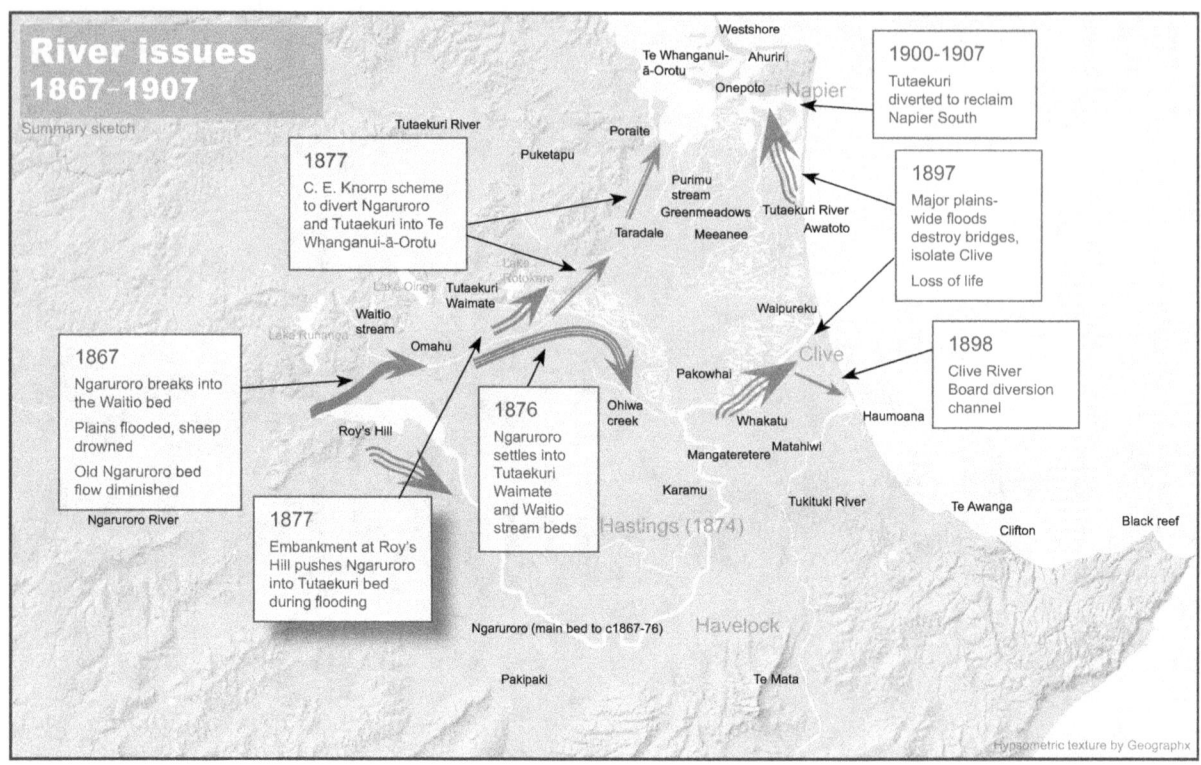

Old pastoral money joined the new power of the mid-sized farmers to make Hawke's Bay one of New Zealand's key centres of meat and wool production. The Heretaunga Plains, divided between town and small-holding, offered new opportunity to diversify. Agriculture — belatedly — flourished across the Heretaunga plains, helping turn the district around Napier and Hastings as the economic hub of the region. Further south, dairy companies cemented southern Hawke's Bay — with Taranaki — as one of New Zealand's important dairying centres.

Soldiers, society and separatism

River control dominated Hawke's Bay's local politics during the first years of the twentieth century. The meandering waterways of Heretaunga — Tukituki, Ngaruroro and Tutaekuri, with feeders and streams such as the Mangaone, Waimate and Waitio — had been a bugbear to the settlers for decades. As early as 1862 the Ngaruroro was 'threatening to swamp large tracts of land.'[7] Unprecedented rains five years later flooded the plains, drowned 1200 of Thomas Tanner's sheep, and prompted the 'devious'[8] Tutaekuri to flood into the Tutaekuri-Waimate stream bed. Meanwhile the Ngaruroro swung into a new bed that used part of the old Waitio stream.[9] Efforts to resolve the issue ran foul of settler-age attitudes to public works. Public meetings in 1868, though amicable, came out against a Canterbury-style rating system.[10] Ormond pushed a river control bill to the House,[11] but practical efforts were localised and merely pushed danger points from one place to another. Meanee was almost flooded in 1875 as a result.[12] Railway work at Roy's Hill further changed the flows that decade, but an official Public Works Department report put the cost of permanent embankments at £180,000 — some $20.6 million in early 21st century money.[13] Neither that or a cheaper alternative were adopted.[14] Napier, too, came in for periodic drenchings — and 'Carr's Cut', a channel to divert the Tutaekuri away from the town — was not wholly effective.

The crisis broke in April 1897. Heavy autumn rains prompted warnings in the *Hawke's Bay Herald* of a 'disaster which must result from the haphazard banking', urging locals to 'cast aside petty village jealousies and work in unison'.[15] Douglas MacLean — Donald's son, despite the different spelling — convened a meeting; but massive floods that Easter inundated the district. Men drowned trying to go to the rescue of Clive residents.[16] It was a salutary lesson; yet as late as 1902 there were protests

The remains of the Waitangi bridge near Clive after the 1897 floods.

Photographer unidentified,
Athol Williams Collection,
Alexander Turnbull Library,
F-61689-1/2

The dredge "C.D.K." on the Tutaekuri River, which was diverted to flood part of the Whare-o-maraenui block, reclaiming land near Wellesley Road, Napier. It was named after engineer Charles Kennedy, one of the movers-and-shakers behind the Napier South reclamation scheme. He also gave his name to one of the main roads in that suburb.

Photographer unidentified, Hawke's Bay Museum, 8129

over 'separate river boards fighting against one another'.[17] Arguments still ran hot in 1912, when the newly-formed Hawke's Bay Rivers Board, chaired by Ormond, secured the rights to dig a diversion channel to the sea from Pakowhai.[18]

Only Napier came out ahead. Silt deposited with the floods gave engineer C. D. Kennedy and associate William Langlands the idea of creating new town lands with the help of the Tutaekuri. The Harbour Board were disinterested in a solo effort, so Kennedy floated a partnership with George Latham, George Nelson and William Nelson, leased 1,780 acres of the Whare-o-maraenui block,[19] and began what school inspector Henry Hill called a 'grand work'.[20] The project was as audacious as it was risky. To reclaim the intended triangle of land, the Tutaekuri had to be diverted across it — ultimately above the level of downtown Napier, which was protected only by a stop-bank. Naming one of the longer streets after mayor John Vigor-Brown was perhaps politically sensible under the circumstance.[21] Other main roads drew names from the syndicate and leading townsfolk. And despite some touch-and-go moments when the river threatened to burst the elevated stop-banks and gush into Napier, they got away with it, using draft horses and drags to scoop the new suburb into shape. They re-diverted the river into a straight bed along the line of George's Drive and sold the first sections in 1908.[22] Houses shortly followed, joining a smithy built to shoe the horses.[23]

These ventures played out to a background of new social priorities. Hawke's Bay — like New Zealand — plunged into the social militarism that swept the country in the last years of the nineteenth century. Fuelled by a new sense of pro-British patriotism, this social ideal found expression in regulations requiring school cadetship and territorial service. Schools were a particular breeding-ground for the ethos, driven in part by new focus on secondary education. Private schools were all the rage for those who could afford them, most finding homes in Havelock North, where Heretaunga school moved in 1912.[24] A new Presbyterian girls' boarding school, Iona College, opened in the town in 1914 — pushed along by local landowner Hugh Campbell who was apparently concerned by the predominance of nearby Woodford House, an Anglican school.[25]

Social militarism was certainly on display when HMS *New Zealand* visited Napier in 1913. This 18,500 ton battlecruiser[26] was New Zealand's gift to Britain, product of an effort to take the high ground in Australasian defence politics.[27] Her 1913 tour of New Zealand was months in planning and used as an excuse to introduce electric lighting to Napier's waterfront and municipal theatre. Special trains brought up to 12,000 visitors to Napier to see this 'mighty engine of warfare',[28] which arrived on 25 April and anchored in the Ahuriri roadstead. That morning a thousand school children boarded the government steamer *Tutanekai*, braving heavy swells to visit the battlecruiser. The whole town was in holiday mood. Some 300 sailors were led around town by the Napier Pipe and City Bands, before heading to a slap-up lunch at the Drill Hall. Vigor-Brown entertained the officers, and during the afternoon there were sports events. Evening brought a public display of the new electric lights, while the officers went to dinner in the Hawke's Bay Club's new building on the Marine Parade. Visitors were still queuing to get on board the warship next day, before she sailed for Gisborne.[29]

Jingoistic sentiments came to the fore in August 1914 when, as Guthrie-Smith put it, the 'old world crashed and passed away'.[30] When Napier nurse Louisa Higginson reached England with her friend Mary Collins in the hope of volunteering for war work, they could not understand the apparent lack of English patriotism.[31] Yet Imperial loyalty was not the sole motive for volunteering. When war came in 1914, Napier reporter Aubrey Tronson joined for 'pure love of adventure and travel', pestering the recruiting office twice a week.[32] Hawke's Bay's leading soldier of the day was Napier-born Andrew Hamilton Russell (1868–1960) — Guy to his friends, 'our General' to the men of the Hawke's Bay Battalion.

> "Special trains brought up to 12,000 visitors to Napier to see this 'mighty engine of warfare', which arrived on 25 April and anchored in the Ahuriri roadstead."

> "Social-militarist ideas of war as a superior sports ground were destroyed at Gallipoli."

Like his father and grandfather, Russell had been trained as a professional soldier, in his case at the Royal Military College near Sandhurst, and while he abandoned a promising career to run the family farms in 1892, he retained a close involvement in New Zealand's military. He 'Wired offering services' a few days after war broke out, and three days later was made commander of the New Zealand Mounted Rifles Brigade.[33] 'It is a great compliment,' he confided to his diary, 'must do my best'.[34] He led the brigade at Gallipoli, and as Major-General went on to command the New Zealand Division in 1916, leading them through a harrowing campaign on the Western Front.[35]

Social-militarist ideas of war as a superior sports ground were destroyed at Gallipoli.[36] Many Hawke's Bay soldiers lost their lives, among them Mason Chambers' son Selwyn, killed by random fire while behind the lines. 'I am so sorry for you,' Russell wrote to Mason and Margaret Chambers, 'for I knew and felt how you hated parting with him. One hardly cares to reckon any chance of getting out of this alive, or even untouched'.[37] Mason Chambers' other son Hugh survived despite joining the Royal Flying Corps in 1916. He won the Distinguished Flying Cross.[38] Other Hawke's Bay men caught up in the struggle included George Bollinger, who was with the Hawke's Bay contingent on Gallipoli. Later he served on the Western Front,[39] a hellish world of shellfire, wire, bodies and stench.[40] Harry Bourke reached the front in 1918, finding 'dead men and horses lying about'.[41]

These experiences were shared by a socially significant proportion of Hawke's Bay's youth. Every family was touched, directly or otherwise. Even those whose sons survived, who did not receive the dreaded government condolence telegram, remembrance cards and linen pouch of personal effects,[42] found the returning soldiers were not the young men who had left. Some, as Doug Stark declared, were 'restless, gas-drenched wrecks'.[43] Others returned crippled. A dismaying number died during the 1920s, many succumbing to the lasting effects of gas, their numbers never fully captured by the official statistics. The influenza pandemic of 1918–19 added depth to the agonising sense of loss and tragedy felt by many families across Hawke's Bay during the period.

These experiences, shared with the country as a whole, accelerated and coloured the way society developed during the war years and afterwards — changes reflected, with characteristic conservatism, in Hawke's Bay. The shift had been building for decades, and it found expression in the doctrine of 'social purity', a moral crusade that became as powerful, judgemental and encompassing in its time as the ideals of the 'politically correct' 80 years later. Social purity had its origins in Victorian-age

Art classes at Iona College, Havelock North. This Presbyterian-based girls boarding school was founded in 1913–14 with the help of local pastoralist Hugh Campbell, who offered land on the basis that that the Anglican-based Woodford would otherwise attract all the girls of the district.

Photographer unidentified, Iona College Collection, Alexander Turnbull Library, F-101837-1/2

idealism, in the middle-class values of the tight nuclear family, in settler-age religious zeal and in the denial of hedonistic pleasures. During the nineteenth century that led to the double standard, but as the century ended, social pressure grew to live according to the ideal. As always, the notion was pursued to extremes in some circles, framed by new ideals of order, regulation and even eugenics.

The ethos found expression across the young Dominion in the Scout movement and in Plunket with its initial effort to regulate babies by the clock. War exigencies added momentum. Government squashed 'objectionable posters' in cinema foyers, including the 1331-seat Hastings Municipal Theatre.[44] Alcohol, always an issue for the more puritanically minded settlers, became a key problem amid this new mind-set. Hawke's Bay folk, like those of New Zealand generally, had taken a bipolar attitude to the 'demon drink' for decades. 'Of course I could not go into the liquor trade,' George Maunder declared when looking for opportunities around Napier in 1867.[45] Mangawhare station manager David Balfour intoned his children to 'beware drink, it is a treacherous thing'.[46] Such sentiments stood at odds with the male-dominated frontier world of hard drinkers, but the drive against liquor coalesced as the century ended. It was a national affair that Hawke's Bay shared; the Hawke's Bay Temperance league was formed in March 1892.[47] Alliance with women's movements gave momentum. Legislation introduced 'wet' and 'dry' districts — in Hawke's Bay the latter included Makotuku, Ormondville and Norsewood — and in 1911 the first vote for prohibition was introduced.

War gave further social momentum to restraint. Measures against drink included an act to make 'shouting' illegal, and the elimination of barmaids on the curious argument that they were women of loose morals who induced men to drink. Six o'clock closing followed in 1917. It has been argued that this was designed to support family life by forcing men to go home[48] In reality it underscored a 'bloke' culture, well established in the settler period, that exalted the speed and quantity of consumption along with the ability to 'hold' it afterwards. The practical outcome was that men went home drunk. Alcohol, New Zealanders were advised in 1919, was 'one of the chief causes of cruelty, crime and vice'.[49] And that year a law change swung the balance. Prohibition was in by 3,263 votes — but the country remained 'wet' when the soldiers' votes were counted. Puritanically-minded civilians cried 'debauched',[50] but threats of eternal damnation counted for little among those who had fought on the Western Front.[51] It was a slender margin nonetheless; and 47 percent of New Zealand voters remained in favour of prohibition as late as 1925.[52]

Race relations continued to foster myths of brotherhood. Māori were recovering from the lows of the 1890s. The population in 1921 was back where it had been in 1858.[53] In Hawke's Bay there were communities at Pakowhai and Waiohiki. Work was available rurally, often shearing, or as labour in timber-felling operations. But the injustices of the settler period persisted. A disproportionate Māori death toll at the hands of the influenza pandemic of 1918–19 highlighted their marginalisation, economically and, ultimately, physically. In practice the tight, centrally controlled world of New Zealand was exclusively pākehā, and heavily urbanised. A largely rural Māori — 82.7 percent in 1936, the first year for which figures are available[54] — had almost no voice. This was as true for Hawke's Bay as elsewhere. Despite the sustained poltical effort of the 1870s and beyond, Ngāti Kahungunu were simply not a significant force in the pākehā world.

The particular thorn in the side of Hawke's Bay's race relations remained the Te Whanganui-ā-Orotū lagoon. Ngāti Kahungunu believed it had not been sold in 1850. When Kennedy and his partners reclaimed land for Napier South, river flows shifted to the point where the Ahuriri lagoon became useless for collecting fish.[55] Traditional gathering and fishing grounds around the Westshore spit fell prey to Napier's effluent, pumped out to sea at the harbour mouth — aptly nicknamed 'Perfume Point' — where it joined the detritus of the South British freezing works.

Māori persisted. Petitions in 1875, 1894 and 1907 were followed by approaches to the land court in 1916, another petition in 1919, and an approach to the Native Lands Commission in 1920. This ruled that the lagoon had, in fact, changed hands.[56] Te Wahapango of Ngai Te Ruruku petitioned parliament again in 1924, but investigation the following year merely reiterated the finding of the 1920 Commission. The issue was still open in February 1931 when the magnitude 7.8 quake changed the scene again.

Such agitation did not disturb the pākehā notion that New Zealand enjoyed the best race-relations in the world. Sentiments were highlighted by the Springbok tour of 1921, when Māori and Springboks duked it out in Napier's McLean Park.[57] The *Daily Telegraph* reported in period terms on the Springbok dismay at 'thousands of Europeans cheering on [a] band of coloured men to defeat members of their own race'.[58] News of the South African attitude to Māori provoked further sharp reaction. The South Africans had visited a marae, and if they 'so despised the Natives', then 'why did they accept their hospitality as they did?'[59] An

Admiral of the Fleet Sir John Rushworth Jellicoe (1859–1935), Governor-General of New Zealand, at Omahu, July 1923. Although Wellington-based during his four-year term, this quiet-spoken man with a repute for personal kindness was no stranger to Hawke's Bay; two of his daughters went to Havelock North's Woodford House.

Henry Norford Whitehead,
H. N. Whitehead Collection,
Alexander Turnbull Library,
G-19310-1/1

editorial made attitudes clear; New Zealand could 'take pride in the fact' that Māori, 'this noble people, so far from being exterminated by war or disease, are a virile and increasing community'.[60] From a historical perspective, the enthusiasm and brotherhood that pākehā displayed for Māori when confronting a foreign power underscored period attitudes. New Zealand, at the time, fancied itself as having the best race relations in the world. The reality was that by the early twentieth century New Zealand was, for all practical purposes, separatist. The nation was divided between an impoverished, dispossessed and ruralised Māori, and a more prosperous and largely urban pākehā. Hawke's Bay was no exception. Māori were well aware of the injustice. Given this context, the *Telegraph* editorial, ultimately, highlighted the rose-tinted view pākehā had of New Zealand's race-relations in the early twentieth century.

Alternative thought and the Havelock Work

The dullness of socially pure Hawke's Bay had its counterpoint in 'our village' — Havelock North. Here, as Ngaio Marsh put it, the 'esoteric found a fertile soil'.[61] It was a place, Eleanor Adkins declared in a 1940 verse, where townsfolk engaged in 'every kind of cult & stunt/to elevate our minds.'[62] From tiny enclaves on the hills above Hastings, an extraordinary cluster of independent social thought emerged during the first decades of the twentieth century. The fringe philosophies pursued by ardent villagers attracted interest from like-minded individuals across New Zealand. They included anthroposophy, theosophy, Robert Sutcliffe's School of Radiant Living, and an Order of the Table Round.[63] All were eclipsed by a secret hermetic order, Stella Matutina, subject of 'dark rumours' and whispered innuendo,[64] which at its peak reputedly involved up to a third of the townsfolk.[65]

These developments raised eyebrows — and the historical question is why such philosophies took hold in a district that defined itself by its conservative, pro-establishment views. There were suggestions by adherents that it flowed from a supposed 'spirtual force' that was somehow embedded in Havelock North's geography,[66] but of course such claims were sophistry. In reality the driving forces were a product of people and society, and the principal movements were well founded in the prevailing ideological framework — particularly

> "The fringe philosophies ...attracted interest from like-minded individuals across New Zealand."

the Anglican church. By contrast with the 'hippie' movement of the 1960s and 1970s, Hawke's Bay's alternate thought of the early twentieth century endorsed the conservative establishment, but still gave practical expression to its bohemian underside.

The movement gained social ground because of Havelock North's close community spirit of the late nineteenth century. Any potential that the township had to grow was lost when the railway was routed through Karamu and Hastings was set up. Havelock North — popularly dubbed 'our village' by its thousand-odd inhabitants — instead developed a sense of tight community spirit that was framed at least in part by perceived rivalry with the 'jewel of the plains'. The township also developed a reputation as a retirement centre for wealthy pastoralists, many of whom had eclectic and far-reaching interests. Like attracted like; and the world of alternate thought grew from their intellectual hunger and sense of enquiry. It was, Marsh declared, 'one of those curious runnings-together of affinities'.[67]

Much flowed from the energies of one man, Henry Reginald Gardiner, a lay reader with the Anglican church.[68] He was very much the right man in the right place, a remarkable character who 'sought always to draw people together', whose 'influence was felt in many intangible ways'.[69] Born in New South Wales in 1872, this 'imposing figure — full, broad shouldered, with a deep resonant voice'[70] — first arrived in Hawke's Bay in 1885. He moved to Havelock North in 1907, where he met Harold Large, an 'idiosyncratic gentleman'[71] who had resigned from the Theosophical Society. The two decided to begin a small literary group,[72] but when over a hundred townsfolk gathered to discuss culture, Gardiner and his brother, Reverend Allen Gardiner, founded the Havelock Work,[73] seeking — among other things — an 'infinity of opinion on the common theme "The Fatherhood of God and the Brotherhood of Man"'.[74] Before long the group outgrew its format of weekly Shakespearean and Dickensian readings, and in 1909 pushed for a new hall with stage, dressing rooms, and 300 seats. This opened in 1910 on Anglican church land, and the group organised performances and events such as the Old English Village Fete of November 1911. That was dwarfed by the Shakespearean Pageant the following year, intended to raise enough money to pay off the hall.[75]

Gardiner also played a role in the Stella Matutina hermetic order that appeared a few years later. Few admitted to belonging, though at one time it appears to have had a membership of 300 — albeit drawn to some extent from across New Zealand — but still reaching that figure when the town populace numbered no more than a thousand.[76] Secrecy fuelled speculative talk of rituals and monastic cells.[77] As always, reality was more

> "Secrecy fuelled speculative talk of rituals and monastic cells."

James Chapman-Taylor (1878–1958).

James Chapman-Taylor, Judy Siers Collection, Alexander Turnbull Library, F-31666-1/2

mundane; the order began as private group exploring their conviction that the Anglican church had 'lost the esoteric teaching which they believed that Jesus had given to His disciples'.[78] The wheels were set rolling by Gardiner and his wife; by Harold Large, and Exchange Hotel owner Mary McLean, who created a 'Society of the Southern Cross' to infuse rituals into their meditation meetings. In 1911, Reverend J. Fitzgerald introduced them to the 'Golden Dawn', Stella Matutina, founded by Robert Felkin in 1880. Fitzgerald then put them in touch with Felkin — who agreed to come to Havelock North.[79]

Felkin was a strict Anglican, freemason and member of the Order of the Table Round. The fact that he was prepared to cross the planet to find new adherents gives due scale to his movement in the wider context of world philosophy.[80] His first visit in 1912 was largely funded by Mason Chambers,[81] drawing in Wellington architect James Chapman-Taylor. Afterwards, Mason and the younger John Chambers established a trust and donated land for a house built to one of Chapman-Taylor's designs, incorporating a secret temple.[82] Felkin went back to Europe, but in 1916 his health collapsed and — at Gardiner's insistence and John Chambers' expense[83] — returned to Havelock North. Here he settled in the Chapman-Taylor house, Whare Ra. His arrival gave the movement a remarkable community focus. The order had its 'inner' and 'outer' circles, with much revolving around the basement temple with its mystic sigils.[84] Felkin's wife Harriot kept the movement running after his death in 1926, with the support of anthroposophist Charles McDowell.[85] In the late 1930s they purchased land near Taupō for a new centre. The Havelock North side of the order continued to operate for many years.

Other fringe ideologies flourished in Havelock North alongside Stella Matutina, essentially present through the same intellectualised torrent of emotional need that Gardiner had done so much to focus. Some were controversial. Robert Sutcliffe's School for Radiant Living prompted rumours of public nudism.[86] The most enduring of these alternative ideologies was anthroposophy, which the Austrian independent thinker

Rudolf Steiner developed in part out of Helena Blavatsky's 'theosophy' around the turn of the twentieth century. Steiner believed he was inspired by occult powers that spoke through him, styling his pronouncements 'spiritual science', although his asssertions bore no resemblance to any known scientific principle. Indeed, by the science of his day and later, Steiner's teachings presented as over-intellectualised and deeply anthropocentric gibberish. Nonetheless, Steiner's doctrine covered the full range of human endeavour, framed in period thinking — notably his declarations about supposed human racial heirarchies, in which Aryan Germans apparently occupied top spot — along with his techniques for educating children, making homeopathic remedies, gardening methods, dance, spiritualism and assertions about reincarnation. The religious aspect of his teaching was explicit: 'No-one [sic] need be estranged from his religious life through spiritual science,' he declared in 1916.[87]

In New Zealand, Steiner's proselytes found fertile ground initially among Wellington fringe thinkers, who spread his doctrines to Havelock North during the First World War.[88]

Hollywood lifestyles

Hawke's Bay took time to settle down after the First World War. Government efforts to rehabilitate veterans included soldiers' settlements in the back-country. Some 63,648 acres of Hawke's Bay's more remote areas were in use for this purpose by May 1918, with a further 14,346 acres to hand.[89] In practise these 'starvation joints' were unlikely to succeed at the best of times. Most of the money made from them flowed not from returns on the farming enterprise, but out of the speculative bubble in land sales that came on the heels of the policy. It could not be sustained, and the crunch came in 1921 when Britain cancelled its wartime 'commandeer' of all New Zealand's pastoral products.

Downturn prompted renewed commercial rivalry for the shrinking consumer pie. Hastings draper H. W. C. Baird formed the Hastings Retailers Association, joined forces with the Hastings Chamber of Commerce, and began selling Hastings shops to Napier consumers. Signs were even set up in Ahuriri pointing to Hastings.[90] This business war added to the challenges faced by Napier Mayor J. B. Andrew, elected in 1923. Napier certainly seemed to be flagging during the 1920s. A proposed loan of £290,750 — the equivalent of about $24.5 million in early 21st century sums[91] — was soundly rejected by ratepayers, putting

"...the crunch came in 1921 when Britain cancelled its wartime 'commandeer' of all New Zealand's pastoral products."

Opening ceremonty for the hydro-electric power station at Tuai, 1929, part of the Waikaremoana Hydro-Electric Power Scheme. This became part of the national grid — a balanced system designed to provide power for a nation. Hawke's Bay consumers of the day were reputedly told that, once the cost of building this state-owned scheme had been covered, power itself would be free.

A. Hardcastle, Alexander Turnbull Library, F-61443-1/2, PAColl-5671-1/1

paid to proposed extensions of the borough tramways into Napier South, and simultaneously killing sewerage and water plans for that area.[92]

These tensions fed into district politics; there was spiralling demand for road sealing and power reticulation, coupled with the embarrassing matter of flood control. By the mid-1920s most of Heretaunga's main rivers were silted, in part a consequence of Whitmore's enthusiastic advocacy of willow as cheap flood control half a century earlier. Napier engineers had plans to use the rivers to build a better export harbour and reclaim part of the swamp, but the benefits were not likely to be shared by Hastings and county rate-payers. Rival engineers put up plans with price tags ranging from £83,000 to a whopping £240,000, — some $19.9 million in early 21st century money.[93] In 1930, after bitter argument, a scheme was put forward to Parliament as an amendment to the Hawke's Bay Rivers Bill — but was rendered obsolete by earthquake.[94]

Local bodies had better fortunes in their quest to electrify. Dannevirke Borough Council's 1903 proposal foundered on the estimated £100,000 cost of a hydro-electric scheme at the Waihi Falls.[95] However, both

Napier and Hastings set up their own diesel-driven systems before the First World War. Havelock North tapped into the Hastings supply until wartime shortages prompted a crisis of confidence during 1916.[96] The 'Waikaremoana Hydro-Electric League' wanted a regional system and by 1918 had brought 25 local bodies into the picture; but sentiment in Havelock North was less inclusive. In the end the Havelock North Town Board built its own system on the Maraetotara river, raising a £12,500 loan for the purpose — some 1.2 million in early 21st century values, and a significant sum for a town of just on a thousand individuals.[97] The rest of the district joined the Waikaremoana scheme, and by the end of the decade most towns were integrated with the national grid, drawing power variously from Waikaremoana and Mangahao. Southern Hawke's Bay residents mooted a connection in 1920, but it took five years and a £175,000 loan before Minister of Works Gordon Coates ceremonially connected Dannevirke — focus of distribution around the district — in May 1925.[98]

Sealing the district's roads became another priority in the face of rising car ownership. The twentieth-century world motoring revolution began early for both New Zealand and Hawke's Bay. Thoroughbrace coaches and five-horse teams swiftly vanished in the face of such modern contraptions as the nine-seater Cadillacs that the Hawke's Bay Motor Coach Company began running up the Taupō road in 1913 — slashing a three-day journey to just one, if all went well.[99] The last commercial stage coach in Hawke's Bay, reputedly, made a final run to the Gentle Annie in 1918.[100] Firms took up motor-lorries, among them the Heretaunga Co-Operative Dairy Company whose first trucks arrived in 1914-15. The Hastings Borough Council even purchased a Straker electric truck for local work.[101] The First World War introduced most soldiers to motorised transport, accelerating the revolution when they returned home. Some 12,000 vehicles were imported in 1920 alone,[102] and New Zealand swiftly became one of the most motorised nations in the world. By the end of the 1920s horses had virtually gone from Hawke's Bay's roads, and the Hastings Borough Council tacitly recognised the shift by requesting the removal of public hitching posts.[103]

Motor transport swiftly provoked a fresh political crisis. Individual roads boards objected to maintaining roads used by 'foreign' traffic. Lobbying eventually led to the Main Highways Act of 1922, which absorbed around 6000 miles of roading into state control and provided funding for county councils to seal them, though nobody knew what the best surface was. Napier's Mayor, John Vigor-Brown, experimented with tar outside his Westshore home in 1909. In 1925 the County

> "Sealing district roads became another priority in the face of rising car ownership."

Employees at the Whakatu freezing works, probably late 1920s.

Henry Norford Whitehead,
H. N. Whitehead Collection,
Alexander Turnbull Library,
G-19279-1/1

Council agreed to experimentally seal a stretch of road between Awatoto and Napier in concrete at the cost of £5234, comparing it with another area sealed in bitumen.[104] Although bitumen won, the concrete test road proved enduring.[105]

Pastoral production was bolstered by freezing works at Pakipaki and Whakatu. By 1927–28 the Whakatu plant, owned by the Hawke's Bay Farmers' Meat Company, had an annual through-put of some 1,239,600 animals.[106] To this was added a sawmilling industry, which by the early twentieth century was focused on the slopes of the Ruahine Range, Puketitiri, and bush around Te Pohue. The charge into Puketitiri was led by the Hawke's Bay Timber Company, which opened a mill there in 1896. Others followed, including Robert Holt and Sons and Hastings company McLeod and Gardiner. The latter's Puketitiri mill was capable of sawing up to 10,000 linear feet of timber per day and employed around 30 people. Sawmills operated in the district until 1940–41.[107]

Puketitiri flourished on the back of a significant stand of native bush which, to eager nineteenth century settlers, seemed ripe for milling. The first sawmill opened in Puketitiri in 1896 and the locality became a significant milling centre from the early twentieth century. By the 1920s the area was home to several major sawmills, principally those of McLeod and Gardiner and Robert Holt and Sons. The township became a thriving local centre on the back of that industry, but dwindled after 1940 when the bush was largely cut out. Only a small stand of the Puketitiri Bush, Ball's Clearing, was saved.

Myra Skinner, Matthew Wright Collection

High Street, Waipawa, late 1920s; a bustling central Hawke's Bay service town. Trucks and cars underscore the speed with which motor transport replaced horse-and-cart in the years after the First World War.

Sydney Charles Smith,. S. C. Smith Collection, Alexander Turnbull Library, G-45823-1/1

Hawke's Bay gained another string to its economic bow as Heretaunga's orcharding and horticultural industries matured. The industry had small beginnings. William Guthrie planted an orchard near Havelock North in 1872.[108] John Goddard's Havelock Nurseries shortly featured 'apples, pears, cherries, peaches, nectarines, apricots, prunes, currants, mulberries, figs, medlars, lemons.'[109] Liberal land reforms punted the whole enterprise along; in 1905, Thomas Horton purchased land from the Frimley estate and set up a tree nursery, John Rich took up 31 acres of Te Mata and planted the Karoola orchard in apples.[110] In 1914, Horton secured a deal with Brazilian merchants to sell 20,000 cases of apples a year for five years.[111] War intervened, but local orcharding expanded at the rate of about 80 acres per annum, driven in 1917 when John Ormond — now 87 years of age and the grand old gentleman of the district — subdivided his Karamu property. By the early 1920s the plains were well placed to take advantage of demand for fruit,[112] and in 1925 produce reached 20,436 cases.[113] By 1928 some 30 percent of the crop — which totalled 195,630 cases of apples and pears — was being exported, making Hawke's Bay the second largest fruit-growing district in New Zealand.[114]

Farmer Backbone's Engine

Droving sheep near Poukawa during the 1920s. Provincial wealth still rested on pastoral exports, but indifferent British markets that decade left New Zealand bumping along in the economic doldrums.

Henry Norford Whitehead,
H. N. Whitehead Collection,
Alexander Turnbull Library,
G-19310-1/1

For those who could afford it, Hawke's Bay of the 1920s was a world of sports, leisure, fun and entertainment that ran in tension with ideals of socal purity. It was understandable. A generation had risked themselves on the Western Front, particularly; and against all the odds they had survived. Now it was time to party. This was the decade of daring jazz music, of fashions that cast off the vestiges of the Victorian age, an era of 'streamline' architectural shapes. And if these years did not quite roar for New Zealand, they were at least a palliative for the lingering agonies of war and the 'lost generation'.

Cars offered mobility to the wealthier set. White-collar businessmen took their families on Sunday drives and picnicked from well-stuffed wicker hampers. It was an age of dances and dates, of blue-collar 'socials' where entry was by 'plate', of complex morning and afternoon teas where the socially ambitious aspired to the genteel lifestyle of the colonial era. Newspaper columns were given over to describing the world of local socialites. A Hastings dance was attended by women 'in a smart model in black charmeuse'; a 'becoming Nubian brown lace frock'; or a 'parchment

A bus operated by P. Callaghan of Hastings. In the early decades of the twentieth century, when cars were largely a white-collar province, wider access to motor vehicles came through public transport — some of it, as in this example, rather makeshift.

Henry Norford Whitehead,
H. N. Whitehead Collection,
Alexander Turnbull Library,
F-67751-1/1

white crepe du chene'.[115] One Hastings woman prepared for her wedding in 1924 with a succession of ritual gatherings — a 'morning tea', where guests provided recipes; a 'white afternoon' in a Duke Street house where 'each guest bought a white gift'; and a 'toilet afternoon' where guests variously wore a 'henna costume and mole hat', 'egg blue knitted silk' and 'deep jade jersey silk', all with hats 'to tone'.[116]

Hawke's Bay's Mediterranean climate struck a particular chord in this age of outdoor pursuits and sports. The Hawke's Bay Lawn Tennis Club flourished; so did the Hastings Golf Links at Bridge Pā and A. J. Shaw's nine-hole course at Beatson Park.[117] The Waipawa Lawn Tennis Club ran four courts until 1924.[118] Swimming clubs exploded into life, led in 1919 by the Heretaunga Club, based on the Maddison Baths, which had grown to 270 members by 1929.[119] This same climate drew comparison with Hollywood, a world of larger-than-life stars, gossip and a sun-drenched lifestyle that — superficially at least — matched the sunny climes of the Bay. It was the golden age of the cinema, an era when Hawke's Bay families could while away a Saturday afternoon at a shilling a head for the 'stalls' and two shillings tuppence for the 'circle'[120] — about $4.10 and $9 in early twenty-first century sums.¹²¹ Crowds flocked to Napier's Gaiety cinema; the Hastings Municipal Theatre, the Cosy Theatre, the King's Theatre and other cinemas to see Douglas Fairbanks, Mary Pickford and other stars.¹²²

Radio opened another window on the world. The 1920s were the 'golden age' of wireless; and everybody wanted it, straining to hear music and voice through the static. Early broadcasts from Wellington prompted Hawke's Bay residents to rig 30-metre aerials from roof to back fence. The Hastings Radio Society emerged in 1926, giving members 'lectures and demonstrations' to explain the 'mysteries of radio problems.'¹²³

Architecture matched the ethos. The styles of the twentieth century had their origins in the late nineteenth-century rejection of Victorian themes and the possibilities of steel and concrete. Modernism encompassed a whole range of styles — Bauhaus, Spanish Mission, Chicago School, futurist, constructivist, cubist, expressionist, streamline and ultimately moderne. This thinking reached Hawke's Bay around the turn of the century, carried by the enthusiasm of local architects and — in the case of Havelock North — by the social ferment of the village. Mason Chambers brought Auckland architect W. H. Gummer to the district in

Modernist architecture flourished in Hawke's Bay during the 1920s; this This is the new Napier nurse's home, completed in 1930 — a magnificent example of Spanish Mission style, yet structurally flawed. When the quake hit in 1931, the building collapsed with tragic loss of life.

Storkey Collection

The fact that Napier's inner harbour — nicknamed 'Scapa Flow' — was almost deep enough for large ships provoked debate over the economics of building a breakwater harbour adjacent to Bluff Hill. The debate was given force by the 1931 earthquake; both inner harbour and breakwater were shallowed by uplift, and there were suggestions that all efforts should focus on deepening the inner harbour as the main port.

Dave Williams, Dave Williams Collection, Hawke's Bay Museum, W200b

1915, creating houses such as Tauroa, Arden and a magnificent home near Craggy Range for the van Asch family.[124] *Avant-garde* thinker and architect James Chapman-Taylor designed the Transformer House and Clock Tower, among other Havelock North buildings.[125]

Hastings began its flirtation with Spanish Mission before the First World War, when the style was adopted by Henry White for the new Municipal Theatre. William Rush used the same style for the Iona College buildings of 1913, infusing the same themes into Bernard Chambers' home of 1922. Alfred Garnet adopted the modernist look for Hastings' Kilford and Ebbett building of 1917 and the Fitzpatrick & Co Bulding of 1924. Napier architect J. Louis Hay brought 'prairie' styling to the district with his Soldiers' Club of 1920 and his Women's Rest building in Clive Square.[126] Eric Phillips preferred 'classical revival' for the Napier Public Trust Office of 1926, one of the first large reinforced concrete buildings of the district. Other modernist structures that went up in a flurry of urban renewal during the late 1920s included E. A. Williams' Dalgety Building and motor garages such as Fred Lowe Motors and the Lerew Garage.[127] Spanish Mission appeared here and there, notably in the attractive but structurally flawed Nurse's Home atop Napier's Barrack hill. By 1930 both Napier and Hastings were well down the path to modernism in the ordinary course of urban renewal — and then, without warning, disaster struck.

From quake to depression

Napier 'after the quake, before the fire'. As the last tremor subsided, photographer A. B. Hurst rushed from his Napier studio and captured a succession of images — not realising that this record would become even more remarkable after fire ripped through the shattered buildings, completing the destruction.

Storkey Collection

The morning of 3 February began as any other Hawke's Bay summer day. The sea was unusually calm after two days of turbulence,[128] but few paid much attention as the region settled into another glorious summer's morning. The New Zealand Naval Division sloop HMS *Veronica* arrived for a scheduled visit and moored at the Ahuriri quayside. Children went to school. Bernard Chambers left his home near Havelock North to buy parts for his water system.[129]

Suddenly, just after 10.47 a.m., two spasms of violence brought the district to its knees. In just three minutes Hawke's Bay was cast into ruin by one of the largest earthquakes ever recorded in New Zealand, leaving more than 250 dead and thousands injured. Everybody who lived through it remembered the moment. For some it was the noise. K. C. Sinclair thought the sound 'indescribable'.[130] Llewellyn Mitchell des Landes, working in the Napier Gas Company, compared the sound to 'an express train.'[131] Others recalled the violence. W. A. Ashcroft, sitting in his Napier office, compared the movement to a terrier shaking a jack-rabbit.[132] A young woman near Napier's Nelson Park was writing to a friend; ink splattered the page, then she was slammed to the floor.[133] Others saw water gush into the air as shock waves squeezed the aquifer.[134]

In the Napier Technical School, boys 'rushed back to extricate their pals' between the two shocks, and were 'buried under the fallen walls'.[135] One woman in the Masonic hotel ran for the door as 'huge blocks of masonry' crashed around her.[136] On board the merchant *Taranaki*,

The history of Hawke's Bay

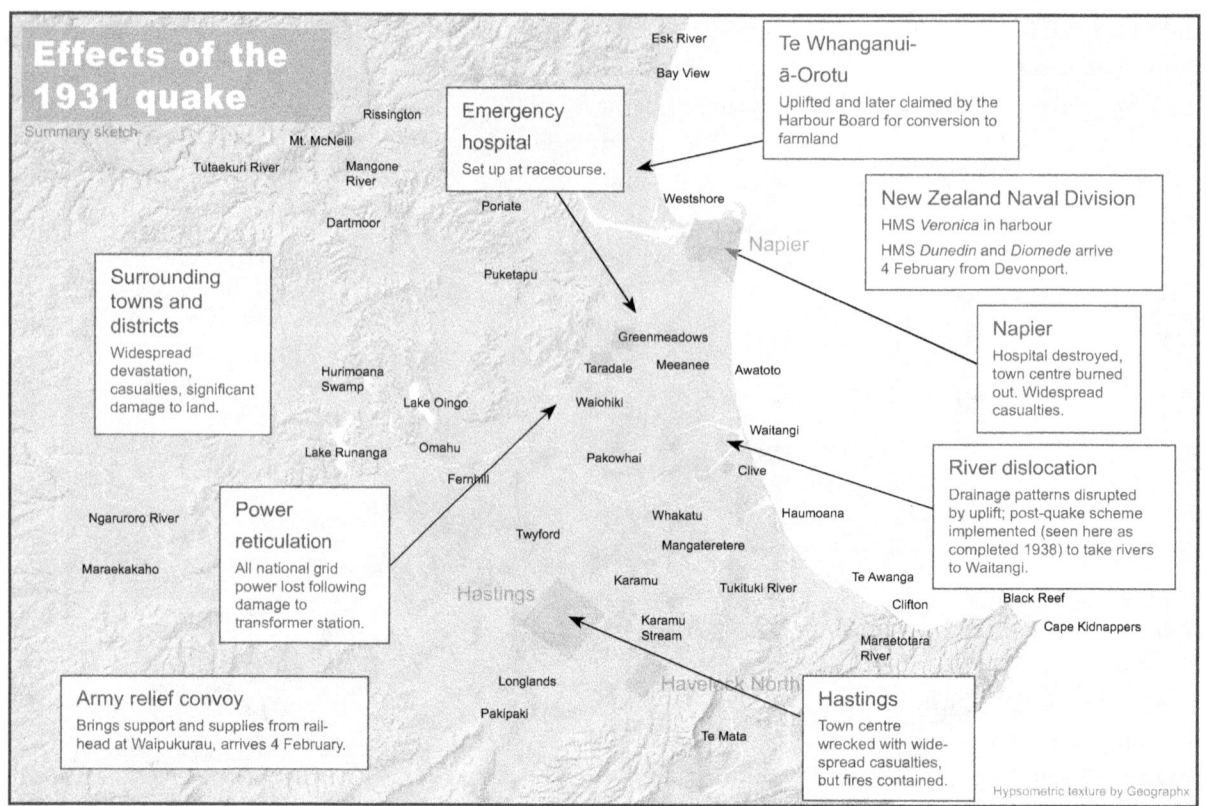

anchored in the roadstead, J. J. Grundy saw 'the whole of Napier' seem to 'elevate itself and then subside' in a cloud of dust.[137] The new nurse's home collapsed 'like a house of cards' with an 'appalling' noise and a cloud of dust.[138] One nurse dashed from the front door as the building fell,[139] but others asleep after night duty were killed. Mary Hunter tried to leave her flat on the hill, scrambled up the steps to the road, and saw 'hundreds of spiral yellow dust clouds going up in the air from the fallen chimneys of every house in sight.'[140]

The whole province was devastated. Hastings' business district became a 'gully of destruction beneath whose ruins could be heard the cries of women and children.'[141] Reginald Gardiner stopped a woman rushing out of the *Herald Tribune* office — saving her life as the pediment crashed down over the entrance. Fifty people were caught inside G. F. Roach's collapsing drapery store,[142] Ernie Weston saw a woman killed by a falling pillar and realised he had 'missed death by inches'.[143] The Cosy Theatre crumbled 'as though its foundations had been swept from underneath it'.[144] In Havelock North, school pupil Gwen Moran was showered with water from the school pool, while somebody cried 'it's the end of the world — the end of the world'.[145] Near Mohaka, Darry McCarthy watched 300 acres collapse into the sea.[146] Two people died in Wairoa, where chimneys collapsed and hogsheads of beer were catapulted from a gantry in the Wairoa Wine and Spirit Company 'as if by giant hands.'[147]

Rescue came swiftly. Some citizens were stunned and shocked; but others — many with military training — rallied at once. So did the navy. Commander H. L. Morgan put parties ashore from the *Veronica* as soon as he had secured the ship. Medical services were hampered by the wreck of the Napier hospital, but there was a 'complete absence of panic'[148] among hospital staff, who rescued patients from the devastated buildings and set up emergency facilities to treat the injured under direction of Dr A. G. Clark. One persistent myth, widely circulated at the time, was that anaesthetics were not used.[149] Wanganui nurse M. D. McNab was even told that doctors were operating 'with pocket knives and razor blades'.[150] None of this was true; antiseptic and anaesthetic procedures remained in force, as doctors were at pains to emphasise a few days later.[151] Casualties flooded in,[152] and hospital authorities activated a plan for an emergency hospital on the Napier racecourse, organised years earlier when a train wreck at Opapa overwhelmed local facilities. Some 454 injured survivors were eventually treated in Napier and Hastings.[153]

Blazes followed the quake, but fire-fighting efforts in Napier were hampered when the water ran out on the back of a complete power

> "Ernie Weston saw a woman killed by a falling pillar and realised he had 'missed death by inches'."

Opposite below: Napier Fire Superintendent W.J. Gilberd and his men tackle a major blaze at the rear of Henderson's Pharmacy, 30 minutes after the quake. This fire, combined with another from the nearby Masonic Hotel, spread to Napier's business district. Initial water pressure was excellent; however, brigade pumping and cracked pipes emptied the Cameron Road reservoir, and power to the borough pumps had failed. Figures centre-frame are thought to be bookshop owners Ernie and Maggie Storkey.

(Storkey Collection)

> "By 7 February some 4,873 people had gone in an exodus that reminded many of war-torn France."

failure: the shock destroyed connections to the national grid and wrecked the borough's standby generators. It was a fatal blow. At first there was a 'good working supply and pressure of water',[154] but once the Cameron Road reservoir had been drained — partly through cracked pipes, mostly by the brigade pumps — there was no more. Efforts to pump seawater were foiled by loose shingle,[155] but Fire Superintendent W. J. Gilberd and his men never gave up. A fortuitous turn of wind helped as they pumped from old sumps and dynamited buildings to make fire-breaks.[156] The 'deafening explosions' sent 'bits of iron' whirling 400 metres or more into Nelson Park.[157] Over the next 24 hours, without respite, the firemen and volunteers laboured to keep fires out of the wooden housing district. However, more than 11 blocks of Napier's business district had to be left to burn,[158] showering survivors with 'very disagreeable' smuts.[159] Fires in Ahuriri were less rampant, despite being fuelled by 4000 casks of tallow.[160] Hastings was more fortunate; the borough power house remained intact and council engineers had the big General Electric diesels running within 90 minutes, keeping the water pressure up and helping the local fire department contain the Hastings blazes in ways that the Napier department could not.[161]

New Zealand rallied to help. Morgan signalled Devonport naval base by Morse a few minutes after the shuddering subsided, and at 11.20 the *Northumberland* broadcast the first general alarm, followed by the *Taranaki*. A little later, Napier 'ham' radio operator G. E. Tyler, running on batteries, signalled contacts in the South Island.[162] New Zealand rallied. The two cruisers of the New Zealand Naval Division, HMS *Dunedin* and HMS *Diomede*, were preparing to leave harbour for exercises that morning and had steam up. When the news came in, Commodore Geoffrey Blake cancelled the manoeuvres and called Auckland hospital. Eleven doctors and 17 nurses reported to the quayside within 90 minutes. Medical supplies, stores, rescue equipment and tents shortly arrived, and by 2.30 p.m. the cruisers were at sea, working up to best speed for an overnight dash to the disaster zone.[163] Meanwhile Cabinet — alerted by the *Northumberland*'s signals — met in emergency session in Wellington and took swift decisions. That afternoon a special train left for Napier with men and equipment from Trentham army camp. The train could only get as far as Waipukurau, but the gear was trans-shipped to trucks in the early hours of 4 February and the convoy arrived in Napier around 6.15 a.m., a few minutes before the cruisers reached the harbour roadstead.[164]

Local authorities met Cabinet representatives in the Napier Borough Council chambers. Decisions were taken to ensure public health,

F. C. Wright amidst the rubble, a little after the quake, possibly in front of the damageed Women's Rest building in Clive Square, looking north towards the devastated town centre.

Storkey Collection

distribute food and water, re-establish law and order, and then evacuate everybody who could be moved — largely for fear of disease in the face of broken sewerage systems. In Napier, a relief and evacuation camp was set up in Nelson Park, eventually housing more than 2000 people. By 7 February some 4,873 people had gone in an exodus that reminded many of war-torn France. 'The traffic on the road to Palmerston North was tremendous,' one reporter wrote. 'Cars, lorries, everything on wheels seemed to be there. They were full of furniture, bedding, mattress, babies prams, and all sorts of household utensils.'[165] Mary Hunter was driven south at night in a line of vehicles that 'looked like a fiery serpent when we got to the bends in the road.'[166] This was no exaggeration: the vehicles were counted. Some 27,000 cars were marshalled through Waipukurau on 5 February alone, underscoring both the scale of the exodus, and the degree to which New Zealand had motorised by then.[167]

A definitive death toll was never reached despite every effort at the time. F. R. Callaghan's official 1933 figure of 256, given in his report on the calamity, was actually a glitch; some 258 names were recorded on the earthquake memorial in Napier's Park Island cemetery.[168] However, that included people whose bodies were never found and were presumed dead, and question marks remained. Among other uncertainties were persistent stories of a woman known to be in the Masonic Hotel, whose body was never found after the fire; and rumours of a car buried under rubble near Bluff Hill. This last was not dispelled until the slip was cleared in the 1960s. Unofficial efforts to revise the total produced figures of more than 260 — in one case, adding deaths from a Wairoa air crash a few days later, which seemed to be stretching the definition. A 2016 effort by genealogists to produce a final number lowered the total to 253, although this too was shortly disputed.[169]

All the deaths were tragedies for the people and families involved; but from the broader historical perspective the debate over whether there were a few more or less than the official total did not alter the general scale of what had happened. It was New Zealand's most lethal natural disaster, and to the death toll must be added over 400 hospitalisations with serious injuries, and at least 2500 others suffering bruises, cuts, contusions, breaks, sprains and burns — though not all bothered to report their injuries to over-worked authorities.[170]

The strength of the quake was also revised. At the time, California-based seismologist Charles Richter calculated the main shock at 7.9 on his eponymous scale, slightly ahead of the 1929 shock near Murchison and exceeded in historical times only by the huge Wellington quake of 1855 and, potentially, by another Hawke's Bay shock of 1863. In 1981, New Zealand seismologists re-calculated the intensity on the 'Moment Magnitude' scale, which offered a more accurate measurement of the energies involved. The new calculation produced a slightly lower result than Richter's, and the disaster officially became the 'Magnitude 7.8 1931 Hawke's Bay, New Zealand' earthquake.[171] It was still popularly called the 'Napier' earthquake;[172] but such distinctions did not reduce the fact that, from the historical perspective, the quake was a calamity for the whole of Hawke's Bay and well beyond. Although felt most intensely in the Heretaunga region, it collapsed buildings from Gisborne to Dannevirke, dropped chimneys in Wanganui, swayed others in Wellington,[173] and was felt across the whole of New Zealand. Virtually everybody in Hawke's Bay was affected by it; and indirectly, the disaster affected everybody in the country, one way or another. Virtually every family knew somebody caught up in it— or offered help to the victims, strangers or not.

This human response to the catastrophe highlighted the character of Hawke's Bay's inter-war society, and was evident from the moments after the main shock subsided. Much flowed from war experience. Many of

F. C. Wright peeling potatoes for an out-door meal at the home of Ernie and Maggie Storkey in Faraday Street, Napier, a few days after the quake. A former professional soldier, he also worked at the Nelson Park refugee camp, lending aid and assistance, after the quake.
Storkey Collection

Hawke's Bay's men had served on the Western Front, they knew how to handle themselves in a crisis; and when disaster struck, they knew what had to be done.

Former British regular soldier F. C. Wright was working on Bluff Hill when the quake struck. He began walking home, then found a panic-stricken woman who had rushed from a house as the hillside fell from under the foundations — leaving her baby in the teetering building. Ignoring the risks, he hastened into the house and rescued the child. A little further on he found others who needed assistance. Although he knew his wife and son would be worried, he could not abandon those who needed help, and in the end spent the rest of the day helping in town.[174] He was not alone. Reginald Gardiner worked all day to help in Hastings, not returning to Havelock North until late afternoon, to the 'great joy and relief' of his family.[175] Others worked on despite personal tragedy. Constable Tripney knew his wife and son had been killed, but 'continued to work... ... with rescue and search parties.'[176] Dr A. D. S. Whyte 'worked in the operating room for hours after he knew his daughter had been killed'[177]

Military structures based around earlier First World War army arrangements also provided a framework for rescue and relief. In Hastings, former Colonel H. H. Holderness was appointed head of a citizens committee, rallying many of his former soldiers, to help[178] while Major W. A. G. Penlington got the task of raising 150 'special police'.[179]

Those without military experience found the disaster traumatic; some even suffered what E. F. Scott called 'an attack of excitement hysteria.'[180] One woman caught in Roach's store later reported that 'the most terrible feeling was that of helplessness.'[181] Another survivor declared that 'Aunty was hysterical absolutely.'[182] One Hastings woman was found 'aimlessly wandering the wrecked streets and asking people indiscriminately if they had seen her husband or children.'[183] Many had trouble sleeping, particularly in the face of apparently endless aftershocks. Ernest St. Clair Haydon found himself 'roaring with laughter' and 'crying like a baby', which he recognised as 'nerves'.[184]

The quake certainly generated fresh community spirit; 'neighbour helped neighbour,' and 'for the time being, at least, there is a greater human understanding of each other than ever there was before. May it continue!'[185] When the milkman turned up on the Napier hill on the day of the quake he gave away his stock.[186] Sailors searching 'in all directions for food, bedding and stores' found most owners 'only too willing to assist

"Many drew on war experience in an effort to comprehend the destruction."

> "Despite an outstanding Māori claim dating back to 1851, when Donald McLean negotiated the Ahuriri block, much of the former lagoon was claimed by the Harbour Board as a 'gift from the sea'. That was fighting talk to local councils and Māori alike…"

us in any way possible.'[187] Most of the goods were accounted for.[188]

Many drew on war experience in an effort to comprehend the destruction. 'Scenes reminiscent of the war time in France,' read one caption in the *Daily Telegraph*'s 1931 book *Before and After*.[189] Ruined Napier was openly compared to shell-ravaged Ypres, and a sailor from the *Veronica* thought the experience was 'far worse' than the war.[190] The struggle of 1914–18 also provided an anchor for the social response. 'Too much cannot be said of the splendid spirit of the Napier people,' a reporter wrote. 'There is something in big catastrophes that brings out the best in everyone, as did the Great War, and the way in which people are forgetting themselves to others strikes the stranger forcibly. Property is nothing. Fatigue and personal feelings do not count.'[191] One newspaper suggested afterwards that the blow 'entirely failed to crush the spirit of Napier's community'.[192] This was true in one sense: but in other ways it compounded the problems of economic depression and drought. Although W. Olphert found people 'wonderfully cheerful',[193] visiting doctor Agnes Bennett saw 'dumb misery… even the children seemed toneless and wearied'.[194]

For Hawke's Bay, already hammered by drought and the economic downturn that began in 1930, the quake threatened collapse. 'Farming was in a very bad way before this came along,' Ernest St. Claire Haydon wrote to friends soon afterwards 'and it now seems to have put the finishing touch to it all.'[195] Thoughts turned to reconstruction, but government was not forthcoming. Part of the issue was practical; the depression that hit Britain in 1930 dried up New Zealand's primary market. Local farm and factory production dropped nearly 20 percent, by value, between 1929-30 and 1930-31.[196] As Tutira's Herbert Guthrie-Smith remarked, the 'harassed government' had lost its sources of income.[197] However, there were also ideological issues. Forbes returned from the Imperial Conference of August 1930 fuelled with notions of book-balancing, given impetus by the fiscal 'sanity and sobriety' prescribed by visiting British banker Sir Otto Niemeyer.[198]

The Hawke's Bay Earthquake Act of April 1931 provided just £1.5 million, about $132 million in early 21st century equivalent money,[199] of which the majority went to businesses and local bodies. Local MP H. M. Campbell condemned it as a 'feeble start'[200] in the face of estimated losses that topped £3,685,450.[201] This was no over-reaction; a 1995 analysis revealed that average repair costs in Napier amounted to £64 per house,

Looking south along Napier's Tennyson Street, late 1930s. The Public Trust building, left foreground, survived the quake largely due to heavy reinforcing.

David Williams, Dave Williams Collection, Hawke's Bay Museum, W44a

mostly for chimneys, of which relief funds — including donations — covered only about 60 percent.[202] The local mood was at times despairing. 'The newspapers use the old slogans "Business as usual"', Dorothy Campbell wrote, '"A newer & better Napier will rise from the ashes of the old", but oh the pitifulness of it all.'[203] Napier's 1935 swing to Labour almost certainly emerged from this treatment.

Government penury put paid to early plans for grandiose reconstruction of Napier on Spanish Mission lines.[204] The town emerged instead with a collection of small modernist buildings, leavened by occasional larger structures such as the Masonic Hotel, the T & G Building and a stylish Municipal Theatre. Reconstruction also fuelled fresh debate in Napier and Hastings over practical matters of street width and town planning. This was resolved in Napier by a three-man government commission given power to slash red tape. Streets were widened, corners splayed, and some 586 building permits granted,[205] with a value to the end of March 1933 of £612,000.[206] Rubble from the old town centre was deposited on the waterfront, making way for a Hollywood-inspired soundshell, colonnades and park extending north to the city baths, echoing the modernist look of contemporary Santa Barbara. The town centre was officially reopened in January 1933,[207] though reconstruction continued into the Second World War — and some buildings, such as the

Picnicking at the annual Hawke's Bay Agricultural and Pastoral Society Show, 1930s style. The cars are noteworthy. By this time the transition to cars is virtually complete, underscoring the fact that by this time New Zealand had become absolutely reliant on imported fuels. The depression reduced the spread of car ownership to blue collar workers, but did not dislodge the fact that cars had become relatively commonplace, and that vehicles in general had almost wholly replaced horse-drawn traffic by this time, aside from suburban milk-floats and a few other hold-outs.

David Williams, Dave Williams Collection, Hawke's Bay Museum, W11b

Anglican Cathedral, were not renewed until the 1950s.[208] The slip under Bluff Hill, which as we have seen was widely thought to have entombed a car with its occupants, was not cleared until the 1960s.

In Hastings, reconstruction included 422 permits for new buildings worth £341,000.[209] However, the effort was marred by a spat between former mayor George Ebbett and standing mayor G. F. Roach.[210] The latter, following nearly 65 percent of his rate-payers, wanted the streets widened, setting his new building off the street in anticipation. Ebbett had enough clout to force the council to abandon the plan.[211]

The disaster was never forgotten and, for those who lived through it, remained an immediate memory. As late as the 1960s and 1970s, when New Zealand's large-scale seismic activity had temporarily subsided and large quakes seemed to be history for a new generation, many Hawke's Bay people spoke in hushed tones of 'the quake', as an immediate event that divided past from present. And in many ways, it was a significant arbiter, certainly socially, for those who lived through the crisis. Their experience included the subsequent aftershock sequence — a relentless series of tremors that continued to shake the district but which were somehow lost to history.

The quake also had a substantial physical effect, well beyond the immediate destruction, and one that shaped the fortunes of Napier

Beach life near Clifton in the 1930s.

David Williams, Dave Williams Collection, Hawke's Bay Museum, W277

through to the end of the century and beyond. In a reversal of the fifteenth-century subduction, the uplift drained much of the Te Whanganui-ā-Orotū lagoon and raised the raupo swamplands to the south of the town. Despite an outstanding Māori claim on it dating back to 1851, when Donald McLean negotiated the Ahuriri block, much of the lagoon was claimed by the Harbour Board as a 'gift from the sea'.[212] That was fighting talk to local councils and Māori alike, but the more urgent problem for the councils was the fact that the same uplift altered drainage patterns across the district, and there was a high risk of flooding.[213] As always with river control schemes the issue was cost. Debate was as bitter as ever, although this time the issue had to be resolved; and in 1932 F. C. Hay proposed a dramatic plan to divert the Tutaekuri wholly down its overflow channel to Waitangi, matching that with other work on the Ngaruroro. The scheme came with a £360,000 price tag, some $36.8 million in equivalent early 21st century money.[214] Government passed legislation to fund it, and work began in March 1934. The diversions were

Napier's Marine Parade gardens on a blazing summer's day in the late 1930s. The Soundshell was modelled by borough council architect J. T. Watson on the Hollywood Bowl and went up in 1935. The fountain was a 1936 gift by Napier businessman Tom Parker, apparently inspired by a similar fountain in Bournemouth. The Soundshell and Sun Bay are in place, but the surround lacks Watson's New Napier arch of 1940, dating this image to the immediate pre-war years.

Photographer unidentified, Alexander Turnbull Library, F-60950-1/2

finished just in time. Flooding in April 1938 tested the new system to its limits, damaging the bridge at Waitangi.[215]

There was a small plus to this otherwise unrelieved gloom. The Harbour Board had plans for turning a profit from the land they had claimed, using depression labour to turn former lagoon-bed into productive farms. The new territory also offered potential to resolve Napier's space problems, and in April 1934 the Harbour Board agreed to relinquish 475 acres of raupo swamp south of the town to the Napier Borough Council. A bridge was put across the old Tutaekuri River bed, Kennedy Road was extended, and the streets of a new suburb — Marewa — were laid out with the help of unemployment relief gangs.[216] Everything about it spoke of modernity, even down to the daring way some streets broke with the grid, hooking instead in wide zig-zags to match the northern curve of the suburb. Street names commemorated war heroes, post-quake administrators and town luminaries. California was an overt architectural influence, and one street — Tom Parker Avenue — mimicked the tree-lined roads of Hollywood's movie-star district. In a further nod to 1930s ideals even a suburban shopping centre was envisaged, a novelty in New Zealand of the day. Construction was nonetheless slow. Just 17 houses were available by April 1939, far less than Napier's estimated shortfall of 500.[217]

District reconstruction took place amid the worst economic depression of the twentieth century. Although domestic prices fell sharply — and, as John Mulgan put it, the 'lovely and satirical' daughters of Auckland's Remuera aristocracy did well[218] — farmers were hit hard as export volumes and prices fell. The effects were particularly dire for provinces such as Hawke's Bay, where the whole local economy rested on pastoral prosperity: a downturn on the farms had knock-on effects into the urban areas, particularly service towns such as Hastings.

Guthrie-Smith's experiences with Tutira station highlight the challenges that Hawke's Bay's pastoral sector had to face. He made a profit of £5,722 in 1929, a dead loss of £331 in 1930, and then in 1931 — partly because of the quake — his losses spiralled to £4,276, around $377,500 in early 21st century money.[219] But the following year was not much better at a loss of £2,336.[220] He was not alone. Even farmers working relatively fertile down-country areas such as the Takapau plains, or parts of Heretaunga not yet turned over to horticulture were challenged. Back-country stations were often in dire straits. One Kuripapango family managed to keep their farm running in the depths of the depression on the proverbial oily rag, one year spending just £70, around $7200 in equivalent early 21st century money.[221] Others simply abandoned their properties.

These difficulties flowed through the rest of society. Fortunes were particularly bad for townsfolk. Most farmers could feed themselves to some extent. The urban unemployed could not, though the domestic quarter-acre with its vegetable garden and chicken coops helped. But some people were so beset with gloom at the loss of their jobs and prosperity that they did not have the enthusiasm even to till their own back yards. National unemployment peaked in 1933 at 79,425, a percentage and number not exceeded until 1992,[222] and Hawke's Bay shared the

Mothers with their children in Hastings' Cornwall Park, late 1930s.

David Williams, Dave Williams Collection, Hawke's Bay Museum, W1a

> "Rock-bottom morale disguised the fact that Coates — popularly reviled by his support of Forbes' 'ill-starred necessities' — was clawing the country back from the brink."

crisis. Children were sent to school cold and often hungry. Despite the mythology of a post-quake boom in Hawke's Bay, reconstruction money did not infuse much into the local economy.[223] Towns such as Wairoa, Waipawa, Waipukurau, Dannevirke and Norsewood missed out on most of it anyway, but even spending in Napier and Hastings was only a drop in the wider bucket.

To give that point due numbers, the district normally fielded around 6 percent of the national construction total. That rose to 13 percent in mid-1934 but fell again in 1935. Although only estimates are available, the total economic effect of reconstruction was apparently equal to about two percent of pre-quake gross domestic product.[224] There was certainly no real effect on unemployment. Around 300 new jobs were created in 1932–33,[225] but the unemployment rate did not materially fall. By April 1931 there were 817 unemployed in Hastings borough, although only about half of the 278 applications for emergency relief between March and July 1931 were attributed to the quake.[226] Relief employment was handled by local bodies, but minimal wages and often humiliating conditions did not help. The Napier Borough Council set up a committee to find youth work in 1932.[227]

The depression was as much a moral crisis as an economic one: economic measures point to a relatively sharp 18-month downturn, after which New Zealand began to recover, guided largely by Gordon Coates. However, the psychological and moral effects were deeper and longer-lasting. The penurious nature of government relief schemes, which by nature implicitly blamed those reliant on those schemes for their own misfortune, was a particular trigger which struck home in Hawke's Bay during the bleak winter of 1933, when the Hawke's Bay County Council tried to use relief gangs to dig the Tutaekuri diversion. This prompted a strike among Hastings relief workers which escalated when the local business community threatened to cut off their 'week end sustenance' — meaning their families would go hungry.[228] This ideological collision underscored the most crucial impact of the depression — the destruction of hope, which was driven to a large extent by government policies that appeared to punish the unemployed for being so. The experience of the work gangs, the cries of hungry children, the worry about where the next meal might come from, became doubly demoralising for men who had lived through a war that matched the Dantean vision of hell — and who had been promised a life fit for heroes afterwards. Their families shared their misery, and these emotions seared the depression experience into the minds of two generations. Local body

efforts to alleviate public sufffering in Hawke's Bay included a popular carnival in 1932[229] and the New Napier celebrations the following January. At the end of 1933 — the Hastings Borough Council set up a 'good cheer depot'.[230]

Rock-bottom morale disguised the fact that Coates — popularly reviled by his support of Forbes' 'ill-starred necessities'[231] — was clawing the country back from the brink. By 1934 he was able to restart public works projects and hoped to introduce state-funded milk in schools to nourish New Zealand's hungry children. But this came too late to restore faith. Public sentiment turned away from a government whose aim, in the mind of the unemployed and their families, appeared to be finding new ways of punishing people whose ill-fortune was no fault of their own.

Labour offered alternatives. Although feared during the 1920s for their radical economic ideas, they swung closer to the economic centre after the death of leader Harry Holland in 1933, and under the avuncular leadership of Michael Joseph Savage, promised a 'way out of chaos to a land fit for heroes' in the 1935 election. The electorate responded with a landslide, 53 seats to 19, destroying the Coates-Forbes coalition. Hawke's Bay shared the swing. largely through dissatisfaction over the government's earthquake response. Conservative Hastings member H. C. Campbell was gone, replaced by Labour candidate E. L. Cullen.[232]

Crowds at the Wairoa railway station mark the opening of the line from Napier, 8 July 1939. The Standard class railcar RM-30 'Aotea', apparently swamped by the crowds, carries the official ministerial party. Restarting the long-delayed Napier-Gisborne line was an initiative of the first Labour government

Photographer unidentified, Evening Post Collection, Alexander Turnbull Library, F-61441-1/2

A Daily Telegraph advertisement for Westinghouse refrigerators sold by Lockyer's appliances, 6 October 1938.

Despite conservative fears, Labour in its post-Holland guise intended to harness capitalism, not destroy it.[233] Finance Minister Walter Nash — whose grandchildren, as it happened, lived in Napier[234] — developed plans with assistance from Coates' former advisor William Sutch, among others.[235] They arrived to a fast-rising economy, which to a large part was Coates' doing; but Labour had their own vision for what to do with that recovery. The new approach began with a vigorous public works programme, which for Hawke's Bay included renewed work on the railway to Gisborne, a project launched from Napier in 1912, but which by 1936 had not even reached Wairoa.

National self-sufficiency was also the order of the day, coupled after 1938 with an initiative that Savage called 'applied Christianity'[236] — government welfare, health-care and old-age policies geared to help those whose misfortune was not of their own doing.

These policies carried a financial cost, one that became clear when the economic recovery dipped in the late 1930s and provoked a debt crisis with Britain. However, that did not affect the recovery of morale, or the way in which New Zealanders in general enjoyed a sudden jump in prosperity and hope, and where local authorities were able to push ahead with long-delayed works.

This last was certainly true in Hawke's Bay, where Borough Councils and Town Boards pressed ahead with road sealing and other public works. By 1939, Hastings drivers could use some 33.08 miles of bitumen seal, 12.33 miles of tarmac, and pedestrians had over 68 miles of sealed footpaths. Plans were afoot to improve water mains and sewage systems.[237]

Hawke's Bay fruit made up just under a quarter of the national crop exported to Britain in 1938.[238] Horticulture was also growing, driven from the mid-1930s when James Wattie opened a jam-making plant in Hastings, then expanded to canned peas, tomatoes and vegetables. In 1937

Napier's Finch and Westerholm-designed State Theatre, probably in August 1939. Note the displaced last 's' in the sign advertising The Little Princess, *a Technicolor period drama directed by Walter Lang and starring Shirley Temple.*
Photographer unidentified, Alexander Turnbull Library, F-57333-1/2

he began buying his own horticultural farms across the plains to supply his factory.[239] By the late 1930s even back-country sheep farmers began making money. Guthrie-Smith received a blessing from his bank manager when the Tutira account went into credit.[240]

The rise in prosperity fuelled a consumer boom. 'Step up to the V8 class', one advertisement urged motorists.[241] Everybody wanted household appliances. In Hastings, the number of electric ranges quintupled between 1934 and 1939 — by the time war broke out, just under one in six Hastings homes had one,[242] while the number of homes with electric water heating shot up from 19 in 1934 to 777 in 1939.[243] Refrigerators joined the widening range of home appliances, although the idea of home refrigeration still had to be sold as a concept in the late 1930s. Lockyer's appliances of Napier and Hastings pushed the modernist-style 1938 Westinghouse for its 'kitchen-proved meat-keeper' — a covered tray sitting beneath the freezer box — promising 'big food savings' — and novelties such as ice cubes in just 56 minutes.[244] One Napier example, albeit with replacement motor, was still in use into the 1980s.

Although chains such as Woolworths, Hallenstein's and Humphries' Cash Groceries made an appearance in Hawke's Bay, most shops were still owner-operated, trading on the repute of local storekeepers who were well known and respected around town. 'Why walk when you could ride in comfort on a Jim Etheridge bike'?[245]

Hotels from Waipukurau's Tavistock to Napier's Criterion competed for diners' custom. Hastings' Olympic Grill offered 'meals at all hours', including 'rabbits and poultry'.[246] Movies had been a reliable and cheap standby even in the depths of the depression, and never lost their charm. One night in October 1938, Hawke's Bay cinema-goers could choose between *Lily of Laguna* at the Plaza — and the 'sepia toned' Otto Preminger-directed flick *Kidnapped*, at Napier's new Spanish Mission-style State theatre. Or families could while away the afternoon at the Mayfair cinema, thrilling first to the serial adventures of Flash Gordon, then the *Air Devils* and finally *Midnight Menace* — a tale set in what the newspaper promotions described as the 'sensation-seething atmosphere' of Europe.[247]

Such claims about Europe's state of affairs might have seemed little more than the hyperbole of period advertising, but they struck true in the late 1930s. Hawke's Bay newspaper headlines that October weekend were dominated by the Czechoslovakian crisis as an impoverished Britain tried to keep a resurgent Nazi Germany at bay. Tensions spiralled over the next months; and in early September 1939, for the second time in a quarter century, Hawke's Bay's people found themselves at war.

CHAPTER SIX
Suburban paradise

The Second World War experience and its consequences gave Hawke's Bay — like New Zealand as a whole — much of its mid-twentieth century shape.

War shortages brought echoes of the depression, but there was no lack of work. Draconian 'manpower' regulations ultimately maximised New Zealand's war effort. Hawke's Bay escaped the infusion of American GI's who influenced life in Wellington and Auckland, but district families still had to face wartime shortages of labour and materials, the threat of a Japanese invasion; and as always, the stress of knowing that many of their sons and fathers faced death in foreign lands. The generation who went to fight between 1939 and 1945 — these 'mature men … quiet and shrewd and sceptical'[1] — came home knowing what they wanted.

The war cast a pall over New Zealand's centennial celebration. The Hawke's Bay effort focussed on a contribution to national events near Wellington's Lyall Bay, but there were other events in Hawke's Bay, including 'Māori entertainment', sports meets, gatherings of 'old identities', and — inevitably — shopping promotions.[2] The moment was marked in print by J. G. Wilson's narrative provincial history, a three-year committee project.[3]

New tensions with Japan during 1940 prompted government efforts to establish a Home Guard, drawing in 5,654 Hawke's Bay men — including First World War veterans — by March 1941.[4] Lack of a national instruction manual was met by Hawke's Bay territorial officers, who

Emerson Street, Napier, probably 1939–40. Post-quake construction is virtually complete. By these middle decades of the twentieth century, both Napier and Hastings were assuming a dominating role in Hawke's Bay, economically, politically and socially — much of it by virtue of population.

David Williams, Dave Williams Collection, Hawke's Bay Museum, W216a

wrote one.[5] Lack of weapons was less easy to overcome: and although government commandeered all privately-held small arms, some units still had to practise initially with broom-sticks. The government also set up a civilian Emergency Precautions Service (EPS), a national effort based on systems set up in wake of the Hawke's Bay earthquake, organised around local body structures, though this brought rivalries into fresh focus.[6] Lobbying for a military base in Hawke's Bay came to nothing,[7] but practical defences set up during the early war years included trenches and air-raid shelters — in Hastings, enough to house 900 people.[8] Concrete bunkers were built along the Napier shoreline north and south of the harbour; but here the populace seemed less inclined to share the load. A March 1942 call to dig an air-raid shelter near Browning Street produced a dismal response.[9] Despite a 'stay put' order by the government,[10] some Napier families also laid plans to get away into the back country if trouble brewed.[11]

The actual threat Hawke's Bay faced is debatable. United States researchers working through Japanese archives in 1947 discovered an occupation scheme for New Zealand,[12] but no explicit plan for the invasion that had to precede it. In 1940–41 the official assessment of the threat to New Zealand varied wildly from full-scale invasion to raids, and US analysts observed as early as 1942 that isolation alone would serve Japan's military purposes.[13] Coastal raids and assaults on local shipping were nonetheless a possibility in 1942. The Imperial Japanese Navy

deployed submarines into the South Pacific before war broke out in December 1941. One ran into a New Zealand auxiliary cruiser off Fiji in January 1942,[14] and three submarines operated close to the New Zealand coast during the year — even launching float-planes.[15]

However, despite popular fears, enemy action in Hawke's Bay was unlikely. Although Napier's harbour was the largest on the East Coast, the district had no other tactical significance; and planners in Tokyo prepared only conceptual plans for invasion, revolving around New Zealand's main centres.[16] Plans to invade Australia were developed; but both competed with schemes to take Hawaii. In the end Japan pushed east across the South Pacific islands to Polynesia in an effort to cut off Australasia and create a perimeter the United States would find hard to break. That stalled in the Solomons after the battles of Coral Sea and Midway in mid-1942, ending the threat of military attack on New Zealand.[17]

In the event, Hawke's Bay felt the practical impact of war in more subtle ways. German merchant raiders prompted compulsory blackouts from February 1941,[18] mainly to eliminate sky glow.[19] Napier residents nailed cloth and tar paper over windows — the marks still visible on the frames decades later[20] — and endured gloomy streets and blinkered headlights. It did not go down well.[21] Fears that enemy agents were planting propaganda among the populace triggered calls for 'rumour wardens'.[22]

These developments underscored the ubiquity of twentieth century total war. Radio — 'wireless', in period terms — kept Hawke's Bay's

Lower Heretaunga Street, Hastings, 1939–40. The car in right-front is a 1938 Ford Ten —effectively new, underscoring the recovery from depression. Perhaps more noteworthy are the bicycles. Despite growing prosperity, pedal-power was still an affordable transport option for many families, and hill-less Hastings was particularly well suited to them. By this time the borough was cemented as Hawke's Bay's key rural service centre.

David Williams, Dave Williams Collection, Hawke's Bay Museum, W318

Classic Kiwi camping, Clifton beach.

David Williams, Dave Williams Collection, Hawke's Bay Museum, W238c

families in touch with world events, and cinema newsreels were leavened with war coverage — documentaries such as 'Into Tripoli', 'In the Rear of the Enemy', and 'Russia fights for freedom'.[23] Patriotic Committees flourished; Hawke's Bay branches collected more than £100,000 worth of goods for the war effort, distributing more than 20,000 parcels for servicemen.[24] Hastings businessman Harry Poppelwell raised funds on a relatively large scale through his 'Fun Sessions' — variety shows by local entertainers. The idea was swiftly picked up by the Napier Patriotic Committee in a spirit of 'wholehearted co-operation' which, inevitably, was joined by 'hearty rivalry'.[25] Other social events and dances — including 'Jitterbug' contests — variously celebrated victories or raised money for the 'Māori War Effort'.[26]

War shortages brought echoes of the depression. Fuel was rationed, and restrictions were placed on train travel. Other imports, notably radios, were either unavailable or requisitioned by the government for the war effort. 'No more good new machines available until the end of the war,' Loach and Price declared by way of advertising their radio repair services.[27] Other goods were equally in short supply. 'Remember!' one Poppelwell's advertisement intoned in 1943, 'There will be no further stocks of double-breasted overcoats'.[28] 'Be measured for your suit NOW while we still have a smart range of English worsted suiting,' tailor Jack Snaddon warned Napier clients in 1942.[29] Some goods were nonetheless still available; one shop offered 'American skunk fur necklets'.[30]

Hawke's Bay industry swung to support the war effort. J. Wattie Canneries' output included some 145,000 dozen 'M & V' ('Meat and Vegetable') rations for the troops. Most of this went to the Pacific via the Joint Purchasing Board of the United States. A lend-lease canning plant and dehydration tunnel arrived at Wattie's plant in 1943.[31] By 1944 some 2700 acres were in fruit and 2000 acres in crops across the Heretaunga Plains, producing more than a million cases of apples and 1500 tons of peas, among other things — and production could apparently have been higher had more labour been available.[32] Other food was provided by donation. One major volunteer effort that spanned the war collected honey for the people of Hastings, Sussex. Deliveries were supplemented in 1944 by donations of toys, tomato soup from J. Wattie Canneries, and sweets offered by ice-cream maker F. C. Rush Munro.[33]

German and Japanese forces were notable by their absence off the Hawke's Bay coast. In the early 2000s there was speculation in Hawke's Bay media that the Japanese had landed a spy by submarine in 1943.[34] This was over-blown. Popular spy mania certainly ran hot during the war — Home Guard flash-signals between Napier and Mohaka were mistaken for espionage by the uninformed in 1941.[35] However, a wireless interception network and decryptions from the United States kept New Zealand military officials informed of Japanese submarine movements.[36] Coast-watchers and patrols completed the net; even floating mines were detected. There were submarine attacks in the Tasman during early 1943, and another national alert in November,[37] but it was 1945 before Hawke's Bay encountered the enemy more directly. In January, the German Type IX-D2 submarine U-862, under Käpitanleutnant Heinrich Timm, slipped into the bay.

The moment was thoroughly mythologised; later there were suggestions that Timm entered Napier's breakwater harbour;[38] or even that the crew came ashore and milked cows. That last had its origins, apparently, in a practical joke Timm played on Air Marshal Sir Rochford Hughes when both were serving in NATO forces in the 1950s, and Timm spun a tall tale of his own wartime exploits. However, the story gained a good deal of currency in 1990s Hawke's Bay, prompting one Meeanee farmer to insist that dry cows he recalled from late in the Second World War must have been caused by German submariners. The alleged landing and raid on Hawke's Bay's cow herds even spurred a stage play in the 1990s. But it was all wishful thinking; the voyage was well documented — not least by Timm himself, in the boat's official war diary: and the facts are more mundane.

'See Napier and Live!' — a 1944 riff by the government tourism board on the catch-phrase allegedly coined in the 1780s by Goethe: 'See Naples and Die'. The Italian city was in the forefront of the New Zealand mind for other reasons in 1943–44.

Artist unidentified, coloured print, Alexander Turnbull Library, Eph-A-TOURISM-Napier-1944-01

Crowds on Napier's waterfront, late 1930s.

David Williams, Dave Williams Collection, Hawke's Bay Museum, W243c

In May 1944 Timm sailed from Narvik for the Far East, reaching Penang in September, then went on to Australasian waters. He found no opportunities off Gisborne and Wairoa, and at dusk on 16 January 1945 motored across Hawke Bay to Napier. He knew about the beacons marking the route into the breakwater harbour, but although new wharves were opened in 1939 and 1943,[39] the harbour was still relatively shallow in 1945 and ships had to quit the place in certain tides and swells. Timm had no chance of entering; and even if he had, there was no room to manoeuvre. Nor was there any chance of landing.

The only vessel in harbour that night was the coaster *Pukeko*, but Timm knew none of this as his boat idled through the sea near Napier. Blackout was long over. The German sailors saw what they thought were well-lit street cafes, watching couples dancing to jazz that echoed across the quiet water.[40] It was a curiously European way of looking at the town; Napier had no such facilities in 1945, though given their line of approach the Germans were possibly looking at the Joylands cabaret at Westshore. The Soundshell was a popular roller-skating venue — but there was nothing formal scheduled that evening, though the swimming baths, on the waterfront a few hundred metres south of the breakwater harbour, were jammed with spectators watching a championship. At any event, Napier's people were clearly enjoying themselves.[41]

As the hours wore on the *Pukeko* left harbour, fully illuminated. Timm followed, attacked as dawn came on 17 January — and missed. A lone sailor on deck saw the torpedo as it streaked past, but it was such an unlikely sight in Hawke's Bay — at any stage in the war — that he thought he must be mistaken.[42] Timm continued to stalk the little vessel, but when she began signalling the Portland Island signal station, he decided they had been seen and sheared off to the south. Next day he was ordered to abandon the cruise.[43] His presence was never suspected ashore; and in one of the ironies of the day, this moment of drama — the district's sole close encounter with the enemy in the whole of that long and bitter war — went virtually unremarked for nearly fifty years.

Suburban sprawl and the pastoral revolution

By war's end much of the Hawke's Bay back-country lay under a shaggy coat of gorse and scrub, highlighted that summer when wildfires threatened Puketitiri.[44] Once again the district faced a difficult period of adjustment. Returned servicemen had to be settled, a process helped

Roller-skating on Napier's Marine Parade was popular during and after the Second World War.

David Williams, Dave Williams Collection, Hawke's Bay Museum, W168

Napier's breakwater harbour in the late 1940s, with the Blue Star cargo-liner Royal Star, *formerly the Clan Line's* Empire Wisdom, *on the left. The harbour was primary outlet for Hawke's Bay's exports — but still relatively shallow.*
David Williams, Dave Williams Collection, Hawke's Bay Museum, W208b

only slightly by a months-long wait for shipping home.[45] Others were 'manpowered' into Hawke's Bay's industries before war ended, part of a government effort to reorganise the economy for peace. Depression-era housing shortages had not been alleviated when war broke out, and a national crunch was widely expected. This was particularly true in Hawke's Bay, where a significantly higher proportion lived in urban areas by comparison with the rest of New Zealand.[46]

Fears that New Zealand might plunge into a new depression were, however, unfounded. The Labour government — cynically but practically — capitalised on the war situation to restore New Zealand's economic position;[47] and the Korean War that broke out in 1950 put wool at a premium. Prices rose from 37.98 pence per pound in 1949–50 to 87.47 pence per pound the following year.[48] The fleece that had spiralled Hawke's Bay to such prominence a century earlier was suddenly back in favour, and the district — which with the Wairarapa and parts of the Gisborne district carried just over a quarter of New Zealand's sheep flock,[49] was in a unique position to exploit it. The boom was further fuelled by the 'second pastoral revolution', the use of new technologies such as aerial topdressing and giant discing to bring marginal back-country into production. Some

1450 farmers formed a co-operative to establish a large fertiliser works at Awatoto, south of Napier, which opened in 1951.[50] That was distributed across wide areas of back-country initially by war-surplus Tiger Moths. Later the task was picked up by larger aircraft, including Lockheed Model 18 Lodestars and Douglas DC-3's operated by Gisborne-based Lawson Field, whose aircraft became a familiar sight in Hawke's Bay skies.

The effects were decisive: district stock-holding rose by about half in the 20 years from 1949.[51] Curiously, this was one of the lowest percentage increases in the country, suggesting that Hawke's Bay — as a pastoral district — was already running efficient farms.

Horticulture also flourished around Napier and Hastings, a relatively small region which nonetheless held one one-eighth of New Zealand's total area in orchard and market gardens.[52] J. Wattie Canneries went from strength to strength on the back of it, drawing much from the drive and character of its founder.[53] Dairying flourished in the south of the region. Most of this bounty flowed through Napier harbour, which became New Zealand's third largest export port by value by 1950.[54] As elsewhere, work came to a halt in February 1951 when watersiders struck. During the 151-day action, Napier's harbour was kept going by military personnel, mostly Air Force, who loaded cargoes bound for Britain and South Africa.[55] The town avoided much of the violence that flared elsewhere,[56] but shared the outcome. The National government of Sydney Holland used the moment to alter the power balance with the unions, and the new compact lasted until the 1990s.

Nuhaka, July 1949.

W. Wilson, Alexander Turnbull Library, National Publicity Studios Collection, F-39771-1/2, A 13389

A cycle race in Hastings, captured by Clive-based photographer Dave Williams probably during the late 1940s.

David Williams, Dave Williams Collection, Hawke's Bay Museum, W295

Traditional Hawke's Bay farming was joined during the 1950s by a new venture — forestry. This was a consequence of policies established during the First World War, when William Massey set the wheels in motion for better forest management through the Lands Department. Plans were given further shape in 1919 when Francis Dillon Bell called for a permanent Forest Service, initially to manage the remaining saleable tracts of bush. That role changed during the inter-war economic downturn and Depression era when plans to establish exotic forests were introduced as a make-work scheme. The first of them was set up on the central plateau and others followed, mostly planted in *Pinus radiata*, locally called either simply Radiata or sometimes Monterey or California pine. Douglas fir, Ponderosa and Corsican pine were introduced later, along with eucalypts, the latter in an effort to avert problems with a monoculture.

Hawke's Bay's first state forest was established near Tangoio in 1938, but the scale of the district state forest operation grew dramatically after the end of the Second World War. Significant areas of back-country fell into disrepair during the conflict because of labour shortages: gorse began to take over, and a succession of droughts emphasised the vulnerability of these districts to fire. At the same time, government was pushing to expand its forests, both for domestic timber and for export. Gwavas State Forest was set up in 1944, and Kaweka, Esk and Mohaka State Forests followed over the next few years. They brought controversy. The land selected for these enterprises was arguably not suited for farming even with the new techniques of the day, but that point was disputed by some of those who had farmed the land taken up for the new state forests. Opposition from some quarters to the forest development remained bitter even a generation later. The counter-argument was that even pine needed reasonable ground to flourish.

Exotic forestry had a significant impact on Hawke's Bay even before its own forests matured. Much of the output from the Kaingaroa State Forest was trucked down the Napier-Taupō Road to Napier, and efforts to improve this highway were largely driven by the trade in logs. A new bridge over the Mohaka River opened in 1966, helping slash travel times. The settler-era coach journey to Taupō had been a three-day affair. Early motor buses and better roading brought that down to a day. By the early 1960s it was a two or three-hour drive — and by the turn of the twenty-first century that had been slashed to just 90 or 100 minutes. Logging

Staff examining peas in the Hastings plant of J. Wattie Canneries, January 1948.

Photographer unidentified, New Zealand Free Lance Collection, Alexander Turnbull Library, F-160227-1/2, PAColl-5469-1/2

An iconic Hawke's Bay landmark; Pania of the Reef in June 1954, with May Robin of Hukarere Māori Girls College, who modelled for the face.

Photographer unidentified, New Zealand Free Lance Collection, Alexander Turnbull Library, PAColl-6585-88

trucks were ubiquitous by the 1970s. Many were operated by the Pan Pacific pulp and timber plant at Whirinaki, a joint venture between Carter Consolidated Ltd and Japanese firms Oji Paper and Kokusaku Pulp that opened in 1973.[57]

Hawke's Bay's state forests were managed from New Zealand Forest Service offices in Napier, and were entering production by the late 1980s when the government disbanded the Forest Service and sold the felling licenses to private enterprise, robbing taxpayers of the anticipated direct return on a generation-long investment.

The second pastoral revolution that began in the late 1940s breathed new life into Hawke's Bay's towns from Wairoa to Woodville, fuelling the simmering rivalry between Napier and Hastings. Impelled by the Thirty Thousand Club — whose name embodied booster aspirations for scale of population — Napier won the race to become a city in 1950.[58] Greater Hastings Incorporated responded that year with a Blossom Festival, designed to mark spring.[59] This struck a remarkable chord, and the event became a local institution that lasted around 20 years, drawing national interest.[60] At its peak in 1956, some 83,000 visitors came from around the North Island to see the Blossom Parade and associated Highland Games.[61] Hastings officially became a city that year, nearly three-quarters of a century after the term was first used to describe it, celebrating the moment with parades, speeches and an overflight of RNZAF Vampires.[62]

Despite its civic status and long-standing image as a seaside resort, Napier could not compete with the Blossom Festival. That did not stop the Thirty Thousand Club pushing for civic amenities and parks, including a beautification programme along the former Tutaekuri river bed, adjacent to Georges Drive. A statue of Pania of the Reef, the eponymous focus of a local Māori legend, was unveiled in 1954.[63] It became a local icon — and drew national attention when somebody stole it in 2006. A floral clock followed in 1955. Guy Natusch's War Memorial Hall — a long-delayed centennial project[64] — opened next to the clock in July 1957.[65] Work also began on a new Anglican cathedral, a belated replacement for the brick

Central Hawke's Bay towns grew under the impetus of the second pastoral revolution; this is Dannevirke's High Street in 1952.

Photographer unidentified, New Zealand Free Lance Collection, Alexander Turnbull Library, F-29564-1/4

Riverslea School float in the Blossom Festival, 1958.

Photographer unidentified, New Zealand Free Lance Collection, Alexander Turnbull Library, C-27125-1/2

Marewa shopping centre around 1951 — a novelty in mid-century Hawke's Bay. Although the suburb was planned in the late 1930s, the buildings here are still under construction and the grassed area in the foreground was subsequently built over. The fish and chip shop became a Marewa tradition, still serving up dinners for hungry Kiwi families over half a century later.

David Williams, Dave Williams Collection, Hawke's Bay Museum, W186(b)

structure that had collapsed during the 1931 earthquake. It took time: although the foundation stone was laid in 1955 and part of the structure dedicated in 1960, the building itself was not completed until 1965.

All this played out to unabated commercial rivalry. The Hastings Retailers Asssociation launched a fresh offensive in Napier during 1966. 'Hastings opens a week of bargains', one headline announced in Napier's *Daily Telegraph*. 'Hastings retailers show enterprise', declared another.[66]

These developments underscored a social point; Hawke's Bay was becoming increasingly urbanised in reality as well as ideal. Most of the growth came in the two main centres and surrounding districts, which in a social sense became the focus of Hawke's Bay society through sheer weight of numbers and economic power. The impetus was the 'baby boom' that began in the mid-1940s, compounding the legacy of depression-era housing shortages. Napier was in a particularly awkward position at first. The Harbour Board had allowed Marewa to be developed but were reluctant to release more land, and it was May 1945 before an agreement was finally reached with the Borough Council to build a new suburb — Onekawa. Nearby land was set aside for industrial development, and another agreement opened up other land for housing between Marewa and the Napier Boys' High School.[67]

Architect Guy Natusch designed this house in Onekawa, Napier's first post-war suburb. A Mk I Ford Zephyr Six sits in the driveway, a few years old when this picture was taken, but still a mark of status for any Hawke's Bay family.

Duncan Winder, Duncan Winder Collection, Alexander Turnbull Library, F-878-1/2-DW

None of this could be developed in time to meet soaring post-war demand. Some families were put up in huts on the Kennedy Park motor camp. Others had to jam into relatives' homes, some even living in tents pitched in back gardens. It was the end of the decade before the first of 950 Onekawa sites were ready for sale to prospective home-builders. Street names reflected the places that had dominated the lives of two generations; Anzac, Cassino, Tripoli, Alamein, Maadi, Ypres, Flanders and Menin among them.[68] Napier continued to grow amid criticism that the town was taking over valuable agricultural land. South Onekawa and an adjacent suburb, Pirimai, followed in the late 1950s and early 1960s.[69]

Hastings also needed to expand. Here too the issue of encroaching on agricultural land reared its head. But room had to be found for a burgeoning population. In the early 1960s the decision was taken to establish a new suburb, Flaxmere, on low-fertility land south of Omahu. Some 895 acres were set aside in 1964, and the Hastings City Council took out a £200,000 loan — some $6.95 million in early 21st century money[70] — to fund what was envisaged as an 'elite subdivision',[71] a 'new concept in modern living'.[72] Housing embodied the latest themes and designs; ranch-slider doors, patios, fibralite cladding and concreted paths. The suburb grew, expanding by the late 1980s to become nearly a third the size of Hastings.[73]

Councils and citizens of both towns had high hopes for their new suburbs, envisaging a new middle-class nirvana built around mid-century dreams; but in the event both Flaxmere and Maraenui evolved in other

Ice creams on the Napier town beach, January 1953.

W. Walker, Alexander Turnbull Library, National Publicity Studios Collection, F-27460-1/2, A 29945

Hastings' Windsor Park 1957–58.

T. Ransfield, Alexander Turnbull Library, National Publicity Studios Collection, PICT-000047, A53309

ways. The primary reason was that low-cost state housing provided homes for a newly urbanised Māori and low-income pākehā, whose practical engagement with the insular middle-class culture of mid-twentieth century New Zealand was minimal. Once the cycle began it was difficult to break. The Hawke's Bay experience was far from unique around New Zealand, and official thinking turned to avoiding such social problems in future by 'pepper-potting' — distributing state houses among privately owned dwellings. This was tried in Napier's next suburb, Tamatea, which was set out in three stages from the late 1960s. As elsewhere around New Zealand the strategy was not successful, and meanwhile Mayor Peter Tait, apparently shocked by the scale and density of US cities, warned against rapid expansion. Efforts to find room for Napier to expand triggered debate, although early-1970s plans to establish a 1,585 acre 'satellite city' near Wharerangi proved still-born.[74]

Other arguments flared over a provincial airport. Bridge Pā and the two Napier airfields were not suitable for the aircraft being introduced into passenger service by the late 1930s, but where an airfield might go was subject to intense debate. Napier won the first rounds in 1944, and the district airport was developed on former swamp at the Beacons site north of Napier. That did not quell the arguments, which continued

Increasing traffic volumes made better roading essential by the 1950s, and the money was there to push a wide range of national public works projects. Hawke's Bay received its share. Here, construction is under way on the approaches to the road bridge over the Waipawa river in November 1958.

Photographer unidentified, New Zealand Free Lance Collection, Alexander Turnbull Library, F-102207-1/2

to bubble along until 1961 when the Civil Aviation Administration confirmed the suitability of the Beacons site, paving the way for a new runway. Hastings voices responded with calls for a motorway to connect their centre to it, and initial plans were laid in 1961 for what eventually emerged as a two-lane highway, completed after many delays in the early twenty-first century.[75]

These political gyrations did not disguise the fact that the 1950s and 1960s brought to reality the middle-class, suburbanised environment that Hawke's Bay's people had sought for so long. It was a safe, secure world of tight nuclear families, where fathers earned the household wage; where women — despite brief liberation into the workforce during the war — were home-makers. It was safe, secure, and intentionally boring. It was also egalitarian by expectation. Old money still existed across Hawke's Bay — and others across the district made plenty on the back of the wool boom. But few dared flaunt it. The fiction of a universal middle-class of roughly equal income was given weight by rising prosperity; more ordinary people could afford a better lifestyle than ever before.

Cars were in particular demand, though penurious foreign exchange regulations kept car hunger sharp through the 1950s. At times cars even

A Morris Minor being crank-started on a Hawke's Bay road. This is the two-door 1949 model with 850 cc motor. Its eventual successor — the 'Morris 1000' — became iconic.

Matthew Wright Collection

appreciated in value. British vehicles dominated; Hillmans, Humbers, Vauxhalls, Morrises, Austins and Dagenham-designed Fords — Zephyr, Consul, Anglia and Cortina among them.[76] Even blue-collar workers could afford one in the 1950s, and by the 1960s some families were looking to a second vehicle, often the ubiquitous 'Morrie Thou'. Many cars were kept on the roads until they rusted through, 'bogged' and with engines 're-bored' well beyond their designed lifetime. Rising traffic densities prompted the Hastings City Council to set up a 'ring-road' through the central city. It went in over a single weekend in 1972, generating confusion among frustrated motorists. Trade suffered, but it was 1979 before the Hastings Chamber of Commerce finally condemned the scheme.[77]

Television reached Hawke's Bay in the early 1960s. Initial broadcasts from Mount Erin, near Havelock North, repeated the signal from Wharite Peak at the south end of the Ruahine Range. Television sets were expensive to buy at the time — but many families could afford to rent them, and the arrival of a reasonable signal prompted one Napier businessman to set up Hawke's Bay Television Hire in 1964.[78]

Hawke's Bay's people took to television as they had taken to radio a generation earlier. Initial programming included *The Flintstones* and *Thunderbirds*, along with local productions such as *C'Mon* and Selwyn Toogood's *It's In The Bag*. Colour broadcasts began in early spring 1974, around a year after colour was introduced in Wellington. Many families first saw that in the pastel brown hues of the Philips K9, which gained an initial dominance of the New Zealand colour television market. A national television network emerged in 1975, including a second channel, bringing new US-made shows such as *The Six Million Dollar Man* to New Zealand homes. Broadcasts ran around 12 hours a day; this was the age of rainbow channel logos that unfolded to the last bars of Emerson, Lake and Palmer's prog-rock epic 'Trilogy'; and of close-down themes such as 'Goodnight Kiwi', an iconic animated cartoon in which the national bird found a bed in a TV transmission dish.

Hawke's Bay life reflected the national quest for family security, locally carrying an enduring sense of provincialism — the little-admitted but generally held idea that life in Napier, Hastings and district towns was less metropolitan than that of Auckland, Wellington or Christchurch. It was a reflection of the wider 'colonial cringe' that afflicted New Zealand at the time, reinforced by an environment of regulation and exchange control that effectively separated local society from overseas trends. In a reflection of the national 'colonial cringe', with its 'try hard' flip-side, Hawke's Bay countered its local sense of 'double inferiority' relative both to metropolitan Britain and to New Zealand's own main centres with the notion that a quiet provincial life was better than the rushed pressures of the cities.

Retailing took on new styles in the late 1950s and early 1960s. This is Napier's Melody House with self-select record bins of a type later adopted widely across New Zealand.

John Wright, Matthew Wright Collection

In fact there was not a lot to choose between New Zealand's major centres and Hawke's Bay when it came to shared social values, which revolved around the family and a suburban home with three bedrooms, garage, front garden devoted to roses or flowers, and back garden for vegetables, occasional fruit trees, and the ubiquitous blokes' shed. Men were expected to till the vegetable garden, mow the lawns and bring home the wages to run the family home. Women kept house, cooked 'meat and two veg' meals, baked cakes, scones and biscuits — often

Napier's Ellison Street, summer 1957.

John Wright, Matthew Wright Collection.

from the *Edmond's Cookbook* — and tended the front garden. Domestic pride reigned supreme in newer Hawke's Bay housing districts that, with concreted driveways and front paths, were easier to keep trim. The lifestyle was backed with design as local architects explored new ways of 'encouraging gracious unhampered living'.[79] This was the age of 'ranch-slider' doors and of living spaces that broke down barriers between rooms.

Weekends were for organised sports, lawn-mowing, boating, family picnics and outings, and occasional parties — the latter often revolving around bottles of bulk-brewed draught beer delivered in 'crates'. Rising prosperity made more leisured weekends possible; and as always, Hawke's Bay's climate and landscape offered opportunities for outdoor activities, particularly during summer. Some families even owned motor boats. Sunday 'drives' might take a Napier or Hastings family to Dartmoor, or perhaps to Haumoana for a beach walk. Occasionally families descended on riversides or beaches for a 'sausage sizzle', barbequing over open fires built from driftwood. Girl Guides and Boy Scouts flourished: and the Omatua homestead, near Rissington, became a regional venue for Guide camps and organised youth activities.

This life had its dark side. The 1950s and 1960s were also the era of the 'rugby widow' and six-o'clock closing, which usually meant that some fathers rolled home drunk. At a time when men worked and women stayed home, domestic boredom was only occasionally broken by a dwindling number of home-delivery salesmen, their roles made obsolete as the age of the self-service supermarket dawned. Hawke's Bay's first major chain was the Hawke's Bay Farmers Co-Operative, which opened across the district from the early 1960s.

Adolescents emerged as a new social group during the post-war years. They were eventually dubbed teenagers — an American term. While Hawke's Bay's teen culture of the 1950s did not widely embrace the 'scooter' set ideals of the metropolitan 'bodgies' of Auckland and Christchurch, most found havens in local milk bars, among them Napier's Callinicos Milk Bar and Confectionery with its 1930s decor,[80] or the Palm Grove — 'the most up-to-date and largest milk bar in Hawke's Bay'.[81] Many listened to rock'n roll and eagerly waited for Johnny Devlin or the Māori Volcanics to come to the district. A sense that Hawke's Bay was provincial and thus safe from metropolitan social change perhaps helped in 1953 when 60 adolescents were arrested for alleged sex offences around Lower Hutt's Elbe Milk Bar. It was a local issue, but it focussed national concerns and in one of New Zealand's periodic fits of of wild over-reaction to an assumed social problem, government commissioned a report by Oswald Mazengarb. His judgement, blaming 'over-sexed' adolescent girls for a supposed moral crisis among New Zealand's youth, was sent to every household.[82] Pavlova-era New Zealand feared nemesis; but this crisis had been blown up out of very little, and whether the sentiments were shared in Hawke's Bay is moot.

> "For most Hawke's Bay families the 'pavlova' years were an age of meat-and-two-veg meals at home, leavened with a weekly pilgrimage to the suburban fish-and chip shop."

Milk-bar culture highlighted the limits to entertainments. Going out usually meant cinema — by the 1950s, in Technicolour or 'wide screen' Panavision — or a live show. Napier had two dramatic societies; Operatic and Repertory, operating from the Municipal Theatre and the Little Theatre on McGrath Street. And there were concerts by touring artists.

Going out of an evening did not necessarily mean also eating out. For most Hawke's Bay families the 'pavlova' years were an age of 'meat-and-two-veg' meals at home, leavened with a weekly pilgrimage to the suburban fish-and chip shop. 'Greasies' could be got from most of the shopping centres around the district. And a few restaurants flourished, among them Paxie's Cafe, a Napier institution for over half a century.

Lunches were another matter. Sandwich bars offered Neenish tarts, Eccles and butterfly cakes and tea and filter coffee — at least during weekdays. Even after licenced restaurants were introduced in 1961, other choices usually boiled down to the dining room of local hotels such as

Children being evacuated from flood-waters in Onekawa, Napier, 1963.

Photographer unidentified, *Evening Post* Collection, PICT-000039

Waipukurau's Tavistock or the Sawyer's Arms at Tikokino. 'Bistro lunches' were available in Napier's Criterion Hotel Bar at three shillings— about $4.80 in early twenty-first century sums— in 1966.[83] Promotions were explicit. 'Enjoy a glass of Leopard beer or wine with a light meal'.[84]

The 'baby boom' brought fresh demand for education. Between 1948 and 1957, school rolls in Hawke's Bay grew by 9000, and 340 classrooms were built — some replacing older structures. School bus services spiralled from 90 services a day to 220.[85] The quality of teaching remained questionable: Hawke's Bay's mid-century educational institutions had declined from the intent of Clarence Beebe's national reforms of the late 1930s, reverting to a teacher bully-culture built around pseudo-military discipline and institutionally normalised abuse of pupils, including physical assault.[86] This sub-culture continued for Hawke''s Bay primary schools into the 1970s, and matters were little different for higher education, which took the impact of the population boom a few years later. Napier's first co-educational high school opened in the 1960s, followed by others there and in Hawke's Bay's other main centres.[87]

Doing the time-warp

Hawke's Bay's conservative, provincially-framed society bent before the generational winds that began blowing in the 1960s, but did not break or even change very radically at first. Pressure for that change gained hurricane force during the subsequent decade. But the conservative, safe world of mid-century Hawke's Bay was not swept away easily.

Although some commentators have argued that the 1970s began with an effort to develop New Zealand in new directions,[88] 'pavlova' society had immense inertia, particularly in the provinces. Its values spanned two generations, transcending politics with socio-cultural imperatives that were intended to protect New Zealanders from hardship that was not of their own making. Ultimately, though, neither New Zealand nor its provinces could isolate themselves from broader worldwide change forever. By the 1970s the social direction set in the 1930s and 1940s was approaching its use-by date; and New Zealand's cringe-oriented perception of itself amplified the problem. A new generation did not share the upbringing of their parents and grandparents. Television opened windows to a world of apparently accessible café culture and plentiful services and imports.

For Hawke's Bay, the ethos of provincialism — which was expressed in sartorial choices such as 'walk shorts', long socks and Roman sandals by way of business attire — was a powerful drag-anchor. But new ideals still crept — subtly — into district life. Perhaps the biggest social shift of the period came in 1967 when law reform allowed bars to stay open until 10.00 pm. This was significant, and an era of so-called 'drinking barns'— huge public bars with restaurants— followed. But they did not challenge prevailing appetites. Most bars offered roasts, steak-and-chips, or self-service buffets, sometimes dubbed 'smorgasbords' after US practise, deriving function and name, although not detail of cuisine, from Swedish practise. In Hawke's Bay this was typified by what was available in Napier's Onekawa Hotel and Hastings' Stortford Lodge. Meanwhile, Havelock North diners had the Te Mata Hotel with its 'bistro meals'.

These bars and restaurants did not challenge prevailing ideals of the nuclear family. 'Make your wining and dining a family affair at Napier's Leopard Inn', one advertisement declared in 1978. Napier's 'Travelodge' offered a 'dine and dance' every Saturday, and the Criterion Hotel advertised 'a la carte' dining and 'smorgasbord family night', Monday to Saturday. Bars did not, of course, open on Sundays.[89]

> "Like most overseas trends, the 'drop-out' youth trends of the 1960s took time to filter through the staid walls of New Zealand's cosseted mid-century society."

> "Some of the sillier fashion trends, such as 'flares' and 'stubbies', were always going to be transitory..."

For all that, the switch to ten-o'clock closing was more a change of emphasis than of fundamental value. The larger sea-change came from other directions — notably through the 'counter culture'. Like most overseas trends, the 'drop-out' youth trends of the 1960s took time to filter through the staid walls of New Zealand's cosseted mid-century society. Its New Zealand incarnation reached its peak in the early 1970s, taking inspiration from the Haight-Ashbury movement of San Francisco, Jerry Rubin's 'yippies', and the fantasy vision of pre-industrial England peddled by Britain's Glastonbury set. To this extent, Hawke's Bay's hippies were — as the song went — living in the past.[90] Their shallow pop-philosophical ideals were often mingled with misunderstood aspects of Indian tantric philosophy, taken out of context and re-framed to suit the 'free love' imperatives of yet another generation that fondly believed it was the first to discover sex.[91] Elements of the movement identified with the older world of alternative thought that still existed in Havelock North.

Local advocates of this 'counter-culture' believed they offered alternatives to the prevailing society of mid-century Hawke's Bay. Small groups of twenty-somethings took to communal living, rejecting the nuclear family in favour of 'open' relationships. They did so often to a soundtrack of Bob Dylan, joined by British folk-rock bands such as Steeleye Span and Fairport Convention.

The problem was that while evangelists of this life-style imagined that they stood on the cusp of a brave new world, they also relied on the society they claimed to have had rejected in order to survive, often through its welfare system. This underscored another key point: many 'counter culture' values were unsubtle reversals of their parents' ideals, including mid-century tastes in food, social structures, hair styles, clothing and work ethic. This underscored the way that the 'counter-culture', in practise, was closely framed by the world its adherents fondly believed they had rejected. Certainly in New Zealand's conservative provinces, still suffused with 'pavlova era' ideals, the counter-culture did not find deep roots. A few 'communes' flourished briefly in Hawke's Bay, but the movement soon faded. Part of the reason was that by nature it was also a culture of youthful superficiality; the hippies grew up.

However, although the counter-culture was never mainstreamed, it still infused a change of style into wider society. Hawke's Bay followed New Zealand and the Western world into a 1970s of longer hair and more colourful clothing. Some of the sillier fashion trends, such as 'flares' and 'stubbies', were always going to be transitory; but Hawke's Bay youth of the day took to these and other socially defining imperatives of the day with alacrity. Most waited eagerly for *Ready to Roll* with its distinctive theme tune, the Commodores' 'Machine Gun'; or queued around blocks to see *Star Wars* in 1977.[92] 'Disco fever' swept the bay the following year, and Hawke's Bay teenagers did the Brooklyn Hustle. Local nightclubs sprouted illuminated floors on the back of the trend — some fabricated by a Napier electronics firm. *Grease* was the word in Napier and Hastings that October.[93]

Tastes changed with popular styles, again infused with a fair dose of the counter-cultural rejection of prevailing norms. Carpets were sold with long ragged loops dubbed 'shag pile' and lounges gained step-down 'passion pits'. Architects dabbled with a pseudo-colonial look defined by cinder-block walls, sharply pitched roofs and, occasionally, porthole windows. These assertions of designer status disappeared as rapidly as they had come, leaving behind a scattering of intellectually pretentious period structures that dated swiftly, typified in Hastings by the 'Tommo's Family Restaurant' building, which went up in the early 1980s and was demolished in 2015.

> "In the 1950s world of meat-and-two-veg meals, ethnic foods were not merely a novelty but something for which most Kiwis simply did not have an appetite. That changed."

The more lasting cultural change for Hawke's Bay came with the contents of the dinner plate. Napier's first 'Chinese Restaurant' — offering esssentially Westernised versions of Asian cuisine — opened in the early 1970s and did a roaring trade. American-style 'fast foods' arrived in 1972 when a Kentucky Fried Chicken outlet opened in Hastings, shortly followed by another in Napier. Interest in less processed fare was met in Napier by a new café, 'Whole Earth Foods', which opened in Dickens Street. All these choices were a far cry from mid-century 'meat-n-two-veg' and proved enduring, underscoring a mood for change that, perhaps inevitably, was presented as overdue modernisation.

Other forces for social change gathered strength during the 1970s. Perhaps the key shift was a significant Māori renaissance. In 1921, in an opinion that effectively summed up the mind-set of that day, Napier's *The Daily Telegraph* opined that Māori, though a 'virile and increasing community', would 'find it more and more difficult to maintain his racial purity'.[94] Such words were predictable in that era of eugenics; but this vision of inevitable swamping by pākehā stood against the practical reality of early twentieth century New Zealand in a social sense. For all the pākehā conceit of having the best race relations in the world, the fact remained that 'God's Own' New Zealand was separatist. In Hawke's Bay, Māori continued to live principally in rural communities such as Te Haroto, Te Hauke and Nuhaka. Sometimes they were not far from their neighbours; Waiohiki — with its golf course — was just a few kilometres

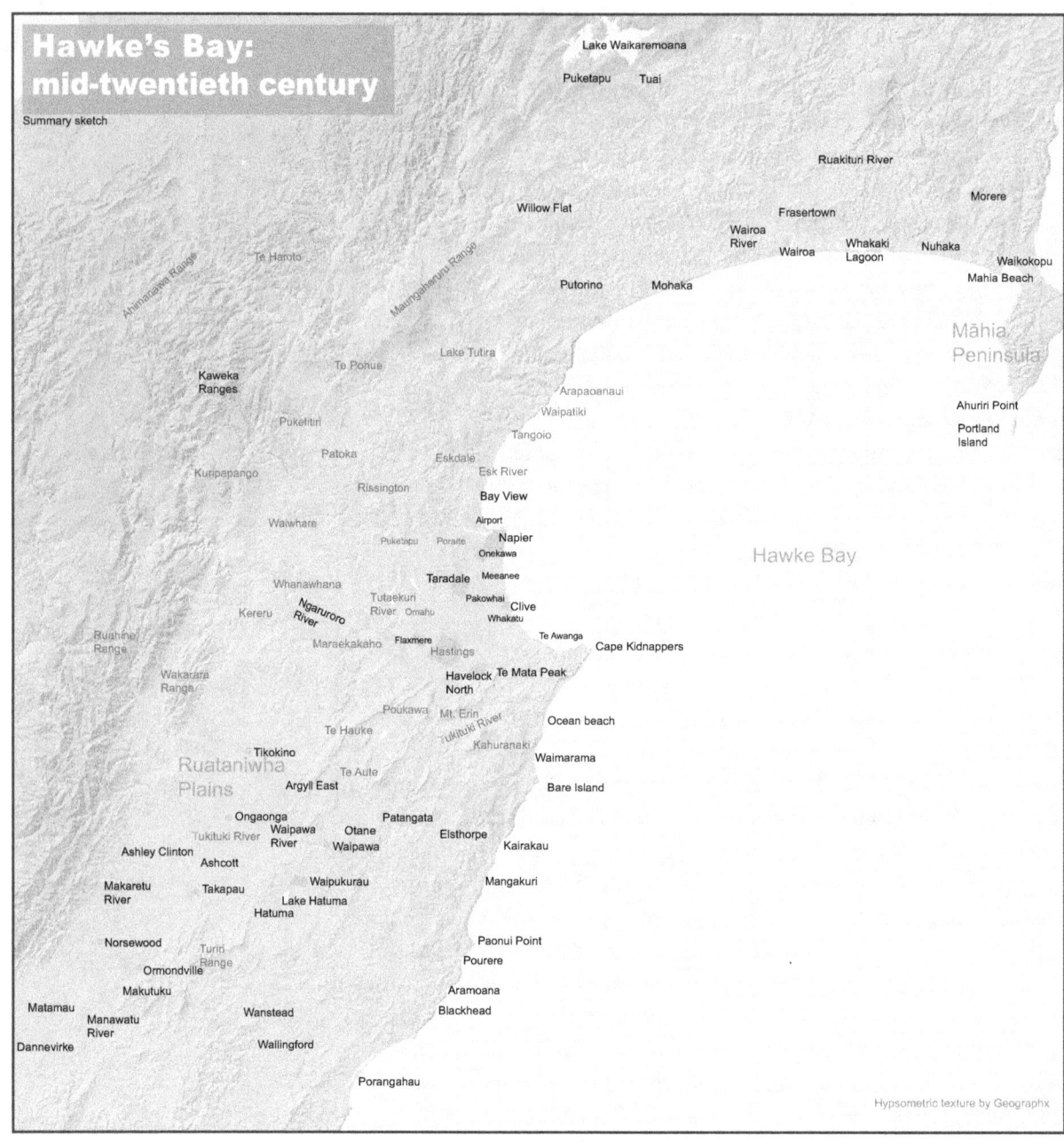

from Taradale. Whakatu was adjacent to Clive and not far from Hastings. Yet in practise, Māori lived out of the way of pākehā, and the majority of the population were well removed from pākehā urban areas. North of Wairoa, in clusters extending through to Poverty Bay and the East Cape, Māori made up more than half the rural population — an area described in one study as a 'most isolated part of the region'.[95] These rural communities, surviving on the proceeds of wheat farming, small dairying operations and kumara gardening, were effectively marginalised.

Part of the early twentieth-century drive by Māori to recover a culture and place that had been suppressed by colonisation came from Te Aute Māori Boys' College, whose alumni included Te Rangi Hiroa (Sir Peter Buck), Sir Apirana Ngata and Maui Pomare. These people and others exerted significant influence through the early decades of the century.[96] The Ratana alliance with Labour from the mid-1930s also helped the cause. However, the more significant change came after the Second World War. In the fifteen years between the censuses of 1951 and 1966, some 63,000 Māori migrated from rural to urban areas. This was more than a third of the 1966 population.[97] It was a remarkable switch, given force by a dramatic rise in Māori population. This was a combined product of a sharp rise in birth rate and an equally sharp fall in the death rate.[98] There has been suggestion that 'push-pull' effects were in play — factors driving young Māori to leave their rural communities and drawing them to the towns. Seasonal labour has been identified as one attraction,[99] though in Hawke's Bay the key employment opportunities of this kind were still closer to the Māori centres of the district than to Napier or Hastings.

For all that, the move by Māori to Hawke's Bay's growing suburbs provoked social difficulties, shared nationally as young Māori moved generally into post-war suburban areas around New Zealand. The education system, in particular, jarred; in 1963, national figures indicated that 93.3 percent of Māori boys left school without qualifications and just 2.6 percent went on to higher education.[100] The outcome was that many urbanised Māori could find employment only as labourers or seasonal workers,[101] becoming reliant on welfare and ending up in a poverty trap from which it was difficult to escape, even over generations.[102] Hawke's Bay's urban Māori were effectively ghettoised in state-housing areas such as Maraenui and Flaxmere. These issues were compounded by the dislocation associated with the loss of whānau support. Even use of Te Reo Māori diminished. Government efforts, which included dropping the period term 'native' from 1947, and legislative measures such as the Māori Welfare Act of 1962, did not address these deeper social problems.

One immediate outcome was intensified racial stereotyping at popular level. Māori were blamed for most of the crime. This had some basis in statistics: by the early 1960s, Māori formed a disproportionate element of the jail population.[103] However, in other respects this was symptomatic of social dissonance — of tensions between societies that, in practice, remained culturally separate.

> "...many forces were pushing change in New Zealand by the late 1970s, and Hawke's Bay, for all its provincial, conservative outlook, was drawn into the tumult."

Many forces were pushing change in New Zealand by the late 1970s, and Hawke's Bay, for all its provincial, conservative outlook, was drawn into the tumult. Matters came to a head over the 1981 Springbok tour. This sporting event prompted the largest public protests since the 'Red Fed' demonstrations of 1912–1913, overtly to show opposition to the apartheid practised by South Africa's white minority government. Such sentiment was genuinely directed towards protesting apartheid, and politically necessary to show that New Zealand's people disagreed with the government; but in other ways the protests also proxied the frustration felt by a wide section of the public towards a New Zealand society that was widely perceived as over-regulated and behind the times. The mood was focussed by the way that the Prime Minister of the day, Robert Muldoon, was trying to preserve that very world through fresh regulation; policies that were increasingly framed for the New Zealand public by Muldoon's abrasive political and media persona.[104]

The Hawke's Bay response to the Springbok tour epitomised the provincial self-image. The local anti-tour protest focussed on a Springbok-versus-Māori match in Napier's McLean Park on 25 August — a curious re-run of 1921. It was a wet day, and the police riot contingent — the 'Red Squad' — were deployed in front of water-filled Burkes bins, along streets adjacent to the park. They were armed with PR-24 long batons, nicknamed 'Minto Bars' after a prominent national protestor who, by coincidence, hailed from that part of Napier.[105] However, although apparently ready for violence, the police were confronted by a quiet protest that included women pushing prams, the elderly, and a few others.[106]

This mood of reasonable assertion in a provincial centre contrasted with the sense of self-righteous personal affront and indignant anger displayed towards the tour by students on some university campuses;[107] and with the open street battles that broke out in some main centres. These last spoke of underlying motives that reflected more than just a due stand against South African politics. In its own way, such objection to New Zealand's apparent social immobility at the hands of an intransigent Prime Minister was also true of the Hawke's Bay style of protest. And so Hawke's Bay — like New Zealand in general — staggered into the 1980s with the winds of change blustering around it.

CHAPTER SEVEN
Metropolitan province

The last years of the twentieth century brought tumultuous times for Hawke's Bay. Far-reaching reforms, pushed by central government from the mid-1980s, swept away the systems that had supported Hawke's Bay's pastoral prosperity, along with many of the state innovations that had defined New Zealand's mid-twentieth century.

In the process, the district underwent changes of a depth and speed not seen at any time in its history.

New Zealand's late-century difficulties began in the 1950s when Britain — the main export market — declared its intent to join the European Economic Union. New Zealand's undiversified pastoral economy was at risk — a particular issue for districts such as Hawke's Bay that relied heavily on wool, meat and dairying. The message was clear, but a nation that still regarded itself as British responded by clinging still harder to the mother country. The late-1966 collapse of wool prices[1] was a wake-up call,[2] but hopes remained pinned on selling to the EEC. The access arrangements concluded in 1972 allowed just butter and cheese.[3]

Back country Hawke's Bay: a Hughes 300 helicopter with one of the ubiquitous HQ Holdens of the day in the background, Te Hoe river valley, late 1984.

Matthew Wright

Incoming Labour Prime Minister Norman Kirk hoped to rectify the problem by diversifying;[4] but in 1973 the first 'oil shock' sent waves rippling through the economy. And then Kirk died, in office.

All this was bad news for Hawke's Bay. However, National Prime Minister Robert Muldoon, elected in 1975 — though recognising the need to adapt — also sought to save the society he knew, an approach wrapped, as we have seen, around his polarising brand of personal politics.[5] One result was policies designed to protect the pastoral sector — a Livestock Incentive Scheme, low-interest rural loans and a Supplementary Minimum Payments system. Muldoon apparently intended these as a stop-gap while farmers developed new markets. Few did. A second 'oil shock' in 1979 prompted a 'think big' energy and industry initiative. That took time to develop, and in 1982 Muldoon turned to regulation, defying calls for regulatory reduction.[6] Then in mid-1984 a fourth Labour government was elected. Three generations of regulatory control, capped by Muldoon's combative brand of personal politics, set the scene for a sharp political reaction,[7] further focussed by the lens of the 'cultural cringe' with its built-in notion that Kiwis had to overcompensate for perceived backwardness.

The results were dramatic, even in a decade when 'power' was a buzzword and displays of it, usually at the expense of others, had become a device for earning personal status. Old regulations were swept away, producers found the state rug was ripped out from under them, and bloat, both real and perceived, was slashed out of public and private sectors. However, while change was clearly needed, the 'reform' period also imposed wide-ranging policies built around zealously framed neo-liberal economic purism that took no account of the complexity of the human condition. The speed and intensity with which change based on this ideology was pushed through from the mid-1980s into the late 1990s, spanning governments on both sides of the political spectrum, became dislocating — as was apparently intended by its architects, who argued that their medicine was the only medicine for New Zealand, and it had to be taken swiftly.

The results were disastrous. While initial deregulation was welcomed by a population who felt imprisoned by fifty years of 'fortress New Zealand',

Napier's Breakwater harbour, mid-1986, with the navy in port.
Matthew Wright.

there was less acclaim for other policies that, in practise, penalised those disposessed by the changes just when the rest of the package put them in need of support. However, debate was reduced to polemic in which criticism of any aspect was demonised as rejection of the whole package and therefore, apparently, support for 'Muldoonism', even if it was not. This attitude, coupled with the simplistic catechisms with which the reforms were sold — and on which they seemed to be based — gave them the appearance of an ideological crusade. And while initial liberalisations were welcomed, the wholesale scrapping of many controls opened the door to cowboy adventurism. The share market ballooned, drawing in everyday 'Mum-and-Dad' investors, before crashing heavily in late 1987. That was the moment when government decided to launch a rapid-fire disposal of taxpayer-owned infrastructure, without referendum and against popular opinion. In wake of the worldwide stock market crash these long-standing public assets fetched only bargain-basement prices.[8]

All was justified by its advocates as short-term pain that would be compensated for through significant and long-term gains for the wealthy that would apparently 'trickle down' on everyday New Zealanders, gains somehow generated in spite of the succession of body-blows the reformers were delivering to the production base. In fact, average growth during the 'reform' period, usually defined as 1984–99, was just half a percent per annum. This was lower than Australia, where similar policies were not pursued so zealously,[9] and below the average of member states in the Organisation for Economic Co-operation and Development (OECD), the usual benchmark for success in those terms.[10] While adjustment to the post-British world had costs, analysts put much of New Zealand's pain down to mis-management by the reformers.[11]

193

The 'Raspberries and Lumpy Custard' clown company in Napier's Emerson Street during a parade in 1990. This group emerged as a private venture from a 'Street Theatre' sponsored for several years by the Napier City Council as a city promotion, public entertainment and make-work scheme in the face of the reform period downturn.
Matthew Wright

There was a massive social cost.[12] Crime rates rose tenfold between 1980 and 1994.[13] By 1992, as the economy shrank and national unemployment soared above Great Depression levels,[14] electorate dissatisfaction was clear. The nicknames given to the main policies — 'Rogernomics', 'Ruthenasia' and, later, 'Jennicide', riffing in classic Kiwi style off the first names of their architects[15] — underscored popular dismay.[16] Yet it was 1999 before, as one commentator put it, New Zealanders 'turned their backs on 15 years of failed reforms',[17] and the fifth Labour government declared the experiment over.[18] It had been a difficult end to the millenium. As one observer argued, New Zealanders had been 'flagellating ourselves at the altar of economic orthodoxy' — a push for 'purity' for which, in practise, country and people had paid heavily.[19]

This was certainly the case in Hawke's Bay, where the late 1980s brought hardship on a scale not seen since the early 1930s. The district did not particularly share the brief burst of youthful hedonism that suffused the main centres.[20] By contrast, provincial fortunes were dismal for a decade or more. Part of this was the cost of adjustment to the loss of traditional markets. The withdrawal of supplementary minimum payments — a decision taken by the Muldoon administration[21] but pushed through by the 'Rogernomes' — had its effects. Between 1984 and 1989, the value of pastoral land in Hawke's Bay dropped by a quarter. Even horticultural land fell by 18 percent.[22] As early as 1986, some farmers were talking about abandoning the back-country. However, the 'reforms' further compounded the downturn. The retraction of government services, including the closure of country post-offices and mass redundancies from state employers, came as a double blow to Hawke's Bay's rural districts in particular. Objections repeatedly fell on deaf ears; although change was imposed on a tacit framework of 'consultation', there was a clear sense among the public that any objection to the neo-liberal juggernaut was a charade.

The public perception that ideology was being asserted over both reasonable position and hard empirical evidence certainly seemed clear when it came to one of the most contentious issues of the day, the closure of Napier public hospital in favour of an expanded regional facility in Hastings. The decision to shut down such a major taxpayer-funded service struck chords on many levels, not least by reigniting aspects of the long-standing civic rivalry between the two centres.

What was perhaps missed was that intra-provincial rivalry took second place to a more fundamental issue. The experience of 1931 had shown that, at times of major natural disaster — a permanent risk for the district — a hospital was needed in both centres. The development of 1990s 'high tech', as it was called at the time, had not changed the fact that connections between the two cities were reliant on roads and multiple bridges — all vulnerable in a large seismic disaster. Populations had increased since 1931, and helicopters were unlikely to make a difference given potential casualty figures.

These arguments were raised; but purist 'small government' ideology was apparently the default official position of the day, and even cogent arguments about the obvious humanitarian issues fell on barren ground. Napier hospital was closed and most of the buildings left to fall derelict. They were demolished in 2016.

The hospital debate and experience underscored the reality of the reform period on Hawke's Bay. For those without independent means, the 'invisible hand' of the neo-liberal free market appeared to be a hostile fist, driven home with destructive intent, and the electorate were powerless to stop the damage to their livelihoods and prosperity. Some 78 percent of all people in the Hastings district earned less than $30,000 per annum by 1990,[23] and 46 percent of the resident working-age population were not employed.[24] The district plunged into what one commentator called

> "A reform-weary electorate responded cynically. 'I came away wondering if the decision had already been made,' one observer suggested to the local paper after one meeting."

Pastoral enterprise diversified during the 1990s on the back of the dislocation of old systems and the quest for new markets. These cows are at Rissington.
Matthew Wright

a 'decade of recession', characterised by 'job losses on a massive scale' as freezing works and other traditional employment closed or relocated to the larger cities.[25] Even long-standing commercial businesses reformed. Wattie's — partly taken over in 1980 by Goodman's[26] — slashed its local tomato growers from 24 to six,[27] sold its canning plant,[28] looked for ways to expand into Australia — and was taken over by Heinz.[29]

These changes were accompanied by local-body restructuring. Efforts to alter the organisation of local government had been rumbling for decades, prompting periodic spats over jurisdiction in Hawke's Bay.[30] The third Labour government's Local Government Bill of 1973 called for change,[31] prompting debate across Hawke's Bay through the mid-1970s.[32] A significant part of the argument revolved around Napier's efforts to build a 'satellite city' at Wharerangi, but as Hastings Mayor J. J. O'Connor remarked at the time, there seemed little need to turn 'local government upside down simply for the sake of changes.'[33] United Councils eventually emerged under the Muldoon government; but a more radical shift came in the late 1980s, buoyed by the period evangelisation of 'small' government and the conceit that anything prior was unsophisticated. The results were dramatic. Old boards were swept away, District Councils replaced County and Borough Councils, and in Hawke's Bay the main argument was whether Napier should retain its political independence. Debate around

From farming to viticulture in the Te Mata valley, near Havelock North, in the early twenty-first century.

Matthew Wright

the formation of a Hastings District Council in 1989[34] — as opposed to a Napier district — was coloured by partisan and parochial sentiment.

The issue was revived in the mid-1990s when the Hawke's Bay Regional Council recommended an amalgamated district council in Hawke's Bay, mainly to rationalise services.[35] A reform-weary electorate responded cynically.[36] 'I came away wondering if the decision had already been made,' one observer suggested to the local paper after one meeting.[37] The Local Government Commission favoured amalgamation; but nearly three-quarters of those who voted in Napier were against it.[38]

The other significant development of the period flowed from the revival of Māori as a people, both culturally and as an important socio-economic force. This was relatively new. The urban migration of the 1950s and 1960s, with its effective ghettoisation of Māori communities — evidenced in Hawke's Bay by the Maraenui and Flaxmere experience particularly — did not end the practical dissonance between Māori and pākehā life. The 1970s were a decade of land protest, including Whina Cooper's 1975 land march and the 18-month occupation of Bastion

Part of the drainage system dug into the former Te Whanganui-ā-Orotū lagoon, post-quake by the Napier Harbour Board.

Matthew Wright

Point.[39] Government cautiously responded; Norman Kirk opened the door, and the Waitangi Tribunal was formed in 1975. However, it was not until the mid-1980s, as a consequence both of the reform period and of a general change of attitude towards indigenous peoples, that the Tribunal gained the power to look at retrospective claims.[40]

One of the highest profile land disputes in Hawke's Bay remained the Te Whanganui-ā-Orotū lagoon, which Ngāti Kahungunu had not sold in 1850–51, but which government believed it had bought. Land lifted from the lagoon by the 1931 quake was claimed by the Napier Harbour Board as a 'gift from the sea', prompting a petition by Hori Tupaea and others in 1932. This led to a hearing in 1934, but it was 1948 before Judge Layne Harvey's report rejecting their claim was completed and publicly released, by which time another petition with more than 250 signatories had been organised. Further approaches by Māori in 1955 and 1965 foundered on Harvey's report, as did efforts in the early 1970s.[41] That changed with the new legislation, and in 1988 seven hapū lodged a claim.[42]

Resolving this was an important issue for Hawke's Bay. It was a complex process which, from the historical perspective, was framed both by prevailing academic-historical sub-culture and by the specific function of historical work done to background the Treaty-related claims. This was

The Tutaekuri river, early twenty-first century.
Matthew Wright

built around legalistic and judicial requirements rather than the more abstract analysis of general history. This focus left the 'industry' historical work open to mainstream criticism of being 'presentist', a problem not helped by the perception produced during Tribunal hearings in Napier in 1999, where one historian was reported as suggesting that researchers were 'fearful of being seen as unsympathetic to Māori'.[43]

Debate over the historical methodology drew attention away from the underlying issue — which was that Māori had been colonised, subjected

Bridge over the Mangaone River near Rissington.
Matthew Wright

A view of the Esk Valley, looking towards north-western Hawke's Bay.

Matthew Wright

to a succession of injustices that reflected the asymmetric power-balances of that colonial process, then denied any real voice or opportunity by which those injustices could be rectified. The Hawke's Bay experience over the Te Whanganui-ā-Orotū lagoon was joined by other local issues stemming from Donald McLean's purchase process of the later 1850s, along with other infringements of Māori rights.

This was recognised in government circles by the late twentieth century, but progress was slow. The Tribunal's initial hearings on the Te Whanganui-ā-Orotū claim, for example, took place in 1993–94, and a report appeared in 1995 — seven years after the claims had been lodged — but concluded that final recommendations were 'not appropriate at this stage'.[44] Such dilatory progress was frustrating to claimants, not least because the issue had been outstanding since 1851. A settlement was eventually reached in November 2016.[45]

Cosmopolitan transformation

For Hawke's Bay the last years of the twentieth century were a time of change, uncertainty and adaptation. The mid-century district with its brown rolling hills, flecked with sheep, was already changing by the 1990s. State forest projects at Gwavas, Te Pohue and Mohaka — among others — had long since changed the look of the back-country. Deer fences rose in the Takapau Plains, where animals once hunted as pests became a marketable source of venison. Wine-making, which had bubbled alongside other Hawke's Bay ventures for nigh on a century, became a major industry. Local demand was driven by new café culture, and there were world markets to exploit. By the early twenty-first century even long-standing horticultural industries, such as apple and pear production, were giving way to more diversified interests.

These changes were framed by new attitudes and lifestyles, facilitated in part by the liberalisations that initially went with the reform period, but driven by deeper shifts in culture. It was no coincidence that this new thinking came just as a new generation grew to adulthood, one that generally rejected the 'colonial cringe' and looked to a more cosmopolitan New Zealand. The children of the baby-boomers wanted variety, technology and freedom from what they perceived as the stultifying world

Craggy Range winery, Tukituki valley, late 2018.
Matthew Wright

Above and below: Waimarama beach remained popular largely because it was the only accessible sandy beach in the dsistrict
Matthew Wright

of their parents — which meant freedom to drink alcohol when they wanted, to eat out when they wanted, to buy whatever consumer goods could be had, and to join a wider world opening up in the face of new communications technology. Hawke's Bay's youth of the late 1990s and early twenty-first century engaged with technology through the internet,

which swiftly produced a social media culture. They were not alone, as New Zealand re-invented itself as a confident small nation on the world stage.

Hawke's Bay shed much of its provincialism along the way. This new mind-set was reflected in many walks of life. The advent of 'café culture' prompted new bars and eating places across Hawke's Bay, riding a wave of prosperity as the district recovered from the reform period. New cuisine highlighted the metropolitan character of early twenty-first century Hawke's Bay; and while the over-priced and under-sized *nouvelle cuisine* of the 'yuppie' period could not last, it certainly paved the way for a range of ethnic restaurants and menus that embodied fusion cooking and a range of new flavours. Hawke's Bay diners had to learn a new vocabulary as bruschetta took the place of toast, panini — Anglicised with the plural 's', although the word was already plural in Italian — replaced toasted sandwiches; and cafés took the place of mid-century pie carts. Coffee was delivered with a range of initially bewildering

Above and below: The conversion of woolstores into restaurants and apartments, coupled with new residential construction, transformed Ahuriri, Napier's former harbour district, into a thriving urban community.
Matthew Wright

Napier's Marine Parade gardens remained a key city attraction into the twenty-first century. The only major structural change from the mid-twentieth century incarnation was the tree growth.
Matthew Wright

Opposite below: Dannevirke, early 2017.
Matthew Wright

options — 'long black', 'short black' and 'Americano' among others. All were well removed from the mid-century choice of 'yes' or 'no', followed — or not — by a slosh of drip-filter brew from a pyrex decanter.

Hawke's Bay's urban landscape changed under the same forces. Napier people brought up on the ideal of the quarter-acre were dismayed at the metropolitanism of the 'town houses' that appeared on the Marine Parade in the late 1960s. By the early twenty-first century such transgressions of twentieth century urban values had become *passé* as apartment culture burst into life, particularly across Napier's old woolstore district. The flip-side of apartment life was the 'lifestyle block', a semi-ruralised setting for urban dwellers which gained momentum at the same time, drawing Hawke's Bay suburbanites into the country as rural owners sold off their land to capitalise on rising interest from the cities. Migration from other centres helped swell a burgeoning Hawke's Bay populace. Older provincial ideas fell by the wayside. It was a significant shift, reflecting a generational shedding of the 'colonial cringe' that had framed much of New Zealand's general twentieth-century thinking.

Homogenous shopping chains overwhelmed the owner-operated shops that had been a mainstay of district commercial life since the 1860s. The advent of the 'mega-store' helped accelerate Hawke's Bay's transformation,

Above: The swamp at Poukawa had been an important resource for Māori, but dwindled when the lake-lands that fed it were drained for farming. Efforts to preserve and restore the wetlands, with their wildlife, gained pace during the early twenty-first century.
Glen Balks

shifting the focus of shopping away from the Napier and Hastings town centres. Other towns lost out in the face of intensified car culture. Few locals in Te Aute, Otane or even Waipawa had qualms about driving to Hastings for groceries. Waipukurau and Dannevirke were far enough away from the main centres to preserve a reasonably vigorous town life, but Woodville had always been subject to the commercial lure of Palmerston North, and that did not diminish in the new century.

Hawke's Bay's cultural de-provincialisation was underscored by a tourist boom that began in Napier in the mid-1990s, ironically in celebration of local architecture. The district had long sold itself to tourists. As the twentieth century drew to a close this was driven — certainly for Napier, and to some extent in Hastings — by the architectural legacy of the 1930s. The revival had small beginnings. In 1981 an OECD deputation remarked on Napier's collection of small-scale modernist architecture, prompting a Ministry of Works-commissioned study of the buildings.[46]

The movement gained pace when two modernist bank buildings on the corner of Hastings and Emerson streets were demolished, along with a modernist chemists' shop in lower Emerson Street. Napier's unique heritage, it seemed, was vanishing. An influential short film by Peter Wells, *Napier — Newest City on the Globe*, underscored the point. A hundred people were expected at the premier showing, but around eleven times that number turned up.[47] An enthusiast group began organising city walks to explore Napier's unique heritage. The City Council listened,[48] and by the 1990s Napier's early-1930s modernist architecture — including Stripped Classical, Chicago Moderne, Prairie and Spanish Mission among other styles — had become the official city theme, retroactively given the 1960s conflation term 'art deco'.[49] Efforts were made to preserve what remained, although this did not stop a decision to rip up the original 1930s-era footpath in Emerson Street and replace it with a boulevard.

The general social shift that went with this new appreciation of Hawke's Bay's urban 'deco' heritage was significant. Napier, particularly, had always sold itself as a tourist destination. The new metropolitan context of cafés, world-class wines and architectural heritage struck a fresh chord. By the early twenty-first century an annual 'art deco' weekend — packed with light-hearted events celebrating the idealised Hollywood lifestyle of the period — was attracting tens of thousands of tourists, many

Above: Packard Six outside Napier's Masonic Hotel during an Art Deco festival.
Matthew Wright

Opposite top: Marewa, Napier's art deco suburb, and part of Napier South.
Matthew Wright

Opposite below: Havelock North's iconic Transformer House, late 2018.
Matthew Wright

Right: Napier's annual art deco festivals featured period aircraft which carried out over-flights and aerobatic displays across the city. They included a North American P-51D Mustang, seen here at the Hawke's Bay Airport in 2016.

Right below: Crowds at the Napier Soundshell during an Art Deco festival.
Matthew Wright

Opposite top: Diners outside Napier's Masonic Hotel during the Art Deco festival.

Opposite below: Vintage car parade during the Art Deco festival.
Matthew Wright

of them international. The celebration was soon extended, gaining the name 'Art Deco Festival', and joined by a similarly-themed and organised mid-winter event. These festivities engaged with Napier's new tourist profile as both the self-assigned 'art-deco capital of the world' and as a resort town amidst a significant wine-making district. However, certainly during the late 1990s and early 2000s, as the idea and concept grew, these events also provided a significant local tonic for a district that had languished under the destructive hammer-blows of the 'reform period' of the late twentieth century. The new concept of local self, and its expression through the Art Deco Festivals, which essentially encompassed the wider district, also fitted the mood of the new generation, just as the Hastings

Metropolitan Province

Blossom Festival had been an encompassing social event that fitted the 'pavlova era' around half a century earlier.

The lifestyles of early twenty-first century Hawke's Bay underscored the dominating theme of district history. As we have seen, although part of New Zealand's wider society, Hawke's Bay also differed from it in subtle but socially meaningful ways that were defined by locality. In the settler period the district was one of several socially related New Zealand expressions of frontier life, a rugged world of cowboy business deals and pretensions to elitism. The do-anything mentality of this world reflected not just the mind-set of the colony in general — but also the fact that this world was often more intense at its fringes. And the fact remains that Donald McLean used the power he derived from the district in the late 1860s to tackle central governmnent. But his colonial world did not last, and when New Zealand plunged into its 'cultural cringe' of the twentieth century, Hawke's Bay followed.

This thinking framed much about Hawke's Bay's twentieth century. The district embodied the same dual mind-set of provincialism and an expectation of world-beating achievement that characterised the national mood, but in reduced form. While on the one hand exalting a quiet life and provincial tourist opportunities, district society also saw itself as culturally 'behind' major New Zealand centres such as Auckland or Wellington, just as they in turn were seen as being 'behind' the desirably urbane heart of an idealised British Empire. That idea applied as a social construct through much of the twentieth century, despite the practical prosperity of mid-century provincial lifestyle in New Zealand, typified by Hawke's Bay, which remained a significant contributor to New Zealand's prosperity and national wealth through pastoral enterprise and the scale of Napier harbour operations, all of which were significant by national measure.

Such deprecating self-perception was, in many respects, a product of New Zealand's pākehā culture and its self-perception of the period. Yet for all the way that those who lived in this world tried to hold on to the positives they saw in it, this inferiority complex did not last. The generation that grew to adulthood in

Dredging work at the entrance to Napier's Ahuriri harbour, April 2019.
Matthew Wright

Opposite bottom: The ocean-going waka Te Matau a Māui *in Ahuriri harbour.*
Matthew Wright

Puketitiri in late 2015.
Matthew Wright

the early years of the twenty-first century instead saw New Zealand as a valid nation on the world stage; not inferior, not 'cringeworthy', but a place with a due sense of self-worth, and one that could also, given time, reconcile the injustices of its colonial past and then properly embrace an indigenous people and culture, who had been long sidelined.

The general social shift was emphasised for Hawke's Bay when, in January 2018, New Zealand became only the twelfth nation in the world to put a satellite into orbit. It was done using a rocket designed indigenously in New Zealand, and launched from a site near the southern end of the Māhia peninsula. The same launch also delivered the 'Humanity Star' to orbit, a temporary satellite and geodesic reflector, designed to make people look at the sky, and so symbolically draw humanity together.[50] Commercial launches began late in the year. This was historically unprecedented. The idea of satellites being launched from New Zealand, still less from Hawke's Bay, would have been science fiction in a twentieth century province that defined itself around pastoral enterprise and the self-image of being socially behind the times. It was still further from the minds of the ambitious pastoralists who had settled the region in the nineteenth century. And yet it was a reality in the new millennium, underscoring just how far Hawke's Bay had evolved in a history that, by world standards, was short by any measure; but where the pace of change was unrelenting, quick, and — always — interesting.

Notes

Chapter One: Land and People

1. J. D. H. Buchanan, ed. D. R. Simmons, *The Māori history and place names of Hawke's Bay*, A. H. & A. W. Reed, Wellington, 1973, p. 1.
2. H. A. Ballara, 'The Origins of Ngāti Kahungunu', PhD Thesis, Victoria University of Wellington, 1991, p. 1.
3. Malcolm McKinnon (ed), *The New Zealand Historical Atlas*, David Bateman, Auckland 1997, Plate 5; also R. P. Suggate (ed), *The Geology of New Zealand*, Government Printer, Wellington 1978, p. 47.
4. R.P. Suggate (ed), *The Geology of New Zealand*, II, p. 91.
5. McKinnon (ed), Plate 7.
6. See, e.g., Ibid, Plate 6.
7. Trevor H. Worthy, 'Two late-Glacial avifaunas from eastern North Island, New Zealand – Te Aute Swamp and Wheturau Quarry', *Journal of the Royal Society of New Zealand*, Vol. 30, No.1, March 2000, pp. 1, 17.
8. McKinnon (ed), Plate 8.
9. Bruce McFadgen, *Hostile shores, catastrophic events in prehistoric New Zealand and their impact on Māori coastal communities*, Auckland University Press, Auckland 2007, pp. 176-177.
10. Matthew Wright, *Town and Country*, HDC, Hastings 2001, p. 13.
11. Geoff Evans, *The Discovery of Aotearoa*, Reed, Auckland 1998, p. 27. See also James Belich *Making Peoples*, Allen Lane, Auckland 1996, p. 36; Nigel Prickett, *Māori Origins from Asia to Aotearoa*, David Bateman, Auckland (no date), p. 23.
12. See McFadgen, pp. 50, 73.
13. See, e.g., Prickett, *Māori Origins*, p. 23.
14. Patrick J. Grant, 'Climate, Geomorphology and Vegetation', in Douglas Sutton (ed), *The Origins of the First New Zealanders*, Auckland University Press, Auckland, 1994, p. 166.
15. Michael King, *The Penguin History of New Zealand*, Penguin, Auckland 2003, p. 51.
16. See, e.g., Prickett, pp. 23–31.
17. Ibid, p. 13.
18. McFadgen, pp. 176–77.
19. Buchanan, p. 6.
20. See Ballara, 'Origins', p. 61.
21. H. S. McGlone, A. F. Mark, D. Bell 'Late Pleistocene and Holocene vegetation history, Central Otago, South Island, New Zealand', *Journal of the Royal Society of New Zealand*, Vol. 25, No. 1, March 1995, pp. 1-22; see also Marcus J. Vandergoes, Sean J. Fitzsimons and Rewi M. Newnham, 'Late glacial to Holocene vegetation change in the eastern Tākitimu mountains, western Southland, New Zealand', *Journal of the Royal Society of New Zealand*, Vol. 27, No.

1, March 1997, pp. 53-66.
22 Atholl Anderson, *Prodigious Birds — Moas and moa hunting in prehistoric New Zealand*, Cambridge University Press, Melbourne, 1989, p. 179; Janet Davidson, *The Prehistory of New Zealand*, Longman Paul, Auckland 1984, p. 57; Belich, *Making Peoples*, p. 35.
23 See, e.g., Atholl Anderson, 'Food from Forest And Coast' in John Wilson (ed) *From The Beginning, The Archaeology of the Māori*, Penguin, Auckland 1986.
24 William Colenso, 'On the Moa', *Transactions of the New Zealand Institute*, Vol. 12, 1879, in http://rsnz.natlib.govt.nz/volume/rsnz_12/rsnz_12_00_000820.html, accessed 19 October 2007.
25 Matthew Wright, *The Reed Illustrated History of New Zealand*, Reed, Auckland 2004, p. 14. Beverly McCulloch and Michael Trotter, *Digging Up the Past, New Zealand's Archaeological History,* revised edition, Penguin, Middlesex, 1997, p. 50.
26 Patrick Grant, 'Climate, Geomorphology and Vegetation': 166.
27 McFadgen, pp. 233–37.
28 King, p. 71.
29 Buchanan, p. 2.
30 Janet Davidson, *The Prehistory of New Zealand*, Longman Paul, Auckland 1984, pp. 193-194.
31 David Lewis and Werner Forman, *The Māori: Heirs of Tane*, Orbis, London 1982, p. 21.
32 Buchanan, p. 3; J. M. McEwen, *Rangitāne, A Tribal History* Reed Methuen, Auckland 1986.McEwen pp. 3–6 and pp. 10–14 gives a historiography of the *Kurahaupo* canoe and geneological records.
33 Buchanan, p. 3.
34 Ibid
35 See, e.g. Eric Schwimmer, 'The Māori Hapū: A generative model', in *Journal of Polynesian Studies*, Vol. 99, No.3, September 1990.
36 H. S. McGlone, A. Anderson, R. N. Holdaway,'An ecological approach', in Douglas G. Sutton (ed) *The Origins of the First New Zealanders*, Auckland University Press, Auckland 1994, p. 156, following Parsonson.
37 Aileen Fox, 'Hawke's Bay' in Nigel Prickett (ed), *The First Thousand Years*, Dunmore Press, Palmerston North 1982, p. 69.
38 Elder, N. L., *Vegetation of the Ruahine Range: An Introduction*, Royal Society of New Zealand, Wellington 1965; Ashley Cunningham, 'The Indigenous Forests of East Coast: Poverty Bay, Hawke's Bay', typescript, author collection; N. Elder, 'Māori Cultivation and the Retreat of Forest', talk given 9 October 1956, typescript, author collection.
39 Patrick Grant, *Hawke's Bay Forests of Yesterday*, CHB Print, Waipukurau, 1996, pp. 219-224.
40 Illustrated in McKinnon (ed), Plate 12.
41 See, e.g., Fox, 'Hawke's Bay'.
42 Matthew Wright, *Town and Country*: 16.
43 H. Guthrie Smith, *Tutira*, 3rd ed, William Blackwood & Sons, London 1951, p. 61, see also Elder, *Vegetation*.
44 M. D. N. Campbell, "The Evolution of Hawke's Bay Landed Society," PhD Thesis, Victoria University of Wellington, 1973, pp.156-57.
45 W. T. Prentice 'The Māori History of Hawke's Bay', in J. G. Wilson *History of Hawke's Bay*, A. H. & A. W. Reed, Wellington, 1939, p. 31.
46 John Keegan, *A History of Warfare*, Pimlico, London 1993, pp. 388-390.
47 William Pember Reeves, *The Long White Cloud: Ao Te a Roa*, George Allen & Unwin, London, 1898, p. 12, in http://www.nzetc.org/tm/scholarly/tei-ReeLong-t1-front-d6.html, accessed 25 October 2007.

48 William Colenso, William Colenso, 'Historical Incidents and Traditions of the Olden Times, pertaining to the Māoris of the North Island, (East Coast), New Zealand; highly illustrative of their national Character, and containing many peculiar, curious, and little-known Customs and Circumstances, and Matters firmly believed by them. Now, for the first time, faithfully translated from old Māori Writings and Recitals; with explanatory Notes. Part II', *Transactions of the New Zealand Institute*, Vol. 14, 1881, http://rsnz.natlib.govt.nz/volume/rsnz_14/rsnz_14_00_000520.html, accessed 19 October 2007, p. 4.

49 Davidson, *The Prehistory of New Zealand*, p. 184.

50 R. O. Crosby, *The Musket Wars*, Reed, Auckland 2000, p. 17.

51 Matthew Wright, *New Zealand's Military Heroism*, Reed, Auckland 2007, pp.23-25; also Keegan pp. 61–76, 388–392.

52 Janet Davidson, *The Prehistory of New Zealand*, Longman Paul, Auckland 1984, p. 190.

53 Buchanan, p. 17.

54 Keegan, pp. 94–120.

55 See, e.g., Davidson, *Prehistory*, 115–47, esp. 146–47.

56 See, e.g., Angela Ballara, *Taua*, Penguin, Auckland 2003, pp. 71-73.

57 Buchanan, pp. 9–10.

58 Buchanan, p. 3 cites 1500; Waitangi Tribunal, *Te Whanganui-ā-Orotū Report* 1995, p. 17 cites 1550-1625 on the basis of carbon dating.

59 See, e.g., *Te Whanganui-ā-Orotū Report*, p. 17.

60 Wright, *Town and Country*, p. 28.

61 Ballara, 'Origins', pp. 99–100.

62 Davidson, Prehistory, p. 49.

63 Ballara, 'Origins', pp. 71–74.

64 McFadgen, pp. 82–85

65 Ibid, pp. 224–25.

66 Brian Fagan, *The Little Ice Age*, Basic Books, New York 2000, pp. 104–05, 117–118.

67 See, e.g., Wright, *The Reed Ilustrated History of New Zealand*, p. 21; Fagan, pp. 101–112.

68 Davidson, *Prehistory*, 36–37.

69 Atholl Anderson, *The Welcome of Strangers: an ethnohistory of southern Māori AD 1650-1850*, University of Otago Press/Dunedin City Council, Dunedin, 1998, p. 17; also Davidson, *Prehistory*, pp. 56-59.

70 Ballara, 'Origins', pp. 71–74.

71 See, e.g., Angela Ballara and Gary Scott, 'Crown Purchases of Māori land in early provincial Hawke's Bay', Waitangi Tribunal Wai 201, Wellington, January 1994, p. 37.

72 Prentice, p. 46.

73 See, e.g., Ballara, 'Origins', pp. 75–78; Buchanan, pp. 10–11.

74 Buchanan, pp. 10–11.

75 *Te Whanganui-ā-Orotū Report*, p. 17.

76 Crosby, p. 143.

77 Buchanan, p. 10.

78 Ballara, 'Origins', p. 549.

79 Noted by Ballara and Scott, p. 38.

80 Matthew Wright, *Fantastic Pasts*, Penguin, Auckland 2007, pp. 60–61. The only two publications were Ballara, *Taua*; and Crosby, *The Musket Wars*.

81 Crosby, *The Musket Wars*.

82 Ballara, *Taua*.

83 Matthew Wright, *Guns and Utu*, Penguin, Auckland 2011.

84 Wright, *The Reed Illustrated History of New Zealand*, p. 42.

85 Wright, *Two Peoples, One Land*, Reed, Auckland 2006, pp. 21-22

86 Michael King, 'Introduction' in Crosby, p. 12.

87 Dom Felice Vaggioli *History of New Zealand and its inhabitants*, trans. John Crockett, Otago University Press, Dunedin 2000, p.51.

88 Michael King, Introduction p. 12, in Crosby.

89   Wright, *Fantastic Pasts*, p. 61.
90   Prentice, p. 106.
91   Belich, *Making Peoples*, p. 159.
92   Ballara, 'Origins', p. 426–30.
93   Ibid
94   See, e.g., Wright, *Two Peoples, One Land*, p. 19.
95   See, e.g.,http://www.niwascience.co.nz/ncc/clivar/pastclimate#y150000, accessed 21 May 2007.
96   Wright, *The Reed Illustrated History of New Zealand*, p. 41.
97   Fagan, pp. 167–69.
98   J. G. Wilson (ed) *The History of Hawke's Bay*, A. H. & A. W. Reed, Wellington 1939, pp. 85-108.
99   See, e.g., Ballara, 'Origins', pp. 428–29.
100 See, e.g., S. Percy Smith, Māori Wars of the Nineteenth Century, Whitcombe and Tombs, Christchurch 1910, at http://www.nzetc.org/tm/scholarly/tei-SmiMaort1-body-d45.html, accessed 19 October 2007, pp. 293-300, also Ballara, 'Origins', p. 432, n.3; my reconstruction of the chronology differs from Ballara.
101 See, e.g., Prentice, p. 100.
102 Wright, *Two Peoples, One Land*, esp. Chapter 5.
103 Wright, *The Reed Illustrated History of New Zealand*, p. 65.
104 Compare, e.g., Buchanan, p. 22 with Ballara, 'Origins', pp. 428–30.
105 Quoted in Smith, p. 293.
106 Ballara, 'Origins', p. 430.
107 Argued by Ballara, 'Origins', p. 466.
108 Ibid, pp. 431–32.
109 Prentice, p. 87; Buchanan, p. 22.
110 Ballara, 'Origins', p. 432–33; Buchanan, p. 22.
111 Smith discusses timing, p. 297–98.
112 Crosby, p. 90–91.
113 Ballara, 'Origins', p. 433.
114 Crosby, p. 91, Buchanan, p. 22; McEwen, p. 133–34, dates the event to 1828.
115 Ballara, 'Origins', p. 437.
116 Ibid, p. 443.
117 J. Wilson, p. 135.
118 Prentice, p. 95.
119 Ballara, 'Origins', p. 451.
120 Prentice, p. 97.
121 Wright, *The Reed Illustrated History of New Zealand*, p. 43.
122 Ballara, 'Origins', p. 456.
123 Observed by Ballara, 'Origins', p. 468.
124 Wilson, p. 135.
125 Helen M. Hogan, *Renata's Journey*, Canterbury University Press, Christchurch, 1994, p. 16.
126 Wright, *The Reed Illustrated History of New Zealand*, p. 47.
127 Expressed by Prentice, p. 108.
128 Wright, *The Reed Illustrated History of New Zealand*, p. 38.
129 Matthew Wright, *Western Front*, Reed, Auckland 2004, pp. 8-9.
130 *Te Whanganui-ā-Orotū Report* 1995, p. 32.
131 Wright, *Town and Country*, p. 23.
132 WTu, MS-1286, Donald McLean Journal (typescript), 18 April 1851.
133 *Hawke's Bay Herald*, 28 April 1860.

Chapter Two: Cowboy Frontier

1   Wtu MS-0584, Colenso, William 1811-1899, Papers, Journal Vol. 3 (typescript) 22 November 1850.
2   John Tasker, *Myth and Mystery*, Tandem Press 1997, pp. 118-131; also Roger Hervé *Chance Discovery of Australia and New Zealand by Portugese and Spanish Navigators between 1521 and 1528*, trans John Dunmore, Dunmore Press, Palmerston North 1983, p. 68; for rebuttal see Wright, *Fantastic Pasts*, pp. 43-47; Kerry Howe, *The Quest for Origins*, Penguin, Auckland 2003, pp. 130-132.
3   Wilson, *History of Hawke's Bay*, pp. 115–25.
4   Ibid, pp.126–29.

5 See, e.g., Wright, *The Reed Illustrated History of New Zealand*, pp. 48–62.
6 See Niall Ferguson, *Empire*, Penguin, London 2004, p. 2, 112.
7 J. L. Nicholas, *Narrative of a Voyage to New Zealand*, Vol. 1, James Black, London 1817, facsimile edition, Wilson and Horton, (n.d.) p. 101.
8 Barnet Burns, *A Brief Narrative of a New Zealand Chief*, R & D Read, Belfast, 1844; Hocken Library reprint, Dunedin 1970, p. 4.
9 John Tattersall, *Lt. Thomas McDonnell and the naming of Ahuriri*, Hawke's Bay Art Gallery and Museum, Napier, 1970, pp. 10-11.
10 Wilson, pp. 132–34.
11 William Colenso, 'Historical incidents and traditions of the Olden Times', *Transactions of the New Zealand Institute*, Vol. 14, 1881, p. 13, at http://rsnz.natlib.govt.nz/volume/rsnz_14/rsnz_14_00_000520.html, accessed 14 October 2007.
12 Wilson, p. 135.
13 Jack Lee, *The Old Land Claims in New Zealand*, Northland Historical Publications Society, Kerikeri, 1993, p. 35. Wright, *Town and Country*, p. 22; Wilson, p. 143.
14 Wilson, p. 143.
15 Cited in Matthew Wright, *Napier: City of Style*, Random House, Auckland 1996, p. 36.
16 Wright, *Town and Country*, p. 22.
17 Wilson, p. 144; see also Dean Cowie, 'Rangahaua Whanui District 11b Hawke's Bay, Working Paper First Release', Waitangi Tribunal, September 1996, p. 19.
18 See Vincent O'Malley *The Ahuriri Purchase*, Crown Forestry Rental Trust, April 1995, pp 21-22.
19 Claudia Orange *The Treaty of Waitangi*, Wellington, Bridget Williams Books, Wellington 1987, p 71.
20 Wright, *The Reed Illustrated History of New Zealand*, p. 53.
21 *Great Britain Parliamentary Papers*, (GBPP) Vol. 3, 'Correspondence with the Secretary of State Relative to New Zealand', Hobson to Secretary of State for the Colonies, 15 October 1840, Enclosure 10, Bunbury to Hobson, 28 June 1840, pp 110–11.
22 Ibid
23 Wilson, p. 140.
24 *Te Whanganui-ā-Orotū Report 1995*, p. 32.
25 A. G. Bagnall and G. C. Petersen, *William Colenso*, A. H. &A. W. Reed, Wellington, 1948, pp. 163-167.
26 Ann Parsonson, 'The Pursuit of Mana' in W. H. Oliver and B. R. Williams, *The Oxford History of New Zealand*, Clarendon Press, Oxford, 1981, p. 142.
27 NAMU, J.H. Joll, 'Impromptu Talk'.
28 William Colenso, 'Historical incidents and traditions of the olden times', Part II, *Transactions and Proceedings of the Royal Society of New Zealand*, Vol. 14, 1881, in http://rsnz.natlib.govt.nz/volume/rsnz_14/rsnz_14_00_000520.html, accessed 14 October 2007.
29 William Colenso, *The authentic and genuine history of the signing of the Treaty of Waitangi, Thursday, February 6th*, Government Print, Wellington 1890.
30 P. J. Goldsmith, "Aspects of the Life of William Colenso", MA Thesis, Auckland University 1994.
31 A. H. Reed *The Story of Hawke's Bay*, A. H. & A. W. Reed, Wellington 1958, p. 76.
32 Colenso Journal 11 April 1845 and 9 April 1846, cited in Goldsmith pp. 41–42.
33 Bagnall & Petersen, p. 262; Goldsmith, p. 62.
34 Goldsmith, p. 64.
35 Cited in ibid, p. 65.
36 Ibid, p. 97–98.
37 Cited in Matthew Wright, *Hawke's Bay— The History of a Province*, Dunmore Press, Palmerston North 1994, p. 29.

38 Goldsmith, pp. 96–97.
39 Bagnall & Petersen, pp. 300–302.
40 Wright, *Hawke's Bay*, p. 28.
41 Goldsmith, p. 96; Bagnall & Petersen, pp. 324–25.
42 See, e.g. William Colenso, 'A description of a species of Orobanche (supposed to be parasitical on a Plan of Hydrocotyle', *Transactions of the New Zealand Institute*, Vol. 21, 1888, at http://rsnz.natlib.govt.nz/volume/rsnz_21.html accessed 19 October 2007; also W. Colenso, 'Incidents Part II'. Colenso published 76 papers with the *Institute*.
43 William Colenso, 'Status quo: A Retrospect.—A Few More Words by way of Explanation and Correction concerning the First Finding of the Bones of the Moa in New Zealand; also Strictures on the Quarterly Reviewer's Severe and Unjust Remarks on the Late Dr. G. A. Mantell, F.R.S., &c., in connection with the same', Transactions of the New Zealand Instiute, Vol, 24, 1891, at http://rsnz.natlib.govt.nz/volume/rsnz_24/rsnz_24_00_003910.html, accessed 19 October 2007.
44 Wilson, pp. 148–49.
45 Wright, *Napier*, p. 39.
46 Wilson, p. 190.
47 See, e.g. correspondence in AJHR 1861 C-1 'Purchase of native lands, reports of the District Commissioners on the'.
48 Wright, *The Reed Illustrated History of New Zealand*, pp. 100–101.
49 Noted by Wilson, p. 258.
50 Colenso journal entry 4 October 1847, quoted in Wilson, p. 247.
51 Wilson, p. 248.
52 Wu MS-Papers-1348-01, Journal of F. J. Tiffen, 'A record of significant events'
53 Ibid
54 GBPP Vol. 3, 'Correspondence with the Secretary of State Relative to New Zealand', Hobson to Secretary of State for the Colonies, 15 October 1840, Enclosure 10, Bunbury to Hobson, 28 June 1840, pp 110–11.
55 Wu MS-Papers-1348-01, Journal of F. J. Tiffen, 'A record of significant events'
56 ANZ ACHK 16563 G7/6, Te Pohipi, Na Hou and Hoani Waikau to Governor Grey, 12 April 1849, translation and transcript; enclosure in Eyre to Grey 21 June 1849.
57 Ibid, Eyre to Grey, 21 June 1869.
58 Ray Fargher, *The best man who ever served the crown? A life of Donald McLean*, VUW Press, Wellington 2007, p.2..
59 Wright, *Two Peoples, One Land*, p. 80.
60 NAMU McLean Inwards Letterbook, Vol 24, Eyre to McLean, 24 September 1849.
61 Wright, *Town and Country*, p. 27.
62 WTu MS-Papers-0032, Folder 674c, Te Hāpuku to McLean, trans. Charles Royal.
63 ANZ ACHK 16563 G7/12, McLean to Domett, 24 August 1850; see also encl. 1, McLean to Eyre, 27 August 1850.
64 ANZ ACFP 8211 NM2/4, Grey to Eyre, 14 September 1850.
65 NAMU McLean Inward Letters and Papers, Vol 28, diary transcript 25 September 1850.
66 ANZ ACFP 8219 NM10/10, Colonial Secretary's General Outwards Correspondence— 5 September 1849–28 March 1851, S. E. Grimstone to McLean 7 October 1850.
67 NAMU, McLean Inwards Letterbook, Vol 28, Journal 14 October 1850.
68 Ibid, McLean journal 17 October 1850.
69 Ibid, 14 November 1850.
70 ACFP 8216 NM 7/1 Minutes of the Executive Council— 24 February 1848-16 August 1853, 15 November 1850, transcript, p. 220.
71 NAMU McLean Inwards Letterbook, Vol 28, 18 November 1850.
72 WTu MS-Papers-1284, McLean diary, 3 December 1850.

73 See, e.g., Waitangi Tribunal Document Bank, Wai 201, A-21 (e), Colenso journal.
74 *AJHR* 1862 C-1, McLean to Domett, 23 January 1851.
75 ANZ ACFP 8213 NM4/2 Despatches from the Lieutenant-Governor to the Governor-in-Chief –1 June 1850 – 3 March 1853, Eyre to Governor, 20 January 1851.
76 WTu MS-1232, McLean diary, 9 April 1851.
77 *AJHR*, 1862 C-1, Enclosure No.1 in No.6, Te Hāpuku to Grey, 3 May 1851.
78 WTu MS-1232, McLean diary, April 1851.
79 Ibid, 3 November 1851.
80 See, e.g., Joy Hippolite, 'Wairoa ki Wairarapa', Waitangi Tribunal overview report November 1991; Dean Cowie, 'Rangahaua Whanui District 11b
81 Michael King, *Being pākehā Now*, Penguin, Auckland 1999, pp. 206-207; Paul Moon, *The Path to the Treaty of Waitangi*, David Ling Publishing, Auckland 2002, p. 11; Andrew Sharp 'Recent Juridicial and Constitutional Histories of Māori', in Andrew Sharp and P. G. McHugh (eds), *Histories, Power and Loss*, Bridget Williams Books, Wellington 2001 esp. pp 30-36.
82 W. H. Oliver 'The Future Behind Us', in Andrew Sharp and P. G. McHugh (eds), *Histories, Power and Loss*, Bridget Williams Books, Wellington 2001, pp. 10, 12, 27, 29; also Moon, *The Path to the Treaty of Waitangi*; Andrew Sharp 'Recent Juridicial and Constitutional Histories of Māori', in Sharp and McHugh p. 31; Alexandra McKirdy, 'Māori-pākehā land transactions in Hawke's Bay 1848-1864', MA Thesis, Victoria University, March 1994, p. 4.
83 Giselle Byrnes, *The Waitangi Tribunal and New Zealand History*, Oxford University Press, Oxford 2004, pp. 188.
84 Ballara and Scott, p. 81.
85 McKirdy, p. 90.
86 Wright, *Town and Country*, p. 31
87 Wilson, pp. 205–206.
88 McKirdy, pp. 4, 90–91.
89 F. E. Maning, *Old New Zealand*, Golden Press reprint, Auckland 1973, p. 79.
90 See, e.g., Colenso's warning in WTu MS-1234, McLean diary, 30 March 1851.
91 Wright, *The Reed Illustrated History of New Zealand*, p. 94.
92 Ibid
93 WTu MS-1232, McLean diary, 19 March 1851.
94 Ballara, *Taua*, pp. 454–57.
95 Wright, *Two Peoples, One Land*, pp. 82–83; Wright, *The Reed Illustrated History of New Zealand*, p. 48.
96 Waitangi Tribunal, Wai 201 Document Bank, M2, 676D, Hāpuku, Puhara, Tareha, Karaitiana, 13 September 1852.
97 Ibid
98 *AJHR* 1862 C-1, 'Commissioners Reports Relative to Land Purchases', No. 20, Cooper to McLean, 29 November 1856.
99 WTu MS-Papers-0032, McLean, Donald (Sir), 1820-1877, Folder 227, Inward Letters, George Sisson Cooper, G.S. Cooper to McLean, 19 April 1856.
100 Matthew Wright *Havelock North - The History of a Village*, HDC, Hasting 1996, p 13.
101 Wtu MS-Papers-0032, Folder 227, Cooper to McLean, 17 March 1856.
102 Ibid
103 Ibid, Cooper to McLean, 19 April 1856.
104 *AJHR* 1862 C-1, Cooper to McLean, 19 August 1857.
105 Ibid, Cooper to McLean, 29 August 1857.
106 Ibid, McLean to Cooper, 29 August 1857.
107 Ibid, Cooper to McLean, 19 August 1857.
108 NAMU Resident Magistrate's Letterbook, Domett to Colonial Secretary, 29 August 1857.
109 *AJHR* 1862 C-1, No. 32, Cooper to McLean, 29 August 1857.

110 Parsonson, p. 145.
111 WTu, MS-Papers-0032, Folder 227, G. S. Cooper, 5 October 1857.
112 *Hawke's Bay Herald*, 3 October 1857.
113 *Hawke's Bay Herald*, 10 October 1857, letter from Tareha, Karaitiana, Renata Kawepo and others.
114 NAMU J.H. Joll 'Impromptu Talk'.
115 *Hawke's Bay Herald*, 24 September 1857.
116 NAMU Resident Magistrate's Letterbook, Curling to Superintendent, 28 January 1858.
117 WTu MS-1298, McLean, Donald (Sir) 1820-1877, 'Report of the Chief Commissioner Mr McLean's Visit to Ahuriri and the Wairarapa and Wellington'
118 Alice Woodhouse, *British Regiments in Napier 1858-1867*, Hawke's Bay Art Gallery and Museum, Napier, 1970, p. 2.
119 NAMU Resident Magistrate's Letterbook, Domett to Colonial Secretary, 19 December 1857.
120 WTu MS-1298, McLean, Donald (Sir) 1820-1877, transcripts of selected papers, Gore-Brown to McLean, 8 February 1858.
121 *Hawke's Bay Herald*, 9 January 1858.
122 *Hawke's Bay Herald*, 13 March 1858.
123 *AJHR* 1862 C-1, Commissioners' Reports Relative to Land Purchases, No. 47, Cooper to McLean, 30 September 1858.
124 *AJHR* 1862 C-1, No. 47 Encl. 1, Te Moananui, Tareha, Karaitiana Takamoana, Renata Kawepo and 7 others to Governor, 29 September 1858.
125 *AJHR* 1862 C-1, No. 30, Cooper to McLean, 19 August 1857.
126 Wtu MS-Papers-0069-050, Williams, Samuel, Observations on Donald McLean and autobiographical note; memo by Samuel Williams, 9 September 1861.
127 See, e.g., correspondence in Ibid

Chapter Three: The land of the shepherd kings

1 *The New Zealand Spectator and Cook's Strait Guardian*, 9 March 1853.
2 Rev. Richard Taylor, *The Past and Present of New Zealand with its Prospects for the Future*, William Macintosh, London 1868, http://www.nzetc.org/tm/scholarly/tei-TayPast-t1-body-d15.html, accessed 19 October 2007, p. 325.
3 Rev. Richard Taylor, *Te Ika a Maui, or, New Zealand and its inhabitants: illustrating the origin, manners, customs, mythology, religion, rites, songs, proverbs, fables, and language of the natives; together with the geology, natural history, productions, and climate of the country, its state as regards Christianity, sketches of the principal chiefs, and their present position*, Wertheim and Macintosh, 1855, http://www.nzetc.org/tm/scholarly/tei-TayTeik-t1-body-d1-d15.html, accessed 19 October 2007, p. 217.
4 Wright, *The Reed Illustrated History of New Zealand*, pp. 63–73.
5 Ibid, pp. 109–111, 233; Belich, *Making Peoples*, pp. 297–306.
6 Cited in Wright, *Napier*, p. 38.
7 Wtu MS-1817, Rich, George fl 1852-1858, Journal kept by George Rich, sheepfarmer of Ahuriri.
8 WTu, MS-1232, Donald McLean diary, 8 April 1851.
9 Wright, *The Reed Illustrated History of New Zealand*, pp. 122–24.
10 WTu, MS-1232, Donald McLean diary, 28 February 1851.
11 Wilson, p. 223.
12 *AJHR*, 1862 C-1, Enclosure No.2 in No.6, Park to McLean, 7 June 1851.
13 Wright, *Hawke's Bay*, p. 39.
14 Wilson, p. 224–25.
15 Rosamond Rolleston, *The Master*, A. H. & A. W. Reed, Wellington 1980, p. 15.
16 Wu MS-Papers-1348-01, Journal of F. J. Tiffen, 'A record of significant events'.
17 Muriel F. Lloyd Prichard, *An Economic History of New Zealand to 1939*, Collins,

Auckland 1970, p. 78.
18 Wright, *Hawke's Bay*, p. 41.
19 Rolleston, pp. 18, 20.
20 Reserve Bank Inflation Calculator, comparing Q1 1862 with Q1 2008. The Calculator begins at Q1 1862, the earliest date for which any pricing information is available. Graham Howard and Matthew Wright, 'The Reserve Bank Inflation Calculator', Reserve Bank of New Zealand *Bulletin*, Vol. 66, No. 4, December 2003; Graham Howard and Matthew Wright, 'A Note on the Reserve Bank Inflation Calculator', Reserve Bank of New Zealand *Bulletin*, Vol. 67, No. 4, December 2004.
21 Wright, *Hawke's Bay*, p. 43.
22 Campbell, 'Evolution', p. 74.
23 Wtu MS-0442, Campbell, Walter Lorne, 1845-1874, Journal Vol. VI, typescript.
24 Quoted in Sydney Grant, *Waimarama*, Dunmore Press, Palmerston North, 1977, p. 39.
25 Ibid, p. 46.
26 Wtu MS-2117 Tanner, Thomas 1830-1918, 'Notes of a tour in New Zealand 1858'.
27 Wright, *Havelock North*, p. 44; also *Hawke's Bay Herald*, 9 February 1867.
28 See Rolleston, p. 41.
29 *Hawke's Bay Herald*, 21 April 1876.
30 WTu, MS-1232, McLean Journal, 8 April 1851.
31 Wright, *Hawke's Bay*, p. 41.
32 *Hawke's Bay Herald*, 5 April 1892; Reserve Bank Inflation Calculator comparing Q1 1892 with Q1 2008.
33 Campbell, 'Evolution', p. 75.
34 Hawke's Bay Museum, D. P. Balfour, *His Life, By Himself*.
35 Campbell, 'Evolution', p. 5.
36 See, e.g, Asa Briggs, *Victorian Cities*, Pelican, London 1968, p. 76.
37 For discussion see, e.g., ibid, pp. 47–48, 76.
38 Cited in W. H. Oliver and Bridget Williams (eds) *The Oxford History of New Zealand*, Oxford University Press, Clarendon Press, Oxford 1981, reprint with corrections 1984, p. 136.
39 Wright, *Havelock North*, p. 41.
40 Campbell, 'Evolution', p. 353.
41 See, e.g. Boyd, Mary. 'Ormond, John Davies 1831? - 1917'. *Dictionary of New Zealand Biography*, updated 22 June 2007, http://www.dnzb.govt.nz/, accessed 16 Novermber 2007.
42 Rolleston, pp. 35–36.
43 Lieutenant-Colonel R. M. Bell, MBE, ED, *The History of the Hawke's Bay Agricultural and Pastoral Society 1863-1983*, HB A & P Society, Waipukurau, 1983, pp. 29–30.
44 Rolleston, p. 1.
45 S. W. Grant, *In Other Days: a history of the Chambers family of Te Mata, Havelock North*, CHB Printers, Waipukurau, 1980, p. 11.
46 Wtu MS-Papers-2883, White, G Marshall 1863-1949, Notes on history of Hawke's Bay; Wright, *Hawke's Bay*, p. 57.
47 Guy R. Scholefield (ed), *The Richmond-Atkinson Papers*, Vol. 2, Government Print, Wellington 1960, p. 347.
48 Wtu MS-Papers-1296, Biggs, Reginald Newton d. 1868, Biggs to Tuke, 6 November 1868.
49 Wtu MS-Papers-0456, Moonson, C M., fl. 1869, 'Letters concerning the Te Kooti Campaign', C.M. Monsoon to his brother, 26 June 1869.
50 Major-General Sir George S. Whitmore, *The Last Māori War in New Zealand*, Sampson, Low, Marston & Co., London 1902, pp. 11-12
51 Wright, *Hawke's Bay*, p.59.
52 *Hawke's Bay Herald*, 6 March 1858.
53 Wtu MS-Papers-7125, Morris, William, 1815-1882, diary, 15 June 1878, Friday 8 August 1878.
54 *Hawke's Bay Herald*, 6 March 1858.
55 See, e.g. B. I. Coleman (ed) *The Idea of the City in nineteenth-century Britain*, Routledge

56 & Kegan Paul, London, 1973, p. 15.
56 WTu MS-1231, McLean Diary, 12 November 1850.
57 NAMU McLean Inwards Letterbook, Vol 24, McLean Journal, 21 November 1850.
58 Wai 201, M2 Hemi Tahau to McLean, 12 January 1851, trans. Te Taite Cooper and Lee Smith.
59 AJHR 1862 C-1, Commissioners' Reports Relative to Land Purchases, Chief Commissioner to the Honorable the Colonial Secretary, Wellington, 9 July 1851, Enclosure No. 1, Te Hāpuku to Grey, 3 May 1851.
60 NAMU, 'Social Progress at the Antipodes'.
61 Wright, *Havelock North*, p. 38.
62 ANZ ACFP 8217 NM 8/51/1247, Colonial Secretary's Inwards Correspondence— 17 March–30 March 1846, McLean to Domett, 16 September 1851
63 ANZ ACFP 8216 NM 7/1 Minutes of the Executive Council— 24 February 1848–16 August 1853, 19 September 1851
64 ANZ ACFP 8219 NM10/11, Colonial Secretary's General Outwards Correspondence, 28 March 1851–24 June 1852, Domett to Park, 22 September 1851
65 Domett to Crown Lands Office, 20 March 1854, cited in Ian Mills, *What's In a Name: a history of the streets of Napier*, Thinker Publications, Napier, 1999, p. 79.
66 Alice Woodhouse, *The Naming of Napier*, Hawke's Bay Art Gallery and Museum, Napier, 1970, frontispiece.
67 Byron Farwell, *Queen Victoria's Little Wars*, Allen Lane, London 1973, p. 26.
68 Ibid, p. 167.
69 Domett to Crown Lands Office, 20 March 1854, cited in Mills, p. 79.
70 M. D. N. Campbell, *Story of Napier*, Napier City Council, Napier 1975, pp. 5-6.
71 Cited in Woodhouse, *The Naming of Napier*, p. 5.
72 Campbell, *Story of Napier*, p. 6.
73 Domett to Featherston, February 1854, cited in Campbell, *Story of Napier*, p. 5.
74 Woodhouse, *The Naming of Napier*, pp. 6–7.
75 Wilson, p. 265.
76 *The New Zealand Spectator and Cook's Strait Guardian*, 5 March 1853.
77 Ibid, 9 March 1853.
78 Lloyd-Prichard, p. 77.
79 Cited in Reed, p. 101.
80 See, e.g., *Hawke's Bay Herald*, 24 September 1857.
81 Reed, p. 102.
82 Ibid, pp. 104–105.
83 *Hawke's Bay Herald*, Extra, 16 May 1859.
84 Cited in Wright, *Havelock North*, p. 20.
85 *Hawke's Bay Herald*, 26 November 1859.
86 Wilson, p. 265.
87 Ibid, pp. 270–72.
88 Wright, *Havelock North*, p. 21.
89 *Hawke's Bay Herald*, 21 January 1860.
90 Ibid, 16 and 30 June 1860.
91 WTu MS-Papers-1298, McLean, Donald (Sir) 1820-1877, transcripts of selected papers, Colenso to McLean, 15 April 1858.
92 *Hawke's Bay Herald*, 30 June 1860.
93 *Hawke's Bay Herald*, 17 March 1860; see also Wright, *Havelock North*, p. 19.
94 See, e.g., *Hawke's Bay Herald*, 11 February 1860.
95 Margaret A. Gray, *Abbott's-Ford, A History of Waipawa*, C. H. B. Print, Waipukurau, 1989, p. 8.
96 Wright, *Havelock North*, pp. 22–23.
97 Thomas Lambert, *Story of Old Wairoa and the East Coast of New Zealand*, Reed NZ Ltd, Auckland 1998 reprint, p. 401.
98 Wilson, p. 270.
99 Ibid, pp. 272–73.
100 Giselle Byrnes, *Boundary Markers*, Bridget Williams Books, Wellington 2001, pp. 51-62.
101 Henry Tiffen is usually credited, however the original map in ANZ AAFV 997/HT 1,

102 Wright, *Havelock North*, p. 22.
103 Briggs, p. 135
104 Noel C. Harding, Hastings (NZ) from Town Board to City 1884-1962, Hastings City Council, p. 9.
105 Briggs, p. 26.
106 Byrnes, p. 58.
107 Briggs, p. 280.
108 Byrnes, p. 60.
109 *Hawke's Bay Herald*, 24 September 1857.
110 Wright, *Hawke's Bay*, p. 61.
111 Wilson, p. 242.
112 Matthew Wright, 'Wild Colonial Ways Editorial Sore Point', *Hawke's Bay Today*, 5 October 2007.
113 Campbell, 'Evolution', p. 353.
114 See, e.g., ibid, p.106.
115 *Hawke's Bay Herald*, 10 and 12 March 1868.
116 NAMU, D.P. Balfour, *His Life, By Himself*.
117 Wright, *The Reed Illustrated History of New Zealand*, p. 111.
118 Wright, *Hawke's Bay*, p. 68.
119 *Hawke's Bay Herald*, 6 May 1878.
120 Wright, *Town and Country*, p. 200.
121 Ibid; also *Hawke's Bay Herald*, 5 September 1879.
122 Campbell, 'Evolution', title of thesis.
123 upplement to the *Hawke's Bay Herald*, 'Kokiri', 'A pig hunt in the early days', 18 January 1896.
124 Ibid
125 See, e.g. A. G. Hopkins, 'Gentlemanly Capitalism in New Zealand', *Australian Economic History Review*, Vol. 43, No. 3, November 2003; Jim McAloon, 'Gentlemen, Capitalists and Settlers: a brief response', *Australian Economic History Review*, Vol. 43, No. 3, November 2003; Jim McAloon, 'Gentlemanly Capitalism and Settler Capitalists: Imperialism, Dependent Development and Colonial Wealth in the South Island of New Zealand, *Australian Economic History Review*, Vol. 42, No. 2, July 2002.
126 See, e.g., Wright, *Havelock North*: 41; also qMS-0414, Chambers, Joseph Bernard 1859-1931, Journal 1874--1883, entries July 1879.
127 Grant, *Waimarama*, p. 39.
128 Wright, *Hawke's Bay*, p. 65.
129 Ibid, p. 45.
130 See, e.g., Wright, *The Reed Illustrated History of New Zealand*, p. 111.
131 Wright, *Hawke's Bay*, p. 58.
132 Wright, *Town and Country*, p. 175–76.
133 Wtu qMS-0414, Chambers, Joseph Bernard 1859-1931, Journal 1874-1883, entries May 1876.
134 See, e.g., Wright, *The Reed Illustrated History of New Zealand*, p. 147.
135 Caroline Daley, 'Taradale meets the ideal society and its enemies', in Judith Binney (ed), The Shaping of History, Bridget Williams Books, Wellington 2001; also Caroline Daley, *Girls and Women: Men and Boys, gender in Taradale 1886-1930*, Auckland University Press, Auckland 1999.
136 Wright, *Havelock North*, pp. 105–112.
137 David Thorns and Charles Sedgwick, *Understanding Aotearoa/New Zealand: Historical Statistics*, Dunmore Press, Palmerston North 1997, p. 40.
138 Ian Pool, Arunachalam Dharmalingam, Janet Sceats, *The New Zealand family from 1840: a demographic history*, Auckland University Press, Auckland 2007, pp. 61-65.
139 Wright, *Hawke's Bay*, p. 64.
140 Wright, *The Reed Illustrated History of New Zealand*, p. 119.
141 See, e.g., Wright, *Two Peoples, One Land*, pp. 82–83.
142 For discussion, see Wright, *The Reed Illustrated History of New Zealand*, p. 32–34.
143 MS-Papers 1231, Donald McLean, Diary 8

April 1851
144 AJHR 1858 E-1, 'Report of the Otaki Industrial School, 1855'; also AJHR 1862 E-9, 'Further papers relative to Governor Sir George Grey's Plan of native Government, Reports of Officers'
145 Wilson, pp. 392–93.
146 See, e.g., See, e.g. AJHR 1858 E-1 'Report of Ahuriri Native Industrial School 1856'.
147 *AJHR,* 1862 E-4, 'Report on the Te Aute Native Industrial School in the Province of Hawke's Bay', 25 June 1862.
148 Wilson, p. 395.
149 NAMU, Resident Magistrate's Letterbook, Alfred Domett to Colonial Secretary, 29 August 1857.
150 William Sutch, *The Quest for Security in New Zealand 1840-1966,* Oxford University Press, Oxford 1966, p 39.
151 *AJHR,* 1862 C-1, Cooper to McLean, 20 June 1861.
152 Belich, *Making Peoples,* p. 88.
153 'Ka tohe tonu ahau ki te hapai i ou ritenga e Kawana, a, i o te Kuini, i o te Atua'. Wai 201 Document Bank, M2, 675H Karaitiana Takamoana, 15 September 1851, trans. Te Taite Cooper and Lee Smith.
154 Ann Parsonson, 'The Pursuit of Mana' in W. H. Oliver *The Oxford History of New Zealand,* OUP, Auckland 1981, p. 156; see also AJHR C-1, 1862, 'Commissioners' Reports relative to land purchases', Cooper to McLean, 29th July 1858; Vaggioli p. 169; Sorrenson, 'Māori and pākehā', p. 180.
155 *AJHR,* 1862 C-1, Cooper to McLean, 12 March 1860,
156 Wtu MS-Papers-1232, Donald McLean, diary, 5 August 1850.
157 Noted, e.g., Ballara, 'Origins', p. 486.
158 Ibid, p. 503.
159 Wtu MS-Papers-0032, McLean, Donald (Sir), 1820-1877, Folder 227, Inward Letters, George Sisson Cooper, Cooper to McLean, 19 April 1856.
160 See, e.g., *AJHR,* 1862 C-1, Tareha, Takamoana etc to the Governor, 29 September 1858.
161 Argued by Ballara, 'Origins', pp. 473-474.
162 See, e.g., Ibid, p. 496–97.
163 *New Zealand Statutes 1862*, Native Lands Act 1862, pp. 195–96.
164 *New Zealand Statutes* 1865, Native Lands Act 1865, Section 23.
165 AJHR 1871 A-2a 'Memorandum on the Operation of the Native Lands Court by Sir William Martin', Monro to Fenton, 12 May 1871, p. 15-16.
166 New Zealand Parliamentary Debates 1862 'Native Lands Act', p. 620.
167 *AJHR,* 1867 A-10c.
168 *AJHR* 1873 G-7 'Hawke's Bay Native Lands Alienation Commission Act, 1872', p.18
169 Cited in Matthew Wright 'Hawke's Bay was home of land rings', *Daily Telegraph,* 18 June 1994.
170 *e Wananga,* 12 February 1876.
171 bid.
172 NAMU, Ormond Papers, Box A2, Sutton to Ormond, 2 March 1870.
173 *JHR* 1873 G-7 'Hawke's Bay Native Lands Alienation Commission Act, 1872', Chairman's Report p 32.
174 AJHR 1873 G-7 'Hawke's Bay Native Lands Alienation Commission Act, 1872', p. 31-32.
175 See Ibid, pp. 4–17.
176 For detail see Wright, *Two Peoples, One Land,* esp. Chs 4–5, 7–8.
177 *Te Wananga,* 9 December 1875.
178 Wright, *Town and Country,* p. 51.
179 See, e.g. AJHR 1871 A-2, 'Native lands court, Memorandum opn the operatio of the, by Sir William Martin'.
180 NAMU, Ormond Papers, Box A2, Fox to Ormond, 12 November 1869, and enclosures.
181 Wright, *Two Peoples, One Land,* pp. 158–59.

182 Ibid, pp. 165–66.
183 Paul Clark, *Hauhau: the Pai Mārire search for Māori identity*, Auckland University Press/Oxford University Press, Auckland 1975, p. 44, quoting McLean to the Colonial Secretary, 5 August 1865.
184 *Hawke's Bay Herald*, 21 February 1865.
185 AJHR 1865 E-4, 'Further papers relative to the spread of the Hau Hau superstition among the Māories', Cooper to McLean, 25 February 1865.
186 *Hawke's Bay Herald*, 25 February 1865.
187 Reported in *Hawke's Bay Herald*, 1 April 1865.
188 Ibid
189 *Te Waka Māori o Ahuriri*, 29 April 1865.
190 James Cowan, *The New Zealand Wars, Volume 2: The Hauhau Wars*, Government Print, Wellington 1923, pp. 129-131.
191 Wright, *Two Peoples, One Land*, p. 168.
192 *Hawke's Bay Herald*, 26 June 1866.
193 *Hawke's Bay Herald*, 21 August 1866.
194 AJHR 1867 A-1, 'Despatches from the Governor of New Zealand to the Right Hon. Secretary of State for the Colonies', McLean to Stafford, 9 October 1860.
195 NAMU, Whitmore Papers, Box 1, Fitzgerald to Whitmore, 11 September 1865.
196 ANZ, ACFK 8164 AGG-HB2/1, Runanga of Heretaunga to McLean, 9 October 1866.
197 AJHR 1867 A1a, Whitmore to McLean, 13 October 1866; ANZ ACFK 8163 AGG-HB1/1 No. 23, 13 October 1866— James Fraser— Detailed report of action at the Petone Spit and Captain Carr's station.
198 John Battersby, *The One Day War*, Reed, Auckland 2000, title and themes.
199 MS-Copy-Micro-0535-008, McLean, Donald (Sir), 1820-1877 (MS-Papers-0032), Official papers—Superintendent, Hawkes Bay and Government Agent, East Coast - Sketch maps, plans etc of operations, Folders 25-27, 'Whitmore's Plan for Ōmaranui'.
200 See, e.g. MS-Papers-2620, Harris, George, fl. 1866-1899, 'Reminiscences of the fanatic Hau-Hau rebellion'.
201 ANZ ACFK 8163 AGG-HB1/1, No. 24 14 October 1866— Mclean, Napier— Congratulating Whitmore on the 'brilliant' action at Ōmaranui.
202 Wright, *Two Peoples, One Land*, p. 174.
203 See, e.g., *AJHR*, 1867 A1a, pp. 62–73.
204 James Belich, *The New Zealand Wars*, Penguin, Auckland 1986, p. 210.
205 Rolleston, p. 80.
206 See, e.g., Wright, *Two Peoples, One Land*, pp. 170–75.
207 AJHR 1867 A1, 'Despatches from the Governor of New Zealand to the Right Hon. Secretary of State for the Colonies', Whitmore to McLean, 13 October 1866.
208 Wright, *Two Peoples, One Land*, p. 166.
209 Judith Binney, *Redemption Songs: A Life Of Te Kooti Arikirangi Te Turuki*, Bridget Williams Books/Auckland University Press, Auckland 1995.
210 Wtu MS-Papers-3808, Firth, Josiah Clifton 1826-1897, Papers relating to Te Kooti and the New Zealand Wars, 1861-1870, Folder 1, Firth to Pollen, 18 January 1870; see also MS-Papers-3394, Wilson, George Hamish Ormond, 1907-1988, Te Kooti's Flag, MS; MS-Papers-2293, Morris, Maria, 1844-1907.
211 Wright, *Two Peoples, One Land*, pp. 190–91.
212 Argued in ibid, pp. 190–91, 208.
213 Whitmore, pp. 8–9.
214 AJHR 1868 A-15c 'Report relative to the pursuit of the escaped Chatham Island prisoners', G. S. Whitmore, 9 August 1868.
215 J. Hawthorne, letter to the *Hawke's Bay Herald*, 29 August 1868.
216 James Hawthorne, *A Dark Chapter from New Zealand History*, James Wood, Napier 1869, Capper Press reprint, Christchurch 1974, p.

217 WTu Micro-MS-535, Reel 93, Folders 596-602. Tanner to McLean, Aug 15, 1869; see also *Hawke's Bay Herald* 13 April 1869.
218 Belich, *Wars*, p. 255.
219 See, e.g. Wtu MS-Papers-0035-5 McDonnell, Thomas 1832-1899, Papers (MS-Papers-0035), William Best et al to McDonnell, n.d.; NAMU, Whitmore Papers, Box 1, McDonnell to Whitmore, 23 September 1868; Wtu MS-Papers-2048, Stafford, Edward William (Sir) 1819-1901, Stafford Papers (MS-2045-2050), Volume 4, Haultain to Stafford, 11 October 1868.
220 *The Wellington Independent*, 10 September 1868.
221 Wright, *Two Peoples, One Land*, pp. 190–92.
222 *Hawke's Bay Herald*, 29 August 1868.
223 Ibid, 19 September 1868; also 29 August 1868.
224 Ibid, 19 September 1868.
225 Whitmore, Introduction, pp. xxxvii–viii.
226 Wtu qMS-0832 'General Government Agency, public meeting 1869, minutes of a public meeting, Oddfellows Hall, Napier, 1869'.
227 Whitmore, Introduction, p. xxxiii.
228 Cited in *Hawke's Bay Herald*, 19 September 1868.
229 *Hawke's Bay Herald*, 29 September 1868.
230 AJHR 1868 A-4, 'Papers relative to the agency of Mr McLean', Memorandum by Mr Richmond, 12 October 1868.
231 See, e.g., Wright, *Two Peoples, One Land*, p. 203.
232 See, e.g. MS-Papers-1296, Biggs, Reginald Newton, d. 1868, Biggs to Tuke, 6 November 1868; MS-Papers-3508, Steddy, John G, fl. 1868, Letter from John Steddy, postmaster at Gisborne giving news of the Poverty Bay Massacre, 10 November 1868.
233 Whitmore, pp. 66–67.
234 Wright, *Two Peoples, One Land*, pp. 208–209; Wright, *New Zealand's Military Heroism*, pp. 54–55.
235 Wright, *Two Peoples, One Land*, pp. 208–212.
236 NAMU, D.P. Balfour, *His Life, by Himself*, typescript.
237 Wright, *Two Peoples, One Land*, p. 221.
238 *Hawke's Bay Herald*, 16 April 1869.
239 NAMU, D.P. Balfour Diary, 30 April 1869, Balfour's italics.
240 Wtu MS-Papers-3067, Northe letters, John and Anne North to Son and Daughter, 20 April 1869.
Hawke's Bay Herald, 13 April 1869.
241 Ibid, 13 April 1869.
242 Ibid, 20 April 1869.
243 Binney, p. 171.
244 Whitmore, p. 177.
245 NAMU, Whitmore Papers, Box 2, McLean to Whitmore, 22 September 1869.
246 Cited in Wright, *Town and Country*, p. 50.
247 AJHR 1870 A-8a, 'Papers relative to military operations against the rebel natives', McDonnell to Ormond, 6 October 1869.
248 Ibid, McLean to Tomoana, 18 November 1869.
249 AJHR 1870 A-8, 'Papers relative to military operations against the rebel natives', Fox to Ormond, 14 October 1869.
250 Ibid, Ormond to McLean, 5 November 1869.
251 AJHR 1873 G-7, 'Hawke's Bay Native Lands Alienation Commission Act, 1872', case reports, 'Report on Case No. XIII' (Heretaunga block), p. 20.
252 Ibid, p. 24–25.
253 Reserve Bank Inflation Calculator, comparing Q1 1870 with Q1 2008.
254 AJHR 1873 G-7 'Hawke's Bay Native Lands Alienation Commission Act, 1872', case reports, 'Report on Case No. XIII' (Heretaunga block), p. 18.
255 AJHR 1873 G-7 'Hawke's Bay Native Lands

Alienation Commission Act, 1872', Minutes of Evidence, Evidence of J. N. Wilson, p. 36
256 Ibid
257 *AJHR* 1873 G-7 'Hawke's Bay Native Lands Alienation Commission Act, 1872', General Report by the Chairman, p. 21.
258 Ibid
259 Ibid
260 *AJHR* 1873 G-7 'Hawke's Bay Native Lands Alienation Commission Act, 1872', Minutes of Evidence, Evidence of Henare Tomoana, pp. 29-30.
261 Ibid, Evidence of Karaitiana Takamoana, p.19.
262 Reserve Bank Inflation Calculator, comparing Q1 18769 with Q1 2008..
263 *AJHR* 1873 G-7 'Hawke's Bay Native Lands Alienation Commission Act, 1872', Minutes of Evidence, Evidence of F. E. Hamlin, p. 79.
264 Ibid, Evidence of Thomas Tanner, p. 87.
265 *AJHR* 1873 G-7 'Hawke's Bay Native Lands Alienation Commission Act, 1872', General Report by the Chairman, p. 23.
266 *AJHR* 1873 G-7 'Hawke's Bay Native Lands Alienation Commission Act, 1872', Minutes of Evidence, Evidence of Henry Martyn Hamlin, p.73.
267 *AJHR* 1873 G-7 'Hawke's Bay Native Lands Alienation Commission Act, 1872', General Report by the Chairman , p. 25..
268 *AJHR* 1873 G-7 'Hawke's Bay Native Lands Alienation Commission Act, 1872', case reports, 'Report on Case No. XIII' (Heretaunga block), p. 17
269 *AJHR* 1871 G-7, 'Trusts Commissioner for the district of Hawke's Bay under "Native Lands Frauds Prevention Act, 1870", Ormond to McLean, 10 August 1871.
270 See *AJHR,* 1872 A-11, pp. 3–5.
271 Ormond to McLean, 6 May 1872, cited in Sharron Mary Cole, 'The repudiation movement— a study of the Māori land protest movement in Hawke's Bay in the 1870s', MA Thesis, Massey University 1977, p. 66.
272 Cole, pp. 51–55.
273 AJHR 1871 G-7, 'Trusts Commissioner for the district of Hawke's Bay under "Native Lands Frauds Prevention Act, 1870", Ormond to McLean, 10 August 1871.
274 Cole, p. 51.
275 Calculated from figures in Cole, Appendix VII, pp. 121–24.
276 Reserve Bank Inflation Calculator, comparing Q1 1870 with Q1 2008.
277 Scholefield (ed), II, p. 346.
278 *Hawke's Bay Herald,* 4 June 1872.
279 Scholefield (ed), II, p. 346. Russell's italics Russell's italics.
280 MS Papers 0032, McLean, Donald (Sir) 1820-1877, Folder 394, Locke to McLean 10 July 1872.
281 *The Daily Southern Cross,* 11 July 1872,
282 *AJHR* 1872 I-2, Petition of Renata Kawepo and 553 others.
283 AJHR 1873 G-7 'Hawke's Bay Native Lands Alienation Commission Act, 1872', General Report by the Chairman, p. 7.
284 Listed in AJHR 1873 G-7 'Hawke's Bay Native Lands Alienation Commission', pp. 2-17.
285 Cole, p. 69.
286 Quoted in Scholefield (ed), II, p. 347
287 AJHR 1873 G-7 'Hawke's Bay Native Lands Alienation Commission Act, 1872', General Report by the Chairman, p. 6.
288 Ibid, p. 9.
289 Ibid, p. 4.
290 Ibid, p. 6.
291 Ibid, p. 3.
292 Ibid, p. 4.
293 Ibid, p. 45.
294 Ibid, p. 52.
295 *Evening Post,* 22 August 1873.
296 MS Papers 0032, McLean, Donald (Sir) 1820-1877, Locke to McLean, 15 April 1873.

297 *AJHR* 1874 G-1 'Notes of native meetings', Meeting held in the Court House, Napier, 29th November 1873.
298 Ibid
299 Noted by Cole, p. 73.
300 *Hawke's Bay Herald*, 17 April 1873.
301 Ibid, 3 May 1873.
302 See photograph in Wright *Hawke's Bay*, p. 99.
303 Ormond to McLean, 7 May 1873, cited in Cole, p. 73.
304 *Hawke's Bay Herald*, 13 June 1872.
305 AJHR 1873 J-6 'Petition of 300 Māoris of Hawkes' Bay, Wairoa, Turanga and Taupō.'
306 AJHR 1874 G-2, 'Reports from officers in native districts', Locke to the Hon,. the Native Minister, 30 May 1874.
307 Cole, Appendix VII, from Mount Herbert Ledger & Cash Books.
308 Cited in ibid, p. 86.
309 Ormond to McLean, 8 February 1871, cited in Cole, p. 63.
310 Reprinted in *Te Wananga*, 11 September 1875.
311 *Te Wananga*, 8 January 1876.
312 Ibid, 15 April 1876.
313 *Te Wananga*, 16 and 23 September 1876.
314 Keith Sinclair, *Kinds of Peace: Māori People after the Wars 1870-1885*, AUP, Auckland 1991. p.116.
315 Ormond to McLean, 6 May 1876, cited in Cole, p. 91.
316 Cole, p. 126, Appendix VII.
317 *The Evening Post*, 12 August 1876.
318 Rolleston, p. 98.
319 *Hawke's Bay Herald*, 19 January 1877.
320 NAMU, H.R. Russell Letterbook, Russell to [illegible], January 1877.
321 Ibid, Russell to H.D. Bell, 12 February 1877.
322 Ibid
323 Noted by Cole, p. 79
324 *Evening Post*, 10 September 1877.
325 R. Dalziel 'The Politics of Settlement', p. 104–105.
326 *Hawke's Bay Herald*, 24 April 1877.
327 Ibid, 15 January 1877.

Chapter Four: Iron Horse Towns
1 WTu, MS-Papers-1348-01, Journal of F. J. Tiffen, 'A record of significant events'.
2 See, e.g. W. B. Sutch, *Colony or Nation?*, Sydney University Press, Sydney 1966, second edition 1968, pp. 3-34; W. J. Gardner, 'A Colonial Economy' in W. H. Oliver and B. R. Williams (eds), *The Oxford History of New Zealand*, Clarendon Press, Oxford 1981, pp. 57-86.
3 Lloyd-Prichard, p. 110.
4 *Hawke's Bay Herald*, 3 November 1868.
5 *Hawke's Bay Herald*, 24 March 1868.
6 Wright, *Hawke's Bay*, p. 104.
7 Figures in Lloyd-Prichard, p. 108.
8 Reserve Bank Inflation Calculator, comparing Q1 1870 with Q1 2008.
9 Quoted in Matthew Wright, *Rails Across New Zealand*, Whitcoulls, Auckland, 2003, p. 15..
10 Argued, e.g. Keith Sinclair, *The History of New Zealand*, Pelican 1957, second edition 1967, p. 153.
11 Wright, *The Reed Illustrated History of New Zealand*, p. 177.
12 Thomas Lambert, *The Story of Old Wairoa and the East Coast of New Zealand*, Reed, Auckland, reprint 1998, p. 400.
13 See, e.g., Wright, *Rails Across New Zealand*, pp. 14, 20–21.
14 Ibid, p. 10.
15 Wu MS-Papers-1348-11, F. J. Tiffen Collection, Correspondence with H. R. Russell and newspaper clippings, Tiffen to Ludman, September 1853.
16 *Hawke's Bay Herald*, 3 March 1866.
17 NAMU, Donald McLean Letterbook Vol 12., McLean to ??, 8 November 1867.
18 *AJHR* 1867 F-4, 'Railway Gauge Committee'.

19 Thorns & Sedgwick, p. 108.
20 AJHR 1871 D-6a, 'Construction of Railways', Ormond to Gisborne, 1 June 1871, enclosure.
21 Ibid, Weber to Ormond, 17 October 1870.
22 Ibid, Ormond to Gisborne, 2 January 1871.
23 AJHR 1871 D-7 'The purchase of the seventy mile bush block', Ormond to Gisborne, 23 September 1870.
24 Ibid, Ormond to Gisborne, 20 April 1871.
25 Ibid, Ormond to Gisborne, 17 June 1871.
2 AJHR 1874 E-3, 'Appendices to Public Works Statement 1874', p. 33.
27 Ibid
28 Cited in M. Wright, *Town and Country*, p. 120.
29 Chambers diary quoted in Miriam McGregor *Pioneer Trails of Hawke's Bay*, A. H. & A. W. Reed, Wellington 1975, p. 58.
30 Wright, *Town and Country*, p. 120.
31 *AJHR* 1874 E-3, 'Appendices to Public Works Statement 1874', p. 33.
32 WTu MS-Copy-Micro-0535-034, McLean, Donald (Sir), 1820-1877 Papers (partial microfilm of MS-Papers-0032), Hāpuku to McLean, encl.
33 Ibid, Ormond to McLean, 7 December 1874.
34 Ormond to *Te Wananga*, 11 May 1876.
35 Wtu MS-Papers-1711, Russell, William Russell (Sir), 1838-1913, Correspondence, Harriett Russell to 'My Dear Ellen', 17 November 1874.
36 *Hawke's Bay Herald*, 30 October 1874.
37 *Hawke's Bay Herald*, 16 February 1877.
38 *AJHR* 1876 B-8, 'Estimated revenue from railways in each province for 1876-7', p. 1; RBNZ Inflation Calculator comparing Q1 1876 with Q3 2007.
39 Wright, *Rails Across New Zealand*, p. 22.
40 *AJHR* 1874 E-3, 'Appendices to Public Works Statement 1874', p. 31; Reserve Bank Inflation Calculator, comparing Q2 1874 with Q1 2008.
41 Wilson, p. 343.
42 AJHR 1879 E-1, Appendix L, Annual Report of Working Railways by the Commissioner of Railways, North Island.
43 F. O. Playle (ed) *101 Years of Ormondville*, Ormondville Centennial Committee, Ormondville 1978, p. 110.
44 *Hawke's Bay Herald*, 15 June 1882.
45 Ibid
46 Wright, *Rails Across New Zealand*, p. 32.
47 Ibid, p. 23.
48 Wilson, p. 315.
49 Quoted in Wright, *The Reed Illustrated History of New Zealand*, p. 186.
50 Scholefield, 1904, cited in G. C. Petersen, *Pioneering the North Island Bush*, in R. F. Watters (ed), *Land and Society in New Zealand*, A. H. & A. W. Reed, Wellington 1965, p. 73.
51 Petersen, p. 66.
52 Margit Brew, *Scandinavian Footprints: a story of Scandinavians settling in New Zealand*, Egan Reid, Auckland 2007, p. 54-70.
53 Wright, *Hawke's Bay*, p. 106.
54 *AJHR* 1874 D-2, 'Emigration to New Zealand', Commissioners' Report on Ship Hovding, 9 December 1873; 'To the Emigration Board, Napier', E. Greiner and 78 heads of families, 1 December 1873.
55 Ibid, Ormond to Vogel, 9 December 1873.
56 A. L. Andersen, *Norsewood: the centennial story*, A. L. Andersen, Dannevirke, 1972, p. 14.
57 See, e.g. M. Thom, *Dannevirke Borough*, Dannevirke Borough Council, Dannevirke 1952, p. 14.
58 Wtu MS-Papers 3595, Mortensen, H. P., 'Reminiscences of the early pioneers in Norsewood'.
59 Wilson, p. 304.
60 Rollo Arnold, *New Zealand's Burning*, Victoria University Press, Wellington 1994,

	p. 38, reproduced in http://www.nzetc.org/tm/scholarly/tei-ArnNewZ-_N1019F.html, accessed 25 October 2007.	91	Ibid, 1 February 1884.
		92	Gray, p. 44.
61	Andersen, p. 55.	93	Wright, *Town and Country*, p. 211.
62	Arnold, *New Zealand's Burning*, Figure 3.1	94	*Hawke's Bay Herald*, 27 November 1885.
63	Thom, p. 15.	95	Ibid, 20 August 1889.
64	Andersen, p. 26.	96	Ibid, 15 July 1879.
65	Rollo Arnold, *The Farthest Promised Land*, Victoria University Press and Price Milburn, Wellington 1981, pp. 18, 103.	97	Ibid, 5 September 1879.
		98	Ibid, 28 September 1879.
		99	Wright, *Town and Country*, p. 185.
66	Arnold *The Farthest Promised Land*, p. 128.	100	Thom, p. 5.
67	NAMU, Extracts from the diary of C.C. Weston, 10–30 April 1888.	101	Wright, *Havelock North*, p. 124.
		102	Reserve Bank Inflation Calculator, comparing Q1 1880 with Q1 2008.
68	Lambert, p. 765.		
69	Raymond Shaffer, 'Woodville, Genesis of a Bush Frontier Community 1874-1887', MA Thesis, Massey 1973.	103	*Hawke's Bay Herald*, 5 August 1885.
		104	*Hawke's Bay Herald*, 3 June 1889.
		105	Wright, *Town and Country*: 188.
70	Wright, *The Reed Illustrated History of New Zealand*, p. 186.	106	*Hawke's Bay Herald*, 19 December 1890.
		107	Ibid, 16 May 1882.
71	See, e.g. C. R. Peak, biography in HCC 448 Francis Hicks 1839-1911.	108	Wright, *Town and Country*, p. 196.
		109	*Hawke's Bay Herald*, 1 February 1884.
72	Noted in Boyd, p. 27.	110	Mary Boyd, *City Of the Plains*, Hastings City Council, Hastings 1984.p. 64.
73	*Hawke's Bay Herald*, 5 May 1873.		
74	Ibid, 1 February 1884.	111	Wright, *Town and Country*, p. 199.
75	Ibid, 7 June 1873.	112	Cited in Reed, p. 193.
76	Wilson, p. 422.	113	H. Hill, 'On the Artesian Well System of Hawke's Bay', *Transactions and Proceedings of the Royal Society of New Zealand*, Vol. 20, 1887, p. 282.
77	See, e.g., *Hawke's Bay Herald*, 5 September 1879.		
78	Reserve Bank Inflation Calculator, comparing Q3 1873 with Q1 2008.		
		114	Wright, *Napier— City of Style*, p. 49; Reserve Bank Inflation Calculator, comparing Q1 1873 and Q1 2008.
79	Wright, *Town and Country*, p. 129.		
80	Ibid		
81	*Hawke's Bay Almanac*, 1875.	115	Campbell, *Story of Napier*, p. 37.
82	Campbell, 'Evolution', p. 101.	116	Wright, *Napier*, p. 49.
83	Coleman, p. 15.	117	Campbell, *Story of Napier*, p. 56
84	G Graeme Davison *The Rise and Fall of Marvellous Melbourne*, Melbourne University Press, Melbourne 1980.	118	Cited in ibid, p. 34.
		119	Hill, p. 283.
		120	Wright, *Napier*, p. 49.
85	Briggs, pp. 180–83.	121	*Hawke's Bay Herald*, 27 November 1885.
86	Byrnes, *Boundary Markers*, p. 55.	122	Campbell, *Story of Napier*, p. 44; Reserve Bank Inflation Calculator, comparing Q1 1878 with Q1 2008.
87	*Hawke's Bay Herald*, 13 October 1885.		
88	Ibid		
89	Ibid, 15 October 1879.	123	Gray, *Abbott's-Ford*, p. 57.
90	Ibid, 28 October 1885.	124	Thom, pp. 20, 26–27.
		125	Ibid, p. 26.

126 Lester Masters, *Tails of the Mails*, private publication, Napier 1959, p. 63.
127 *Hawke's Bay Herald*, 9 December 1880.
128 Ibid
129 Ibid
130 Ibid, 18 December 1880.
131 Ibid, 12 August 1885.
132 Hastings Public Library MSS 1957 A. I. Rainbow 'A Walk though Hastings in the Early Nineties'
133 See, e.g. Wtu MS-Papers 0535-034, McLean, Donald (Sir), 1820-1877 : Papers (partial microfilm of MS-Papers-0032) (MS-Copy-Micro-0535), also *Hawke's Bay Herald*, 25 July 1863.
134 Wright, *Napier*, p. 57.
135 NAMU, Extracts from the diary of C.C. Weston, 10–30 April 1888.
136 *Hawke's Bay Herald*, 2 March 1863.
137 J. H. Joll, 'Impromptu Talk', cited in Wright, *Havelock North, The History of a Village*, p. 25.
138 Wtu MS-Papers, MS-0434, Campbell, Alexander, fl. 1875-1888, Diaries: Hawke's Bay Almanac, 1875.
139 WTU MS-Papers-1711, Russell, William Russell (Sir), 1838-1913, Correspondence, Harriett Russell to 'My Dear Ellen', 17 November 1874.
140 *Hawke's Bay Herald*, 6 May 1878.
141 J. H. Joll, 'Impromptu Talk', cited in Wright, *Havelock North, The History of a Village*, p. 60.
142 *Hawke's Bay Herald*, 27 November 1885.
143 Grey, p. 111.
144 Wright, *Napier*, p. 57.
145 *Hawke's Bay Herald*, 27 November 1885.
146 See, e.g. James Belich, *Paradise Reforged*, Allen Lane, Auckland 2001, pp.32-36.
147 Argued in Ian Hunter, *Age of Enterprise*, Auckland University Press, Auckland 2007, pp. 48-52.
148 Ibid, p. 49.
149 David Thomson, *A world without welfare: New Zealand's colonial experiment*, Auckland University Press/Bridget Williams Books, Auckland 1998, pp. 10-11.
150 Wtu Micro-MS-0425, Maunder, George Henry, Letters written from Auckland and Hawke's Bay to his sister, Jane, and to his mother.
151 NAMU, Extracts from the diary of C.C. Weston, 10–30 April 1888.
152 Lloyd-Prichard, p. 161.
153 Wtu MS-Papers-455, Adam Dawson, letter from Napier, 8 September 1884.
154 Campbell, 'Evolution', p. 16.
155 Wilson, pp. 232–33.
156 *Hawke's Bay Herald*, 17 December 1890.
157 Reserve Bank Inflation Calculator, Q1 1889 compared with Q1 2008.
158 See, e.g., *Hawke's Bay Herald*, 19 December 1890.
159 *Hastings Standard*, 2 December 1896.
160 Wright, *Havelock North*, pp. 47–48.
161 NAMU, J.G. Kinross Letterbook 1858–76.
162 *Hawke's Bay Herald*, 24 March 1868.
163 Ibid, 5 April 1870.
164 Ibid, 15 March 1884.
165 Quoted in S. Grant, *In Other Days*, p. 54.
166 *Hawke's Bay Herald*, 7 September 1885.
167 Ibi
168 Ibid, 22 September and 20 October 1882. Reserve Bank Inflation Calculator, comparing Q4 1882 with Q1 2008.
169 W. Nelson 'The Tomoana Freezing Works' in E. S. Cliff & Co, *Hastings, the Hub of Hawke's Bay New Zealand*, E. S. Cliff & Co, Hastings, c1918
170 Wright, *The Reed Illustrated History of New Zealand*, pp. 228–29.
171 Lloyd-Prichard, pp. 164–65, 168–69.
172 David Greasley and Les Oxley, 'Refrigeration and distribution: New Zealand land prices and real wages 1873-1939', *Australian Economic History Review*, Vol. 45, No. 1, p. 24.
173 Wright, *The Reed Illustrated History of New*

173 *Zealand*, pp. 228–31.
174 Ibid, pp. 120–21.
175 Ibid
176 Campbell, 'Evolution', p. 227.
177 Wright, *Hawke's Bay*, p. 127.
178 Wright, *Havelock North*, pp. 84–85.
179 Wright, *Hawke's Bay*, p. 127.
180 Wtu Micro-MS-0443, Rolleston, John Christopher, 'Orua Wharo', diary extracts from Sydney Johnson, 17 May 1894; 4 October 1895.
181 *Hawke's Bay Herald*, 30 December 1892.
182 Ibid, 19 December 1892.
183 Ibid, 17 March 1897.
184 Wtu Micro-MS-0443, Rolleston, John Christopher, 'Orua Wharo'.
185 Wright, *Havelock North*, pp. 74–77.
186 Matthew Wright, *Cars Around New Zealand*, Whitcoulls, Auckland 2004, p. 16.
187 Wright, *The Reed Illustrated History of New Zealand*, p. 216.
188 Wright, *Hawke's Bay*, p. 137.
189 Quoted in M. D. N. Campbell, 'Hawke's Bay Politics 1890-1914', MA Thesis, VUW 1967, p. 35.
190 Campbell, 'Evolution', p. 430.
191 Wright, *Hawke's Bay*, p. 137; Reserve Bank Inflation Calculator, comparing Q1 1906 with Q1 2008.
192 Douglas MacLean changed the spelling of his surname; his father was Donald McLean.
193 Campbell, 'Evolution', p. 418. Reserve Bank Inflation Calculator, comparing Q1 1905 with Q1 2008.
194 S. W. Grant *Havelock North, 1860-1952*, Hawke's Bay Newspapers, Hastings 1978, p 44.; G. P. Donnelly *Looking Backward, New Zealand Fifty Years Ago, Life in Hawke's Bay Then and Now*, The Christchurch Press Co. Ltd, Christchurch 1913, pp. 2-5.
195 Guthrie-Smith, p. 400.
196 Wright, *The Reed Illustrated History of New Zealand*, pp. 216–19.
197 Quoted in ibid, p. 218.
198 Campbell, 'Evolution', p. 431.
199 Tom Brooking, '"Bursting up" the Greatest Estate of All' in Binney (ed), *The Shaping of History*, Bridget Williams Books, Wellington 2001.
200 Wright, *The Reed Illustrated History of New Zealand*: 221.
201 Donnelly.
202 WTu MS Cha 1911, letter from John Chambers to directors of the *Hawke's Bay Tribune* 23/1/1911.
203 Ibid
204 Eric Olssen, 'Towards a new society' in W. H. Oliver and B. R. Williams (eds), *The Oxford History of New Zealand*, Clarendon Press, Oxford 1981, p. 257.

Chapter Five: Farmer Backbone's Engine
1 See, e.g., Wright, *The Reed Illustrated History of New Zealand*, pp. 366–71.
2 Ibid, pp. 297.
3 Ibid, pp. 232–34.
4 For argument see ibid, pp. 232–49.
5 Ibid, pp. 234.
6 Bell, p. 55.
7 *Hawke's Bay Herald*, 15 August 1862.
8 Ibid
9 Wright, *Town and Country*, p. 158.
10 *Hawke's Bay Herald*, 1 September 1868.
11 Wright, *Town and Country*, pp. 158–59.
12 *Hawke's Bay Herald*, 18 January 1875.
13 Reserve Bank Inflation Calculator, comparing Q1 1875 with Q1 2008.
14 Wright, *Town and Country*, p. 160.
15 *Hawke's Bay Herald*, 3 April 1897.
16 Wright, *Town and Country*, pp. 278–79.
17 See, e.g., *Hawke's Bay Herald*, 23 June 1902.
18 Wright, *Town and Country*, p. 286.
19 Campbell, *The Story of Napier*, p. 83.
20 *Hawke's Bay Herald*, 23 May 1904.

21 Ian L. Mills, *What's In a Name: a history of the streets of Napier*, Thinker Publications, Napier 1999, p. 246.
22 Campbell, *The Story of Napier*, p. 85.
23 Author observation; this building still stood in 2007.
24 Wright, *Havelock North*, p. 114.
25 Wright, *Town and Country*, p. 299.
26 Normal displacement; she was 22,100 tons deep load. See Ian Sturton (ed), *Conway's All the World's Battleships, 1906 to the present*, Conway Maritime Press, London 1987, p. 59
27 Matthew Wright, *Blue Water Kiwis*, Reed, Auckland 2001, pp. 26-30.
28 Cited in ibid, p. 34.
29 Ibid, pp. 35–36.
30 Guthrie-Smith, p. 411.
31 WTu MS Papers 2477-2, Higginson, Louisa 1885-1978: Diaries / transcribed by Mrs R L Wilson (MS-Papers-2477), typescript.
32 Wtu-MS-Papers-2392, Aubrey Tronson, 'A Soldier's Book of Life'.
33 See, e.g. Terry Kinloch, *Echoes of Gallipoli*, Exisle, Auckland 2005, pp. 32-33.
34 Hastings Public Library, R. F. Gambrill (ed), *The Russell Family Saga*, MS, Russell diary, 10 August 1914.
35 Matthew Wright, *Western Front*, Reed, Auckland 2005, p. 141.
36 Matthew Wright, *New Zealand's Military Heroism*, Reed, Auckland 2007, pp. 75-82.
37 Cited in Wright, *Havelock North*, p. 131.
38 Grant, *Havelock North 1860-1952*, p. 122.
39 See Wtu MS-Papers-2350, Bollinger, George W., Diary and letters, 1915-1917.
40 Wright, *Western Front*, pp. 45–57.
41 Wtu MS-Papers-2481, Bourke, Henry O'Donel 1889-1982, Diary and memoirs 1917-1918, (typescript).
42 Matthew Wright, 'Now we lie in Flanders fields', *New Zealand Listener*, 13-19 October 2007; WTu MS-Papers-1504, Folder 5, P. Howden collection, enclosed memorabilia.
43 Wtu MSX 4760 'Dawes Bently, fl. 1920, Manuscript of Doug Stark, Bomber with Otago on the Western Front', Vol 1. See also D. I. B. Smith (ed), Introduction, in Robin Hyde, *Passport to Hell*, Auckland University Press, Auckland 1986, pp. x-xi.
44 HDC, HN 102, Minister of Internal Affairs Circular Letter, 04/05/1917
45 WTu Micro-MS-0425, Maunder, George Henry 1867-1870, Letters written from Auckland and Hawke's Bay to his sister, Jane, and to his mother, 1867-1870.
46 NAMU, D. Balfour, *His Life, By Himself*, p. 101.
47 Wright, *Town and Country*, pp. 342–43.
48 Belich, *Paradise Reforged*, p.171.
49 Poster reproduced in R. M. Burdon, *The New Dominion*, A. H. & A. W. Reed, Wellington 1965, facing p. 119.
50 Burdon, p. 21.
51 Wright, *Western Front*, pp. 42–64.
52 *The Press*, 3 September 1928.
53 Thorns and Sedgwick, p. 55.
54 Ibid, p. 54.
55 Waitangi Tribunal, *Te Whanganui-ā-Orotū report*, p. 104.
56 Ibid, pp. 168–73.
57 *The Daily Telegraph*, 8 September 1921.
58 Ibid, 9 September 1921.
59 Ibid, 10 September 1921.
60 Ibid, 7 September 1921.
61 Ngaio Marsh, *Black Beech and Honey Dew*, Collins, London 1966, p 160.
62 HNL, 'Our Village' greeting card.
63 Wright, *Havelock North*, p. 155.
64 Grant, *Havelock North 1860–1952*, p. 85
65 HNL A/44/1983, J. H. von Dadelszen, 'The Havelock Work', p. 11
66 HNL, H. Felkin *The Wayfaring Man* in *The Lantern* Vol II No.6, pp 8-9.
67 Marsh: 160.
68 HNL A/44/1983, J. H. von Dadelszen,

68 'The Havelock Work', p. 19.
69 The *Hawke's Bay Herald-Tribune*, 21 January 1959.
70 P. Cornford, interview with author 29 June 1996, from Wright, *Havelock North*, p. 106.
71 P. Cornford, interview with author 29 June 1996, ibid, p. 157.
72 Quoted in Quoted in Iris Nolan, *Our Village, Our Story*, Dannevirke Publishing Co., Dannevirke, 1962, p. 62.
73 HNL, *The Forerunner*, No. 1.
74 Ibid
75 HNL, 'The Shakespearean Pageant at Havelock North'.
76 Havelock rose from 374 in 1900 to 1050 in 1926, see Grant, *Havelock North 1860-1952*, p. 98.
77 Wright, *Havelock North*, pp. 156–57.
78 HNL A/44/1983, J. H. von Dadelszen, 'The Havelock Work', p. 11.
79 Felkin, p. 12.
80 Wright, *Havelock North*, p. 158.
81 Ibid, p. 161.
82 Grant, *In Other Days*, pp. 130–31.
83 HNL A/44/1983, J. H. von Dadelszen, 'The Havelock Work', p. 15; Grant, *In Other Days*, p. 131.
84 Author observation, 1996.
85 HNL A/44/1983, J. H. von Dadelszen, 'The Havelock Work', p. 17.
86 Wright, *Havelock North*, p. 169.
87 For details refer, e.g. Rudolf Steiner *The Mission of Spiritual Science* Rudolf Steiner Publishing Co, London 1916, p. 42; see also http://www.skepticreport.com/sr/?p=480, https://spiritualityisnoexcuse.wordpress.com/2015/08/24/rudolf-steiner-racism-nazis-why-anthroposophy-doesnt-grow-up/ , and http://www.waldorfcritics.org/articles/Staudenmaier.html , accessed 1 February 2017; http://www.orgonomie.net/hdoeng12.htm, accessed 2 February 2017; Peter Staudenmaier, *Between Occultism and Nazism: anthroposophy and the politics of race in the fascist era*, Brill, Leiden 2014, pp. 139-143; and https://sites.google.com/site/waldorfwatch/steiners-racism, accessed 26 February 2017.
88 Wright, *Havelock North— The History of a Village*, pp. 168-169.
89 Wright, *Town and Country*, p. 369.
90 Ibid, pp. 400–402.
91 Reserve Bank Inflation Calculator, comparing Q1 1923 with Q1 2008.
92 Campbell, *Story of Napier*, p. 109.
93 Reserve Bank Inflation Calculator, comparing Q1 1925 with Q1 2008.
94 Wright, *Town and Country*, pp. 421–29.
95 Thom, *Dannevirke Borough*, p. 28.
96 Wright, *Havelock North*, pp. 140–41.
97 Ibid, p. 142; Reserve Bank Inflation Calculator, comparing Q1 1918 with Q1 2008.
98 Thom, pp. 52–53.
99 Wright, *Town and Country*, pp. 313–14.
100 Masters, *Tales of the Mails*, p.162.
101 Wright, *Town and Country*, p. 314.
102 Matthew Wright, *Cars Around New Zealand*, p. 31.
103 Harding, p. 38.
104 Kay Mooney, *History of the County of Hawke's Bay* (4 Vols), Hawke's Bay County Council, Napier, 1973-77, Vol III, pp.53-55.
105 Author observation.
106 — *Official Handbook of Hastings for Tourist, Sportsman and Settler*, Hastings Borough Council, Hastings 1929, p. 112.
107 H. Skinner, pers. comm. (1983 interview).
108 – *Cyclopedia of New Zealand*, Weeks Publishing Co., Christchurch 1906-1908, Vol. VI, p. 479. S. W. Grant *Havelock North*, p.41 dated both this and Guthrie's migration to New Zealand to 1874.
109 *Cyclopedia of New Zealand*, Vol. VI, p. 478.
110 Ibid, p. 479.
111 Thomas Horton Ltd 'Wonderful progress of the nursery industry' inCliff, E. S. &

	Co, *Hastings, the Hub of Hawke's Bay New Zealand*, E. S. Cliff & Co c1918.
112	Ibid
113	*Official Handbook of Hastings for Tourist, Sportsman and Settler*, p. 93.
114	Ibid
115	*The Daily Telegraph*, 10 September 1924.
116	Ibid
117	Wright, *Town and Country*, p. 367
118	Gray, *Abbott's-Ford*, p. 166.
119	*Official Handbook of Hastings for Tourist, Sportsman and Settler*, p. 63.
120	*The Daily Telegraph*, 17 September 1924.
121	Reserve Bank Inflation Calculator, comparing Q1 1929 with Q1 2008.
122	Wright, *Town and Country*, pp. 364–65.
123	*Official Handbook of Hastings for Tourist, Sportsman and Settler*, p. 57
124	Wright, *Havelock North*, pp. 84–86.
125	J. Siers *James Walter Chapman Taylor in the Hawke's Bay*, HB Cultural Trust 1991, p 4; see also HN 102, Letters 1918, Chapman-Taylor to HNTB 9 April 1918.
126	Robert McGregor, *The Art Deco City*: Napier, New Zealand, Art Deco Trust, Napier 1998, second edition 1999, p. 24; Peter Shaw, *Louis Hay Architect*, Hawke's Bay Cultural Trust, Napier 1998, p.38.
127	Matthew Wright, *Quake- Hawke's Bay 1931*, Reed, Auckland 2001, pp. 44-45.
128	MS-Papers-5814, Campbell, Dorothy Beatrice, 1903-1975, Letter 5 Mar 1931.
129	NAMU, Earthquake Personal Reminiscences Box 1 (EPR), Bernard Chambers Memoir (diary extracts).
130	*New Zealand Herald*, 6 February 1931.
131	NAMU Earthquake Personal Reminiscences (EPR) Mitchell des Landes Memoir.
132	WTu MS-Papers-2418-4, Ashcroft, William James Cronshaw, d 1981 : Papers (MS-Papers-2418), Napier earthquake and copies of The Apiarist, 1931-1980, Bill Ashcroft to his sister 15/02/1931
133	WTu MS-Papers-2107, Anderson, Jean, Letter to Elsie Young, 3 Feb 1931.
134	Ibid
135	NAMU EPR, W. Olphert Memoir.
136	*New Zealand Herald*, 6 February 1931.
137	—— *Hawke's Bay — Before And After, Daily Telegraph, Napier 1931 (reprint 1981)*, p. 87.
138	Ibid, p. 63.
139	*New Zealand Herald*, 6 February 1931.
140	NAMU EPR, Mary Hunter Memoir.
141	*Hawke's Bay: Before and After*, p. 73.
142	NAMU EPR, Vera Smith Memoir.
143	*Hawke's Bay: Before and After*, p. 81.
144	*New Zealand Herald*, 6 February 1931.
145	HNL A/335/1988, Havelock North Primary School 125th Jubilee 1863-1988, p 42.
146	NAMU EPR, Darry McCarthy, transcript of radio talk, 3 February 1987.
147	*Hawke's Bay: Before and After*, p. 115
148	NAMU EPR, Joe Peel Memoir.
149	*New Zealand Herald*, 05 March 1931
150	WTu MS-Papers-3838, MacNab, Margaret Duirs, fl 1931, Account of experiences following the Napier earthquake, 1931, 'Letter written February 1985 in response to a radio programme'.
151	This rumour persisted: see, e.g., Campbell, *The Story of Napier*, p. 132.
152	NAMU EPR, Mary Eames Memoir.
153	Wright, *Quake*, p. 56.
154	Ibid, p. 51.
155	F. R. Callaghan, 'The Hawke's Bay Earthquake. General Description', in *New Zealand Journal of Science and Technology*, Vol. XV, No.1, July 1933, p. 12.
156	NAMU EPR, Mary Hunter Memoir.
157	WTu MS-Papers-2107, Anderson, Jean, Letter to Elsie Young, 3 Feb 1931.
158	Wright, *Quake*, pp. 59–60.
159	NAMU EPR, Mary Hunter Memoir.
160	*New Zealand Herald*, 9 February 1931.
161	Edwin F. Scott, 'A Report on the Relief

Organisation arising out of the earthquake in Hawke's Bay on February 3rd, 1931', Christchurch Public Utilities Committee, Christchurch, April 1931, p. 7.
162 Ibid, p. 58.
163 *Hawke's Bay: Before and After*, p. 84.
164 Ibid, p. 96.
165 Ibid, p. 77.
166 NAMU EPR, Mary Hunter Memoir.
167 *Hawke's Bay: Before and After*, p. 118.
168 Geoff Conly, *The Shock of 31*, A. H. & A. W. Reed 1980, pp. 232-235; A. H. McLintock (ed) *An Encyclopedia of New Zealand*, Government Print, Wellington 1966, Vol. 1 p. 475.
169 See, Wright, Quake pp. 101-102, also http://www.stuff.co.nz/dominion-post/news/hawkes-bay/76541493/Study-finds-fewer-killed-in-1931-Hawkes-Bay-earthquake-than-previously-thought. accessed 26 February 2017; David Dowrick 'Damage and Intensities in the Magnitude 7.8 1931 Hawke's Bay, New Zealand earthquake', *Bulletin of the New Zealand National Society for Earthquake Engineering*, Vol 31, No. 3, September 1998.
170 Wright, *Quake*, p. 5.
171 Dowrick 'Damage and Intensities in the Magnitude 7.8 1931 Hawke's Bay earthquake'.
172 Robert McGregor, *The Art Deco City: Napier, New Zealand*, Art Deco Trust, Napier, 1998, p. 2.
173 M. Wynn, pers. comm.
174 J. Wright, pers. comm.
175 HNL, S.M.M von Dadelszen Memoir.
176 *New Zealand Herald*, 5 February 1931.
177 Ibid, 6 February 1931.
178 Scott, p. 2
179 Ibid, p. 5.
180 Ibid
181 *Hawke's Bay: Before and After*, p. 78.
182 WTu, MS-Papers-2107, Anderson, Jean, Letter to Elsie Young, 3 Feb 1931.
183 *New Zealand Herald*, 5 February 1931.
184 WTu MS Papers 5283 Ernest St. Clair Haydon Collection.
185 *Hawke's Bay: Before and After*, p. 74.
186 Ibid, p. 76.
187 Ibid, p. 89.
188 Scott, p. 18.
189 *Hawke's Bay: Before and After*, p. 100.
190 Ibid, p. 77.
191 Ibid, p. 69.
192 Ibid, p. 91.
193 NAMU EPR, W. Olphert Memoir.
194 WTu MS Papers 1346 A. E. L. Bennett Collection.
195 WTu MS-Papers-5283, Haydon, Ernest St Claire b 1885, Napier earthquake, an eyewitness description.
196 Lloyd-Prichard, p. 333.
197 Guthrie-Smith, p. 414.
198 Burdon, p. 129.
199 Reserve Bank Inflation Calculator, comparing Q1 1931 with Q1 2008.
200 Quoted in Conly, *Shock of 31*, p. 182.
201 Simon Chapple, *The Economic effects of the 1931 Hawke's Bay Earthquake*, New Zealand Institute of Economic Research (Inc), Working Paper 97/7, Wellington, August 1997, pp. 26, 50.
202 D. J. Dowrick, D. A. Rhoades, J. Babor, and R. D. Beetham, 'Damage ratios and microzoning effects in Napier in the magnitude 7.8 Hawke's Bay, New Zealand earthquake of 1931', *Bulletin of the New Zealand National Society for Earthquake Engineering*, Vol 28, No. 2, June 1995, p. 135.
203 MS-Papers-5814, Campbell, Dorothy Beatrice, 1903-1975, Letter 5 Mar 1931.
204 *The Daily Telegraph*, 16 February 1931.
205 Callaghan, p. 37.
206 Chapple, p. 14 differs from Callaghan's figures.
207 Callaghan, p. 35.
208 Wright, *Napier*, p. 100.

209 Callaghan, p. 37 cites these permits as being worth £339,538, but see Chapple, p. 14.
210 Harding, p. 56.
211 Ibid
212 Noted in Waitangi Tribunal, *Te Whanganui-A-Orotū Report*, p. 116.
213 Dowrick et al., p. 140.
214 Reserve Bank Inflation Calculator, comparing Q1 1934 with Q4 2008.
215 Wright, *Town and Country*, p. 490–93.
216 Campbell, *Story of Napier*, p. 158.
217 Ibid, p. 159.
218 John Mulgan, *Report on Experience*, Oxford University Press, London 1947, pp. 11-12.
219 Reserve Bank Inflation Calculator, comparing Q1 1931 with Q1 2008.
220 Guthrie-Smith, p. 414
221 Matthew Wright 'The History of Farming in Kuripapango', NZFS, Napier 1984, p. 22; Reserve Bank Inflation Calculator, comparing Q1 1933 with Q1 2008.
222 Lloyd-Prichard, p. 379; Thorns and Sedgwick, p. 74, 78, 95.
223 As observed by Boyd, *City of the Plains*, pp. 274–76.
224 Chapple, p. 37–38, citing *New Zealand Yearbooks*.
225 Chapple, p. 44.
226 Boyd, *City of the Plains*, p. 274.
227 Campbell, *Story of Napier*, p. 156.
228 Hastings District Council Archive, HDC 525 Minute Book, 30 June 1933, pp. 70–71.
229 Wright, *Town and Country*, pp. 480–88.
230 Ibid, p. 484.
231 Mulgan, p. 12.
232 Wright, *Town and Country*, p. 497.
233 Brian Easton, *The Nationbuilders*, Auckland University Press, Auckland 2001, p. 93, citing Bruce Jesson *Fragments of Labour*, p. 17.
234 Keith Sinclair, *Walter Nash*, Auckland University Press, Auckland, 1976, p. 362.
235 Ibid, p. 126.
236 King, *The Penguin History of New Zealand*, p. 354.
237 Wright, *Town and Country*, pp. 514, 516.
238 Rose Mannering, *100 Harvests — a history of fruitgrowing in Hawke's Bay*, PSL Press, Wellington 1999, p. 75.
239 Geoff Conly, *Wattie's — The First Fifty Years*, J. Wattie Canneries, Hastings, 1984, pp. 16-21.
240 Guthrie-Smith, p. 418
241 *New Zealand Herald*, 2 March 1937.
242 *Hastings, Health, Wealth and Prosperity*, p. 40.
243 Ibid
244 *The Daily Telegraph*, 6 October 1938.
245 Ibid
246 *Hastings, Health, Wealth and Prosperity*, p. 21.
247 *The Daily Telegraph*, 1 October 1938.

Chapter Six: Suburban Paradise
1 Mulgan, p. 15.
2 Hastings District Council Archive, HBC 67, file contents.
3 See, e.g., Wilson, foreword.
4 Nancy M. Taylor, *The Home Front*, Vol. 1, Government Print, Wellington, 1986, p. 461.
5 Ibid, p. 462.
6 Wright, *Town and Country*, pp. 542-526.
7 Hastings District Council Archive, HBC 41/42 Proposed Military Camp near Hastings 1941, Jones to Cullen 16/06/1941
8 HBC 41/11 Emergency Precautions 1942, 'Hastings and District Emergency Precautions Scheme'.
9 Campbell, *Story of Napier*, p. 175.
10 Taylor, p. 535.
11 J. Wright, pers. comm.
12 HBC 41/11 Emergency Precautions 1942, 'Hastings and District Emergency Precautions Scheme'

13. M. C. Fairbrother (ed), *Documents Relating to New Zealand's Participation in the Second World War, 1939-45*, Volume III, War History Branch, Wellington 1963, New Zealand Liaison Officer (London) to the Chief of the General Staff, Wellington, 27 March 1942, pp. 251-254.
14. Matthew Wright, *Blue Water Kiwis*, Reed, Auckland 2001, p. 116
15. Matthew Wright, *Pacific War*, Reed, Auckland 2003, p. 38.
16. For a speculative description, see Wright, *Fantastic Pasts*, pp. 174–91.
17. Wright, *Pacific War*, p. 46
18. Matthew Wright, (ed), *Torpedo! Kiwis at sea in World War II*, Random House, Auckland 2007, pp. 33-35.
19. Taylor, Vol. 1, p. 497/
20. Author observation.
21. Taylor, Vol. 1, pp. 500-501.
22. *The Daily Telegraph*, 19 November 1942.
23. *Hawke's Bay Herald Tribune*, 11 May 1943.
24. HPL 98/1095 Fun Sessions Souvenir Programme 1942-1945, Municipal Theatre Hastings NZ, Wednesday 24th October 1945.
25. Ibid
26. *Hawke's Bay Herald Tribune*, 26 May 1943.
27. Ibid
28. Ibid, 6 May 1943.
29. *The Daily Telegraph*, 3 November 1942.
30. *Hawke's Bay Herald Tribune*, 6 May 1943.
31. Wright, *Town and Country*: 540.
32. Hastings District Council Archive, HBC 46/64, 'Hastings and district statistical figures and information'.
33. See Hastings District Council Archive, HBC 43/101
34. *Hawke's Bay Today*, 7 April 2007.
35. Taylor, Vol. 1, p. 462.
36. Matthew Wright, *Torpedo!*, Random House, Auckland 2007, pp. 83-90.
37. Wright, *Blue Water Kiwis*: 134–35.
38. http://en.wikipedia.org/wiki/Unterseeboot_862, accessed 3 November 2007.
39. Campbell, *The Story of Napier*, p. 184.
40. David Stevens, *U-Boat Far from Home*, Allen & Unwin, St Leonards, 1997, p. 182.
41. *The Daily Telegraph*, 16 January 1945.
42. Matthew Wright, 'New Details Uncovered— U Boat Attack in Napier', *Daily Telegraph*, 26 June 1997.
43. Stevens, p. 183.
44. Wright, *Town and Country*, pp. 583-584.
45. Matthew Wright, *Italian Odyssey*, Reed, Auckland 2003, p. 168.
46. K. B. Cumberland and J. W. Fox, *New Zealand: a regional view*, Whitcombe and Tombs, Wellington 1958, p. 126.
47. Wright, *Fantastic Pasts*, pp. 209–210.
48. W. B. Sutch, *The Quest for Security in New Zealand 1940 to 1966*, Oxford University Press, London 1966, p. 409.
49. Cumberland & Fox, p. 120.
50. Campbell, *Story of Napier*, p. 182.
51. R. G. Cant and R. J. Johnston, 'Regional Development Patterns' in R. J. Johnston (ed) *Urbanisation in New Zealand*, Reed Education, Wellington 1973, p. 22.
52. Cumberland and Fox, p. 123.
53. E.g. Conly, *Wattie's*, pp.28–29.
54. Campbell, *Story of Napier*, p.185.
55. Ibid, p. 186.
56. e.g. the Cuba Street batoning, Dick Scott, *151 Days*, Reed, facsimile edition, Auckland 2001, pp. 116-117.
57. Matthew Wright, *Working Together*, Pan Pac, Napier 1997, pp. 4-30
58. Campbell, *Story of Napier*, p. 188.
59. Wright, *The Reed Illustrated History of New Zealand*, p. 400.
60. Harding, p. 69.
61. Hastings District Council Archive, HCC 369/247 Annual Reports All Officers 1957, 'Parks Department, Annual Report for year ended 31st March 1957.'
62. Hastings District Council Archive,

HDC 56/43 City Celebrations — Misc. Correspondence. Group Captain C. A. Turner to Harding, 29/08/1956
63 Campbell, *Story of Napier*, p. 181.
64 Ibid, p. 168.
65 Claire Regnault, *The Fifty Fities: Napier becomes a city*, Hawke's Bay Cultural Trust, Napier, 2000 facing p. 30.
66 *The Daily Telegraph*, 20 August 1966.
67 Campbell, *The Story of Napier*, p. 173–75.
68 Mills, *What's in a Name*, p. 255.
69 Campbell, *The Story of Napier*, p. 192.
70 Reserve Bank Inflation Calculator, comparing Q1 1964 with Q1 2008.
71 HDC Archive, Ray Dunlop "Finishing Flaxmere - A Community Psychology Perspective', 175.301 Assignment One.
72 Wright, *Town and Country*, p. 648.
73 Ibid, p. 649.
74 Campbell, *The Story of Napier*, p. 208.
75 Wright, *Town and Country*, p. 616–17.
76 Wright, *Cars Around New Zealand*, p. 80.
77 HCC 52.13 Traffic Ring Road 1977-1986, Hastings Chamber of Commerce to Town Clerk, 12/03/1979.
78 J. Wright, pers. comm.
79 Natusch and Son, 'A House in Hawke's Bay' in Design Review, Vol. 4, No. 2, September-May 1951-52, at http://www.nzetc.org/tm/scholarly/tei-Arc04_02DesR-t1-body-d11.html#n18, accessed 19 October 2007.
80 Regnault, facing p. 39.
81 *The Daily Telegraph*, 2 September 1958.
82 King, *The Penguin History of New Zealand*, p. 431.
83 Reserve Bank Inflation Calculator, comparing Q3 1966 with Q1 2008.
84 *The Daily Telegraph*, 18 August 1966.
85 A. M. Andersen (ed), *Hawke's Bay Provincial Centennial 1858-1958*, Hawke's Bay Provincial Centennial Council, Napier, 1958, p. 83.
86 Author observation. See also James Marshall and Dominique Marshall, *Discipline and Punishment in New Zealand Education*, Dunmore Press, Palmerston North 1997, p. 106.
87 Notably Napier, Hastings and Havelock North.
88 Chris Trotter, *No Left Turn*, Random House, Auckland 2007, pp. 266-267.
89 *Hawke's Bay Herald-Tribune*, 5 October 1978.
90 A phrase also used by, e.g. Jethro Tull, 'Living in the past', *Original Masters*, Chrysalis, 1985.
91 Wright, *The Reed Illustrated History of New Zealand*, p. 419–421.
92 Including the author.
93 *Hawke's Bay Herald-Tribune*, 5 October 1978.
94 *The Daily Telegraph*, 7 September 1921.
95 Cumberland & Fox: 128.
96 Wright, *The Reed Illustrated History of New Zealand*, p. 335–36.
97 M. F. Poulsen and R. J. Johnston, 'Patterns of Māori Migration', in R. J. Johnston (ed), *Urbanisation in New Zealand*, Reed Education, Wellington 1973, p. 154.
98 Thorns & Sedgwick, pp. 40–41
99 Poulsen & Johnston, pp. 162–63.
100 Calculated from Table XLI in W. B. Sutch, *Colony or Nation*, Sydney University Press 1966, second edition 1968, p. 159.
101 See, e.g., Sutch, *Colony or Nation?*, p. 157.
102 King, *The Penguin History of New Zealand*, p. 473.
103 Tony Simpson, *The Road to Erewhon*, Beaux Arts, Auckland 1976, pp. 141-42.
104 Wright, *The Reed Illustrated History of New Zealand*, p. 429.
105 I was at primary school with his brother: my family lived in the same area.
106 Wright, *Fantastic Pasts*, p. 217.
107 Wright, *The Reed Illustrated History of New Zealand*, pp. 428–29.

Chapter Seven: Metropolitan Province

1. Brian Easton, *In Stormy Seas*, University of Otago Press, Dunedin, 1997, pp. 73-74.
2. Ibid, p. 102.
3. Bruce Brown, 'Foreign Policy is Trade: Trade is Foreign Policy' in Ann Trotter (ed) *Fifty Years of New Zealand Foreign Policy Making*, University of Otago Press, Dunedin 1993, pp. 65, note 24.
4. Easton, *The Nationbuilders*, pp. 184–86.
5. Barry Gustafson, *His Way, A Biography of Robert Muldoon*, Auckland University Press 2000, paperback edition 2001, p. 470; also Easton, *The Nationbuilders*, p. 249.
6. Ruth Richardson, *Making a Difference*, Shoal Bay Press, Christchurch 1995, pp. 24-27.
7. See, e.g. The Treasury, *Economic Management*, The Treasury, 14 July 1984.
8. Brian Easton, 'Strange as it seems', *The New Zealand Listener*, 24 January 2004.
9. 'Kiwis turn their backs on failed reforms—academic', *Evening Post*, 05/12/1999; Bruce Jesson, *Only Their Purpose Is Mad*, Dunmore Press, Palmerston North, 1999, pp. 77-78; also Brian Easton, 'The London Economist and the New Zealand Economy", www.eastonbh.ac.nz, accessed 8 August 2007; and Easton, *In Stormy Seas*, pp. 257-258.
10. Len Bayliss, *Prosperity Mislaid*, GP Publications, Wellington, 1994, p. 29
11. Ibid, pp. 25, 28–29.
12. Jesson p. 213-14; Trotter, *No Left Turn*, pp. 327-328.
13. Thorns & Sedgwick, pp. 131–32.
14. Ibid, p. 74.
15. Noted in Brian Easton, 'The London Economist and the New Zealand Economy", www.eastonbh.ac.nz, accessed 8 August 2007.
16. See also Trotter, p. 338.
17. *Evening Post*, 3 December 1999.
18. See, e.g., *Otago Daily Times* 'Economy a Case of Minor Adjustment', 4 January 2000; *Dominion* 'Economic Restructuring Doomed to Fail — Cullen', 4 March 2000.
19. Peter Lyons 'Purity could be costly', *Southland Times*, 1 December 2003.
20. For description see Olly Newland, *Lost Prosperity*, HarperCollins, Auckland 1994, pp. 85-87.
21. See also Jesson, pp. 34–36.
22. Cited in Geoff Conly, *History of the County of Hawke's Bay*, Vol 5, Hawke's Bay County Council, Napier 1989, pp. 68-69.
23. Hastings District Council Archive, *Hastings Our Future 1997–2007*, p. 10.
24. Ibid, p.11.
25. Ibid, p. 8.
26. David Irving and Kerr Inkson, *It Must be Wattie's!: from Kiwi icon to global player*, David Bateman, Auckland 1998, p. 58.
27. Ibid, p. 96.
28. Ibid, pp. 111–12.
29. Ibid, pp. 136–41.
30. See, e.g., *Havelock North News*, 27 October 1962; 23 and 26 January 1963.
31. Cited in Conly, *History of the County of Hawke's Bay*, Vol. V, p. 134.
32. See, e.g., Hastings District Council Archive, HCC 489, 'Statement on suggested regional reorganisation for Hastings and adjacent areas'.
33. Conly, *History of the County of Hawke's Bay*, Vol. V, p. 138.
34. Wright, *Town and Country*, p. 673.
35. Hastings District Council Archive, HDC BI00 Local Government Reorganisation, 'Hawke's Bay Local Government Study Newsletter 5', 27/06/1997.
36. See, e.g., *Hawke's Bay Today*, 12 October 1999, 16 October 1999, 1 November 1999.
37. Ibid, 15 May 1999.
38. Ibid, 1 November 1999.
39. King, *The Penguin History of New Zealand*, p. 476.
40. Orange, p. 250.

41 Waitangi Tribunal, *Te Whanganui-ā-Orotū Report*, pp. 175–84.
42 Ibid, p. 4.
43 *Hawke's Bay Today*, 27 July 1999.
44 Waitangi Tribunal, *Te Whanganui-ā-Orotū Report*, p. 212.
45 https://www.govt.nz/treaty-settlement-documents/ahuriri-hapū/ahuriri-hapū-deed-of-settlement-summary/ accessed 6 February 2017.
46 Robert McGregor, *The Art Deco City: Napier, New Zealand*, Second Edition, Art Deco Trust, Napier 1999, pp. 4–5.
47 Ibid, p. 5.
48 Peter Shaw and Peter Hallett, *Art Deco Napier*, Second Edition, Cosmos, Napier 1990, p. 16.
49 McGregor, *The Art Deco City*, p. 46.
50 https://www.thehumanitystar.com/. accessed 15 December 2018.

Bibliography

Primary sources
Alexander Turnbull Library

Micro-MS-0425, Maunder, George Henry, Letters written from Auckland and Hawke's Bay to his sister, Jane, and to his mother.
Micro-MS-0443, Rolleston, John Christopher, 'Orua Wharo', Diary extracts from Sydney Johnson.
MS-0442, Campbell, Walter Lorne (1845–74), Journal Vol. VI, (typescript).
MS-0584, Colenso, William (1811–99), Papers, Journal Vol. III (typescript), 22 November 1850.
MS-1231-34, Donald McLean, Diary.
MS-1286, Donald McLean, Journal (typescript), 18 April 1851.
MS-1298, McLean, Donald (Sir) (1820–77), transcripts of selected papers.
MS-1817, Rich, George, fl. (1852–58), Journal kept by George Rich, sheepfarmer of Ahuriri.
MS-2117, Tanner, Thomas (1830–1918), 'Notes of a tour in New Zealand 1858'.
MS Cha 1911, Letter from John Chambers to directors of the *Hawke's Bay Tribune*, 23 January 1911.
MS-Copy-Micro-0535-008, McLean, Donald (Sir) (1820–77) (MS-Papers-0032), Official papers, Superintendent, Hawke's Bay and Government Agent, East Coast.
MS-Copy-Micro-0535-034, McLean, Donald (Sir) (1820–77), Papers (partial microfilm of MS-Papers-0032).
MS-Papers-0032, McLean, Donald (Sir) (1820–77), Inward letters.
MS-Papers-0035-5, McDonnell, Thomas (1832–99), Papers.
MS-Papers-0069-050, Williams, Samuel, Observations on Donald McLean and autobiographical note.
MS-Papers-0434, Campbell, Alexander, fl. 1875–88.
MS-Papers-0456, Moonson, C.M., fl. 1869, 'Letters concerning the Te Kooti Campaign'.
MS-Papers-1296, Biggs, Reginald Newton (d. 1868).
MS Papers 1346, A.E.L. Bennett Collection.
MS-Papers-1348-01, Journal of F.J. Tiffen, 'A record of significant events'.
MS-Papers-1348-11, F.J. Tiffen collection.
MS-Papers-1504, Folder 5, P. Howden collection, enclosed memorabilia.
MS-Papers-1711, Russell, William (Sir) (1838–1913), Correspondence.
MS-Papers-2048, Stafford, Edward William (Sir) (1819–1901), Stafford Papers (MS-2045–2050), Volume 4, Haultain to Stafford, 11 October 1868.
MS Papers-2107, Anderson, Jean, Letter to Elsie Young, 3 February 1931.

MS-Papers-2293, Morris, Maria (1844–1907).
MS-Papers-2350, Bollinger, George W., Diary and letters, 1915–17.
MS-Papers-2392, Tronson, Aubrey, 'A Soldier's Book of Life'.
MS-Papers-2418-4, Ashcroft, William James Cronshaw, d. 1981, Papers.
MS Papers-2477-2, Higginson, Louisa (1885–1978): Diaries, transcribed by Mrs R.L. Wilson (typescript).
MS-Papers-2481, Bourke, Henry O'Donel (1889–1982), Diary and memoirs 1917–18, (typescript).
MS-Papers-2620, Harris, George, fl. (1866–99), 'Reminiscences of the fanatic Hau-Hau rebellion'.
MS-Papers-2883, White, G. Marshall (1863–1949), Notes on history of Hawke's Bay.
MS-Papers-3067, Northe letters.
MS-Papers-3394, Wilson, George Hamish Ormond (1907–88), Te Kooti's Flag, MS.
MS-Papers-3508, Steddy, John G, fl. 1868, Letter from John Steddy, postmaster at Gisborne giving news of the Poverty Bay Massacre, 10 November 1868.
MS-Papers-3595, Mortensen, H.P., 'Reminiscences of the early pioneers in Norsewood'.
MS-Papers-3808, Firth, Josiah Clifton (1826–97), Papers relating to Te Kooti and the New Zealand Wars, 1861–70, Folder 1.
MS-Papers-3838, MacNab, Margaret Duirs, fl. 1931, Account of experiences following the Napier earthquake, 1931.
MS-Papers-455, Adam Dawson, letter from Napier.
MS-Papers-5283, Haydon, Ernest St Claire (b. 1885), Napier earthquake, an eyewitness description.
MS-Papers-5814, Campbell, Dorothy Beatrice (1903–75), Letter 5 March 1931.
MS-Papers-7125, Morris, William (1815–82), Diary.
MSX 4760 'Dawes Bently, fl. 1920, Manuscript of Doug Stark, Bomber with Otago on the Western Front', Vol 1.
qMS-0414, Chambers, Joseph Bernard (1859–1931), Journal 1874–83.
qMS-0832, 'General Government Agency, Public Meeting 1869, Minutes of a Public Meeting, Oddfellows Hall, Napier, 1869'.

Appendices to the Journal of the House of Representatives

1858 E-1, Report of the Otaki Industrial School, 1855.
1861 C-1, Purchase of Native Lands, Reports of the District Commissioners on the.
1862 C-1, Commissioners' Reports Relative to Land Purchases.
1862 E-4, Report of Inspectors on Native Schools.
1862 E-9, Further papers relative to Governor Sir George Grey's Plan of Native Government, Reports of Officers.
1865 E-4, Further Papers Relative to the Spread of the Hau Hau Superstition Among the Māories.
1867 A-1, Despatches from the Governor of New Zealand to the Right Hon. Secretary of State for the Colonies.
1867 A-10c, Return of Certificates Issued by Native Land Court, from 1 November 1865 to 30 June 1867.
1867 A-15, Report by Mr G.S. Cooper on the Subject of Native Lands in the Province of Hawke's Bay.
1867 F-4, 'Railway Gauge Committee'.
1868 A-4, Papers Relative to the Agency of Mr McLean.
1868 A-15c, Report Relative to the Pursuit of the Escaped Chatham Island Prisoners.
1870 A-8, Papers Relative to Military Operations Against the Rebel Natives.
1870 A-8a, Papers Relative to Military Operations

Against the Rebel Natives.
1871 A-2, Native Lands Court, Memorandum on the Operation of the, by Sir William Martin.
1871 D-6a, Construction of Railways.
1871 D-7, The Purchase of the Seventy Mile Bush Block.
1871 G-7, Trusts Commissioner for the District of Hawke's Bay under 'Native Lands Frauds Prevention Act, 1870'.
1872 I-2, Petition of Renata Kawepo and 553 others.
1873 G-7, Hawke's Bay Native Lands Alienation Commission Act, 1872.
1873 J-6, Petition of 300 Māoris of Hawke's Bay, Wairoa, Turanga and Taupō.
1874 D-2, Emigration to New Zealand.
1874 E-3, Appendices to Public Works Statement 1874.
1874 G-1, Notes of Native Meetings.
1874 G-2, Reports from Officers in Native Districts.
1876 B-8, Estimated Revenue from Railways in Each Province for 1876–77.
1879 E-1, Appendix L, Annual Report of Working Railways by the Commissioner of Railways, North Island.

Archives New Zealand

ACFP 8211 NM 2/4, Despatches from the Governor-in-Chief to the Lieutenant-Governor, 24 January– 23 December 1850.
ACFP 8213 NM4/2, Despatches from the Lieutenant-Governor to the Governor-in-Chief, 1 June 1850– 3 March 1853.
ACFP 8216 NM 7/1, Minutes of the Executive Council, 24 February 1848–16 August 1853.
ACFP 8217 8/51/1247, Colonial Secretary's Inwards Correspondence , 17 March–30 March 1846.
ACFP 8219 NM 10/10, Colonial Secretary's General Outwards Correspondence, 5 September 1849–28 March 1851.
ACFP 8219 NM10/11, Colonial Secretary's General Outwards Correspondence, 28 March 1851–24 June 1852.
ACFK 8163 AGG-HB1/1, No. 23, 13 October 1866, James Fraser, Detailed Report of Action at the Petone Spit and Captain Carr's Station.
ACFK 8163 AGG-HB1/1, No. 24, 14 October 1866— Mclean, Napier, Congratulating Whitmore on the 'Brilliant' Action at Ōmaranui.
ACFK 8164 AGG-HB2/1, Letters from Māori, 28 May 1865–1 December 1872.
ACHK 16563 G7/6, Inwards Despatches from Lieutenant-Governor Eyre, New Munster, 2 June 1849– 11 July 1849.
ACHK 16563 G7/12, Inwards despatches from Lieutenant-Governor Eyre, New Munster, 27 August–24 October 1850.

Hastings District Council Archive

BI00, Local Government Reorganisation, 'Hawke's Bay Local Government Study Newsletter 5', 27 June 1997.
Dunlop, Ray, 'Finishing Flaxmere: A Community Psychology Perspective', 175.301 Assignment One.
Hastings Borough Council, 41/11, Emergency Precautions, 1942.
———, 41/42, Proposed Military Camp near Hastings, 1941.
———, 43/101, Honey for Hastings England, 1941–45.
———, 46/64, Bridge Pah Aerodrome, 1946.
———, 67, Centennial of New Zealand.
Hawke's Bay County Council, 369/247, Annual Reports All Officers, 1957.
———, 448, Francis Hicks, 1839–1911.
———, 489, 'Statement on Suggested Regional Reorganisation for Hastings and Adjacent Areas'.

———, 52.13, Traffic Ring Road, 1977–86.
Hastings District Council, 525, Minute Book Hastings Retailers Association, 30 June 1933.
———, 56/43 City Celebrations, Miscellaneous Correspondence.
Havelock North, 102, Minister of Internal Affairs Circular Letter, 4 May 1917.
———, 102, Letters 1918.

Hastings Public Library

Gambrill, R.F., ed., 'The Russell Family Saga', Manuscript.
MSS 1957, Rainbow, A.I., 'A Walk though Hastings in the Early Nineties'.

Hawke's Bay Museum

Balfour, D.P., *His Life, By Himself*, typescript.
Earthquake Personal Reminiscences, Box 1.
Joll, J.H., 'Impromptu Talk'.
Kinross, J.G., Letterbook 1858–76.
McLean, Donald, Inwards Letterbook.
Ormond Papers.
Resident Magistrate's Letterbook.
Russell, H.R., Letterbook.
Social Progress at the Antipodes.
Weston, C.C., Diary extracts.
Whitmore Papers.

Havelock North Public Library

A/335/1988, Havelock North Primary School 125th Jubilee, 1863–1988.
A/44/1983, von Dadelszen, J.H., 'The Havelock Work'.
The Forerunner
The Lantern
The Shakespearean Pageant at Havelock North.
von Dadelszen, S.M.M., Memoir.

Newspapers

Evening Post
Hastings Standard
Havelock North News
Hawke's Bay Herald
Hawke's Bay Herald-Tribune
Hawke's Bay Today
Otago Daily Times
Southland Times
Te Wananga
The Daily Telegraph
The New Zealand Spectator and Cook's Strait Guardian
The Press
Wellington Independent

Waitangi Tribunal

Wai 201 Document Bank

Private papers
Author collection

Cunningham, Ashley, 'The Indigenous Forests of East Coast, Poverty Bay, Hawke's Bay'.
Elder, N.L., 'Māori Cultivation and the Retreat of Forest', talk given 9 October 1956.

Secondary Sources

Andersen, A.L., *Norsewood: The Centennial Story*. A.L. Andersen, Dannevirke, 1972.
Andersen, A. M., ed., *Hawke's Bay Provincial Centennial 1858–1958*. Hawke's Bay Provincial Centennial Council, Napier, 1958.
Anderson, Atholl, 'Food from Forest And Coast'. In John Wilson, John, ed., *From The Beginning: The Archaeology of the Māori*. Penguin, Auckland 1986.
———, *Prodigious Birds: Moas and Moa Hunting in Prehistoric New Zealand*. Cambridge

University Press, Melbourne, 1989.
———, *The Welcome of Strangers: An Ethnohistory of Southern Māori AD 1650–1850*. University of Otago Press/Dunedin City Council, Dunedin, 1998.
Arnold, Rollo, *New Zealand's Burning*. Victoria University Press, Wellington. 1994: 38; reproduced in http://www.nzetc.org/tm/scholarly/tei-ArnNewZ-_N1019F.html
———, *The Farthest Promised Land*. Victoria University Press and Price Milburn, Wellington 1981.
Bagnall, A.G. Bagnall & G.C. Petersen, *William Colenso*. A.H. & A.W. Reed, Wellington, 1948.
Ballara, Angela, *Taua*. Penguin, Auckland, 2003.
Ballara, H.A., 'The Origins of Ngāti Kahungunu'. PhD thesis, Victoria University of Wellington, Wellington, 1991.
——— & G. Scott, 'Claimants Report to the Waitangi Tribunal: Crown Purchases of Māori Land in early Provincial Hawke's Bay'. Waitangi Tribunal, Wellington, 1994.
Battersby, John, *The One Day War*. Reed, Auckland, 2000.
Bayliss, Len, *Prosperity Mislaid*. GP Publications, Wellington, 1994.
Belich, James, *Making Peoples*. Allen Lane, Auckland, 1996.
———, *Paradise Reforged*, Allen Lane, Auckland, 2001.
Bell, R.M., Lieutenant-Colonel, MBE, ED, *The History of the Hawke's Bay Agricultural and Pastoral Society 1863–1983*. Hawke's Bay Agricultural and Pastoral Society, Waipukurau, 1983.
Binney, Judith, *Redemption Songs: A Life of Te Kooti Arikirangi Te Turuki*. Bridget Williams Books/Auckland University Press, Auckland, 1995.
Boyd, Mary, *City of the Plains*. Hastings City Council, Hastings. 1984.
———, 'Ormond, John Davies 1831?–1917', In *Dictionary of New Zealand Biography*, http://www.dnzb.govt.nz (updated 22 June 2007).
Brew, Margit, *Scandinavian Footprints: A Story of Scandinavians Settling in New Zealand*. Egan Reid, Auckland, 2007.
Briggs, Asa, *Victorian Cities*. Pelican, London, 1968.
Brooking, Tom, ' "Bursting up" the Greatest Estate of All'. In Binney, Judith, ed., *The Shaping of History*. Bridget Williams Books, Wellington, 2001.
Brown, Bruce, 'Foreign Policy is Trade: Trade is Foreign Policy'. In Trotter, Ann, ed., *Fifty Years of New Zealand Foreign Policy Making*. University of Otago Press, Dunedin, 1993.
Buchanan, J.D.H. & D.R. Simmons, eds, *The Māori History and Place Names of Hawke's Bay*. A.H. & A.W. Reed, Wellington, 1973.
Burdon, R.M., *The New Dominion*. A.H. & A.W. Reed, Wellington, 1965.
Burns, Barnet, *A Brief Narrative of a New Zealand Chief*. R. & D. Read, Belfast, 1844; Hocken Library reprint, Dunedin 1970.
Byrnes, Giselle, *Boundary Markers*. Bridget Williams Books, Wellington, 2001.
———, *The Waitangi Tribunal and New Zealand History*. Oxford University Press, Oxford, 2004.
Callaghan, F.R., 'The Hawke's Bay Earthquake: General Description'. *New Zealand Journal of Science and Technology*, Vol. XV, No.1, July 1933.
Campbell, M.D.N., 'Hawke's Bay Politics 1890–1914'. MA thesis, Victoria University of Wellington, Wellington, 1967.
———, *Story of Napier*. Napier City Council, Napier, 1975.
——— 'The Evolution of Hawke's Bay Landed Society'. PhD thesis, Victoria University of Wellington, Wellington, 1973.
Cant, R.G. & R.J. Johnston, 'Regional Development Patterns'. In Johnston, R.J., ed.,

Urbanisation in New Zealand. Reed Education, Wellington, 1973.

Chapple, Simon, *The Economic Effects of the 1931 Hawke's Bay Earthquake*. New Zealand Institute of Economic Research (Inc), Working Paper 97/7, Wellington, August 1997.

Cliff, E.S. & Co, *Hastings, the Hub of Hawke's Bay, New Zealand*. E. S. Cliff & Co., Hastings, circa 1918.

Cole, Sharron Mary, 'The Repudiation Movement: A Study of the Māori Land Protest Movement in Hawke's Bay in the 1870s'. MA thesis, Massey University, Palmerston North, 1977.

Coleman, B. I., ed., *The Idea of the City in Nineteenth-Century Britain*. Routledge & Kegan Paul, London, 1973.

Colenso, William, 'A Description of a Species of Orobanche (Supposed to be Parasitical on a Plan of Hydrocotyle'. *Transactions of the New Zealand Institute*, Vol. 21, 1888, at http://rsnz.natlib.govt.nz/volume/rsnz_21.html.

———, 'Historical Incidents and Traditions of the Olden Times, pertaining to the Māoris of the North Island, (East Coast), New Zealand; highly illustrative of their national Character, and containing many peculiar, curious, and little-known Customs and Circumstances, and Matters firmly believed by them. Now, for the first time, faithfully translated from old Māori Writings and Recitals; with explanatory Notes. Part II'. *Transactions of the New Zealand Institute*, Vol. 14, 1881, http://rsnz.natlib.govt.nz/volume/rsnz_14/rsnz_14_00_000520.html (accessed 19 October 2007).

———, 'On the Moa'. *Transactions of the New Zealand Institute*, 12, 1879, in http://rsnz.natlib.govt.nz/volume/rsnz_12/rsnz_12_00_000820.html.

———, 'Status quo: A Retrospect.—A Few More Words by way of Explanation and Correction concerning the First Finding of the Bones of the Moa in New Zealand; also Strictures on the Quarterly Reviewer's Severe and Unjust Remarks on the Late Dr. G.A. Mantell, F.R.S., &c., in connection with the same'. *Transactions of the New Zealand Institute*, Vol. 24, 1891, at http://rsnz.natlib.govt.nz/volume/rsnz_24/rsnz_24_00_003910.html.

———, *The Authentic and Genuine History of the Signing of the Treaty of Waitangi, Thursday, February 6th*. Government Print, Wellington, 1890.

Conly, Geoff, *History of the County of Hawke's Bay, Vol 5*. Hawke's Bay County Council, Napier, 1989.

———, *The Shock of 31*. A.H. & A.W. Reed, Wellington, 1980.

———, *Wattie's: The First Fifty Years*. J. Wattie Canneries, Hastings, 1984.

Cowan, James, *The New Zealand Wars, Volume 2: The Hauhau Wars*. Government Print, Wellington, 1923.

Cowie, Dean, 'Rangahaua Whanui District 11b Hawke's Bay, Working Paper First Release'. Waitangi Tribunal, Wellington, September 1996.

Crosby, R.O., *The Musket Wars*. Reed, Auckland, 2000.

Cumberland, K.B. & J.W. Fox, *New Zealand: A Regional View*. Whitcombe & Tombs, Wellington, 1958.

Cyclopedia of New Zealand. Weeks Publishing Co., Christchurch, 1906–08.

Daley, Caroline, *Girls and Women, Men and Boys: Gender in Taradale 1886–1930*. Auckland University Press, Auckland. 1999.

———, 'Taradale Meets the Ideal Society and its Enemies'. In Binney, Judith, ed., *The Shaping of History*. Bridget Williams Books, Wellington, 2001

Dalziel, Raewyn, 'The Politics of Settlement'. In Oliver, W.H. & B.R. Williams, eds, *The Oxford History of New Zealand*. Clarendon Press,

Oxford, 1984.

Davidson, Janet, *The Prehistory of New Zealand*. Longman Paul, Auckland, 1984.

Davison, Graeme, *The Rise and Fall of Marvellous Melbourne*. Melbourne University Press, Melbourne, 1980.

Donnelly, G.P., *Looking Backward, New Zealand Fifty Years Ago: Life in Hawke's Bay Then and Now*. The Christchurch Press Co. Ltd, Christchurch, 1913.

Dowrick, D.J., D.A. Rhoades, J. Babor & R.D. Beetham, 'Damage Ratios and Microzoning Effects in Napier in the Magnitude 7.8 Hawke's Bay, New Zealand Earthquake of 1931'. *Bulletin of the New Zealand National Society for Earthquake Engineering*, 28, 2, June 1995.

Dowrick, David, 'Damage and Intensities in the Magnitude 7.8 1931 Hawke's Bay, New Zealand Earthquake'. *Bulletin of the New Zealand National Society for Earthquake Engineering*, 31, 3, September 1998.

Easton, Brian, *In Stormy Seas*. University of Otago Press, Dunedin, 1997.

———, 'Strange as it Seems'. *The New Zealand Listener*, APN Holdings, Auckland, 24 January 2004.

———, 'The London *Economist* and the New Zealand Economy'. www.eastonbh.ac.nz.

———, *The Nationbuilders*. Auckland University Press, Auckland, 2001.

Elder, N.L., *Vegetation of the Ruahine Range: An Introduction*. Royal Society of New Zealand, Wellington, 1965.

Eldred-Grigg, Stevan, *A Southern Gentry: New Zealanders Who Inherited the Earth*. A.H. & A.W. Reed, Wellington, 1980: 75–79, 89–105.

Evans, Geoff, *The Discovery of Aotearoa*. Reed, Auckland, 1998.

Fagan, Brian, *The Little Ice Age*. Basic Books, New York, 2000.

Fairbrother, M.C., ed,, *Documents Relating to New Zealand's Participation in the Second World War, 1939–45, Volume III*. War History Branch, Wellington, 1963.

Fargher, Ray, *The Best Man Who Ever Served the Crown? A life of Donald McLean*. Victoria University Press, Wellington. 2007.

Farwell, Byron, *Queen Victoria's Little Wars*. Allen Lane, London, 1973.

Ferguson, Niall, *Empire*. Penguin, London, 2004.

Gardner, W.J., 'A Colonial Economy'. In Oliver, W.H. & B.R. Williams, eds, *The Oxford History of New Zealand*. Clarendon Press, Oxford, 1981.

Goldsmith, P.J., 'Aspects of the Life of William Colenso'. MA thesis, University of Auckland, Auckland, 1994.

Grant, Patrick J., 'Climate, Geomorphology and Vegetation'. In Sutton, Douglas, ed., *The Origins of the First New Zealanders*. Auckland University Press, Auckland, 1994.

Grant, Patrick, *Hawke's Bay Forests of Yesterday*, CHB Print, Waipukurau, 1996.

Grant, S.W., *Havelock North, 1860–1952*. Hawke's Bay Newspapers, Hastings, 1978.

———, *In Other Days: A History of the Chambers Family of Te Mata, Havelock North*. CHB Printers, Waipukurau, 1980.

Grant, Sydney, *Waimarama*. Dunmore Press, Palmerston North, 1977.

Gray, Margaret A., *Abbott's-Ford: A History of Waipawa*. CHB Print, Waipukurau, 1989.

Greasley, David & Les Oxley, 'Refrigeration and Distribution: New Zealand Land Prices and Real Wages 1873–1939'. *Australian Economic History Review*, 45, 1.

Gustafson, Barry, *His Way: A Biography of Robert Muldoon*. Auckland University Press, Auckland, paperback edition 2001.

Harding, Noel C., *Hastings (NZ) from Town Board to City 1884–1962*. Hastings City Council, Hastings.

Hawke's Bay Almanac, 1875.

Hawke's Bay: Before And After. The Daily Telegraph, Napier, 1931 (reprint 1981).

Hawthorne, James, *A Dark Chapter from New Zealand History.* James Wood, Napier, 1869; Capper Press reprint, Christchurch, 1974.

Hervé, Roger, *Chance Discovery of Australia and New Zealand by Portugese and Spanish Navigators between 1521 and 1528.* Trans John Dunmore, Dunmore Press, Palmerston North, 1983.

Hill, Henry, 'On the Artesian Well System of Hawke's Bay'. *Transactions and Proceedings of the Royal Society of New Zealand*, 20, 1887.

Hippolite, Joy, 'Wairoa ki Wairarapa'. Waitangi Tribunal Overview Report, November 1991.

Hogan, Helen M., *Renata's Journey.* University of Canterbury Press, Christchurch, 1994.

Hopkins, A.G., 'Gentlemanly Capitalism in New Zealand'. *Australian Economic History Review*, 43, 3, November 2003.

Horton, Thomas Ltd 'Wonderful progress of the nursery industry'. In Cliff, E.S. & Co, *Hastings, the Hub of Hawke's Bay New Zealand*, E.S. Cliff & Co., circa 1918.

Howard, Graham & Matthew Wright, 'The Reserve Bank Inflation Calculator'. *Reserve Bank of New Zealand Bulletin*, 66, 4, December 2003.

———, 'A Note on the Reserve Bank Inflation Calculator'. *Reserve Bank of New Zealand Bulletin*, 47, 4, December 2004.

Howe, Kerry, *The Quest for Origins.* Penguin, Auckland, 2003.

Hunter, Ian, *Age of Enterprise.* University of Auckland Press, Auckland, 2007.

Irving, David & Kerr Inkson, *It Must be Wattie's!: From Kiwi Icon to Global Player.* David Bateman, Auckland, 1998.

Jesson, Bruce, *Only Their Purpose Is Mad.* Dunmore Press, Palmerston North, 1999.

Keegan, John, *A History of Warfare.* Pimlico, London, 1993.

King, Michael, *Being pākehā Now.* Penguin, Auckland, 1999.

———, *The Penguin History of New Zealand.* Penguin, Auckland, 2003.

Kinloch, Terry, *Echoes of Gallipoli.* Exisle, Auckland, 2005.

Lambert, Thomas, *The Story of Old Wairoa and the East Coast of New Zealand.* Reed, Auckland, 1998 reprint.

Lee, Jack, *The Old Land Claims in New Zealand.* Northland Historical Publications Society, Kerikeri, 1993.

Lewis, David & Werner Forman, *The Māori: Heirs of Tane.* Orbis, London, 1982.

Lloyd-Prichard, Muriel F., *An Economic History of New Zealand to 1939.* Collins, Auckland, 1970.

Lyons, Peter, 'Purity could be costly', *Southland Times*, 1 December 2003.

MacNab, Robert, *Historical Records of New Zealand, Vol. I.* Government Printer, Wellington, 1908.

———, *Historical Records of New Zealand, Vol. II.* Government Printer, Wellington, 1914.

Maning, F.E., *Old New Zealand.* Golden Press reprint, Auckland, 1973.

Mannering, Rose, *100 Harvests: A History of Fruitgrowing in Hawke's Bay.* PSL Press, Wellington, 1999.

Marsh, Ngaio, *Black Beech and Honey Dew.* Collins, London, 1966.

Marshall, James & Dominique Marshall, *Discipline and Punishment in New Zealand Education.* Dunmore Press, Palmerston North, 1997.

Masters, Lester, *Tails of the Mails.* Private publication, Napier, 1959.

McAloon, Jim, 'Gentlemanly Capitalism and Settler Capitalists: Imperialism, Dependent Development and Colonial Wealth in the South Island of New Zealand. *Australian Economic History Review*, 42, 2, July 2002.

———, 'Gentlemen, Capitalists and Settlers: A Brief Response'. *Australian Economic History Review*, 43, 3, November 2003.

McCulloch, Beverley & Michael Trotter, *Digging Up the Past: New Zealand's Archaeological History*. Revised Edition, Penguin, Middlesex, 1997.

McEwen, J.M., *Rangitāne: A Tribal History*. Reed Methuen, Auckland, 1986.

McFadgen, Bruce, *Hostile Shores: Catastrophic Events in Prehistoric New Zealand and Their Impact on Māori Coastal Communities*, University of Auckland Press, Auckland, 2007.

McGlone, H.S, A.F. Mark & D. Bell, 'Late Pleistocene and Holocene Vegetation History, Central Otago, South Island, New Zealand'. *Journal of the Royal Society of New Zealand*, 25, 1, March 1995.

McGregor, Miriam, *Pioneer Trails of Hawke's Bay*. A.H. & A.W. Reed, Wellington, 1975.

McGregor, Robert, *The Art Deco City: Napier, New Zealand*. Art Deco Trust, Napier, 1999.

McKinnon, Malcolm, ed., *The New Zealand Historical Atlas*. David Bateman, Auckland, 1997.

McKirdy, Alexandra, 'Māori–pākehā Land Transactions in Hawke's Bay 1848–1864'. MA thesis, University of Victoria, Wellington, March 1994.

McLintock, A.H., ed., *An Encyclopedia of New Zealand*. Government Print, Wellington, 1966.

Mills, Ian L., *What's In a Name: A History of the Streets of Napier*. Thinker Publications, Napier, 1999.

Moon, Paul, *The Path to the Treaty of Waitangi*. David Ling Publishing, Auckland, 2002.

Mooney, Kay, *History of the County of Hawke's Bay* (4 Vols). Hawke's Bay County Council, Napier, 1973–77.

Mulgan, John, *Report on Experience*. Oxford University Press, London, 1947.

Natusch & Son, 'A House in Hawke's Bay', *Design Review*, 4, 2, September–May 1951–52, at http://www.nzetc.org/tm/scholarly/tei-Arc04_02DesR-t1-body-d11.html#n18

Newland, Olly, *Lost Prosperity*. HarperCollins, Auckland, 1994.

Nicholas, J.L., *Narrative of a Voyage to New Zealand, Vol. 1*. James Black, London, 1817; Facsimile edition, Wilson and Horton, n.d.

Nolan, Iris, *Our Village, Our Story*. Dannevirke Publishing Co., Dannevirke, 1962.

Official Handbook of Hastings for Tourist, Sportsman and Settler. Hastings Borough Council, Hastings, 1929.

O'Malley, Vincent, *The Ahuriri Purchase*. Crown Forestry Rental Trust, April 1995.

Oliver, W.H., 'The Future Behind Us'. In Sharp, Andrew & P.G. McHugh, eds, *Histories, Power and Loss*. Bridget Williams Books, Wellington, 2001.

Oliver, W.H. & B.R Williams, eds, *The Oxford History of New Zealand*. Clarendon Press, Oxford, 1984.

Olssen, Eric, 'Towards a New Society'. In Oliver, W.H. & B.R Williams, eds, *The Oxford History of New Zealand*. Clarendon Press, Oxford, 1984.

Orange, Claudia, *The Treaty of Waitangi*. Bridget Williams Books, Wellington, 1987.

Parsonson, Ann, 'The Pursuit of Mana'. In Oliver, W.H. & B.R Williams, eds, *The Oxford History of New Zealand*. Clarendon Press, Oxford, 1984.

Petersen, G.C., 'Pioneering the North Island Bush'. In Watters R.F., ed., *Land and Society in New Zealand*. A.H. & A.W. Reed, Wellington, 1965.

Playle, F.O., ed., *101 Years of Ormondville*. Ormondville Centennial Committee, Ormondville, 1978.

Pool, Ian, Arunachalam Dharmalingam & Janet Sceats, *The New Zealand Family from 1840: A Demographic History*. Auckland University

Press, Auckland, 2007.

Poulsen, M.F. & R.J. Johnston, 'Patterns of Māori Migration'. In Johnston, R.J., ed., *Urbanisation in New Zealand*. Reed Education, Wellington, 1973.

Prentice, W.T., 'The Māori History of Hawke's Bay'. In Wilson, J.G., *History of Hawke's Bay*. A.H. & A.W. Reed, Wellington, 1940.

Prickett, Nigel, *Māori Origins from Asia to Aotearoa*. David Bateman, Auckland, n.d.

Rabb, Theodore K., *The Struggle for Stability in Modern Europe*. Oxford University Press, New York, 1975.

Reed, A.H., *The Story of Hawke's Bay*. A.H. & A.W. Reed, Wellington, 1958.

Reeves, William Pember, *The Long White Cloud: Ao Te a Roa*. George Allen & Unwin, London, 1898, at http://www.nzetc.org/tm/scholarly/tei-ReeLong-t1-front-d6.html

Regnault, Claire, *The Fifty Fities: Napier Becomes a City*. Hawke's Bay Cultural Trust, Napier, 2000.

Richardson, Ruth, *Making a Difference*. Shoal Bay Press, Christchurch, 1995.

Rolleston, Rosamond, *The Master*, A. H. & A. W. Reed, Wellington 1980.

Scholefield, Guy R., ed., *The Richmond-Atkinson Papers, Vol. 2*. Government Print, Wellington, 1960.

Schwimmer, Eric, 'The Māori Hapū: A Generative Model'. In *Journal of Polynesian Studies*, 99, 3, September 1990.

Scott, Edwin F., 'A Report on the Relief Organisation Arising Out of the Earthquake in Hawke's Bay on February 3rd, 1931'. Christchurch Public Utilities Committee, Christchurch, April 1931.

Scott, Dick, *151 Days*. Reed, Facsimile Edition, Auckland, 2001.

Shaffer, Raymond, 'Woodville, Genesis of a Bush Frontier Community 1874–1887'. MA thesis, Massey University, Palmerston North, 1973.

Sharp, Andrew, 'Recent Juridicial and Constitutional Histories of Māori'. In Sharp, Andrew & P.G. McHugh, eds, *Histories, Power and Loss*. Bridget Williams Books, Wellington, 2001.

Shaw, Peter and Peter Hallett, *Art Deco Napier*. Cosmos, Napier 1990.

Shaw, Peter, *Louis Hay Architect*. Hawke's Bay Cultural Trust, Napier, 1998.

Siers, Judy, *James Walter Chapman Taylor in the Hawke's Bay*. Hawke's Bay Cultural Trust, Napier, 1991.

Simpson, Tony, *The Road to Erewhon*. Beaux Arts, Auckland 1976.

Sinclair, Keith, *Kinds of Peace: Māori People after the Wars 1870–1885*, Auckland University Press, Auckland, 1991.

———, *Walter Nash*. Auckland University Press, Auckland, 1976.

Smith D.I.B., ed., 'Introduction'. In Hyde, Robyn, *Passport to Hell*. Auckland University Press, Auckland, 1986.

Smith, S. Percy, *Māori Wars of the Nineteenth Century*. Whitcombe & Tombs, Christchurch, 1910, at http://www.nzetc.org/tm/scholarly/tei-SmiMaor-t1-body-d45.html

Steiner, Rudolf, *The Mission of Spiritual Science*. Rudolf Steiner Publishing Co, London, 1916.

Stephens, P.R., 'The Age of the Great Sheep Runs'. In Watters, R.F., ed., *Land and Society in New Zealand*. A.H. & A.W. Reed, Wellington, 1967.

Sturton, Ian, ed., *Conway's All the World's Battleships: 1906 to the Present*. Conway Maritime Press, London, 1987.

Suggate, R.P., ed., *The Geology of New Zealand*. Government Printer, Wellington, 1978.

Sutch, W.B, *Colony or Nation?*. Sydney University Press, Sydney, 1968.

Sutch, William, *The Quest for Security in New Zealand 1840–1966*. Oxford University Press, Oxford, 1966

Tasker, John, *Myth and Mystery*. Tandem Press Auckland, 1997.

Tattersall, John, *Lieutenant Thomas McDonnell and the Naming of Ahuriri*. Hawke's Bay Art Gallery and Museum, Napier, 1970.

Taylor, Nancy M., *The Home Front, Vol. 1*. Government Print, Wellington, 1986.

Taylor, Rev. Richard, *Te Ika a Maui, or, New Zealand and its Inhabitants: illustrating the origin, manners, customs, mythology, religion, rites, songs, proverbs, fables, and language of the natives; together with the geology, natural history, productions, and climate of the country, its state as regards Christianity, sketches of the principal chiefs, and their present position*. Wertheim & Macintosh, London, 1855. http://www.nzetc.org/tm/scholarly/tei-TayTeik-t1-body-d1-d15.html

———, *The Past and Present of New Zealand with its Prospects for the Future*. William Macintosh, London, 1868. http://www.nzetc.org/tm/scholarly/tei-TayPast-t1-body-d15.html

The Treasury, *Economic Management*. The Treasury, Wellington, July 1984.

Thom, M., *Dannevirke Borough*. Dannevirke Borough Council, Dannevirke, 1952.

Thomson, David, *A World Without Welfare: New Zealand's Colonial Experiment*. Auckland University Press/Bridget Williams Books, Auckland, 1998.

Trotter, Chris, *No Left Turn*. Random House, Auckland, 2007.

Vaggioli, Dom Felice, *History of New Zealand and its Inhabitants*. Trans. John Crockett, Otago University Press, Dunedin, 2000.

Vandergoes, M., S. Fitzsimons & R. Newnham, 'Late Glacial to Holocene Vegetation Change in the Eastern Tākitimu Mountains, Western Southland, New Zealand'. *Journal of the Royal Society of New Zealand*: 27, 1.

Waitangi Tribunal, *Te Whanganui-ā-Orotū Report 1995*. Waitangi Tribunal, Wellington, 1995.

Whitmore, George S. Major-General (Sir), *The Last Māori War in New Zealand*. Sampson, Low, Marston & Co., London, 1902.

Williams, Frederic Wanklyn, *Through Ninety Years, 1826–1916: Life and work among the Māoris in New Zealand: Notes of the Lives of William and Wiliam Leonard Williams, First and Third Bishops of Waiapu*. Whitcombe and Tombs, Auckland, n.d.; Foreword, at http://www.nzetc.org/tm/scholarly/tei-WilThro-t1-front-d3.html.

Wilson, J.G., *History of Hawke's Bay*. A.H. & A.W. Reed, Wellington, 1939.

Woodhouse, Alice, *British Regiments in Napier 1858–1867*. Hawke's Bay Art Gallery and Museum, Napier, 1970.

———, *The Naming of Napier*. Hawke's Bay Art Gallery and Museum, Napier, 1970.

Worthy, Trevor H., 'Two Late-Glacial Avifaunas From Eastern North Island, New Zealand: Te Aute Swamp and Wheturau Quarry'. *Journal of the Royal Society of New Zealand*, 30, 1, March 2000.

Wright, Matthew, *Blue Water Kiwis*. Reed, Auckland, 2001.

———, *Cars Around New Zealand*. Whitcoulls, Auckland 2004.

———, *Fantastic Pasts: Imaginary Adventures in New Zealand History*. Penguin, Auckland, 2007.

———, *Hawke's Bay: The History of a Province*. Dunmore Press, Palmerston North, 1994.

———, 'Hawke's Bay was Home of Land Rings'. *The Daily Telegraph*, 18 June 1994.

———, *Havelock North: The History of a Village*. Hastings District Council, Hastings, 1996.

———, *Italian Odyssey*. Reed, Auckland, 2003.

———, *Napier: City of Style*. Random House, Auckland. 1996.

———, 'New Details Uncovered: U Boat Attack in Napier'. *The Daily Telegraph*, 26 June 1997.

———, *New Zealand's Military Heroism*. Reed, Auckland, 2007.

———, 'Now We Lie in Flanders Fields'. *New Zealand Listener*, APN Holdings, Auckland, 13–19 October 2007.

———, *Pacific War*. Reed, Auckland, 2003.

———, *Quake: Hawke's Bay 1931*. Reed, Auckland, 2001.

———, *Rails Across New Zealand*. Whitcoulls, Auckland, 2003.

———, 'The History of Farming in Kuripapango'. New Zealand Forest Service, Napier, 1984.

———, *The Reed Illustrated History of New Zealand*. Reed, Auckland, 2004.

———, ed, *Torpedo! Kiwis at Sea in World War II*. Random House, Auckland, 2007.

———, *Town and Country*. Hastings District Council, Hastings, 2001.

———, *Two Peoples, One Land*. Reed, Auckland, 2006.

———, 'Wild Colonial Ways Editorial Sore Point', *Hawke's Bay Today*, 5 October 2007.

———, *Wings Across New Zealand*. Whitcoulls, Auckland, 2002.

———, *Working Together*. Pan Pac, Napier, 1997.

Index

A

Abbotsford 56-58, 60, 62, *see also* Waipawa.
Abbott, Frederick S., 47, 56.
Ahimanawa Ranges, 60, 188
Ahuriri, 8-10, 13, 16, 18, 23, 28, 30, 31, 34-38, 46, 53, 55, 56, 60, 74, 88, 91, 94, 96, 97, 110, 115, 124, 127, 130, 135, 145, 148, 152, 155, 188, 198, 203
Alexander, Alexander, 34
American (influence), 50, 54, 57, 64, 108, 163, 166, 183, 187
Amiowhenua, 18, 23
anthroposophists, 134
anthroposophy 132, 134
apartheid, 190
Arapaoanaui 16, 60, 188
Archaeology, 9, 11, 13-15
Ashley Clinton, 188
Astrolabe (ship), 28
athenaeums 102, 108, 112
Auckland 35, 36, 43, 55, 62, 69, 77, 84, 86, 107, 114, 115, 123, 143, 148, 163, 181, 183, 211
Australia, 50, 165, 193, 196
Awatoto, 10, 18, 124, 138, 171
A'Deane, R. B., 117

B

baby-boomers, 201

back-country, 61, 65, 67, 68, 122, 135, 157, 169-173, 194, 201
Balfour, David Paton, 60, 63, 66, 68, 79, 80, 129
Ballance, John 117
Barraud, Charles Decimus, 19, 61
Bauhaus (design), 143
Beacons (Napier harbour), 168, 178, 179
Beatson Park, 142
Bennett, Agnes, 152
Bibby's Store, 103
Billiards (game), 108-109
Birmingham, 50, 58
Blandford, Henry Morton, 57
Bluff Hill (Napier), 144, 149, 151, 154
boiling-down works, 114
boosterism 99, 102, 105, 174.
Bournemouth, 156
Brathwaite, J. B., 60, 72, 86
Brodgen & Co., 94
Brown, Cartwright, 49

C

Callaghan, F. R., 142, 149
Cameron, Sir Duncan, 75
Cameron Road, 146, 148
Canning, J. D., 50
Canterbury, 34, 92, 93
Canterbury Association, 34
Cape Kidnappers, 7, 8, 27, 60, 188

Capitalism, 46, 53, 160
Carlyle Street, 51, 55, 66
Carlyon, George G., 49, 60, 64, 94, 115
Cassino Crescent, 177
Chapman-Taylor, James, 134, 144
Christchurch, 102, 181, 183
Christianity, 25, 32, 73
Clive, 41, 42, 52, 54-56, 60, 67, 75, 94, 106, 109, 110, 124, 125, 144, 149, 187, 188
Coleman, J. H., 86, 113
Colenso, William, 10, 12, 25, 27, 29, 31-34, 35, 37, 53, 56, 57, 63
Corunna Bay, 54, 114
counter-culture, 186, 187
Cretaceous era, 7
Crosse, T. E., 118
Cuff, Joshua, 85
'cultural cringe',123, 181, 185 192, 201, 204, 211, 212

D

Dairying, 99, 110, 124, 171, 188, 191
Dannevirke, 96, 99, 100, 102, 104, 106, 111, 123, 136, 137, 150, 158, 175, 188, 204, 205
Dartmoor,182
debt-for-land deals, 77, 82
deforestation, 9, 11, 12
Dickens Street, 55, 187
Dinosaur (era), 7-8
Dobson, Robert, 105
Domett, Alfred, 36, 37, 42, 47, 49, 53-55, 63
Donnelly, G. P., 116, 120.
Duart House, 118
D'Urville, Dumont, 28

E

Earthquakes, 9, 15, 136, 144, 149, 150, 152, 159, 164, 176
Edinburgh, 108
Eketahuna, 99

Elsthorpe, 60, 188
Eskdale, 60, 188
Esk River, 60, 173, 188
Esk Valley, 200
Etheridge, Jim, 161
Eyre, Edward 35-37, 47, 52

F

Faraday Street, 55, 150
Farndon, 94, 109
Featherston, Isaac, 53, 55, 97.
Felkin, Dr Robert, 134
Field, Lawson, 171
Fitzgerald, T. H., 47, 49, 56, 57, 63, 74,
Fitzgerald, Reverend J., 134
FitzRoy, Robert, 104
Flanders' Avenue, 177
Flaxmere, 118, 177, 188, 189, 197
Fleming, John, 66
Frasertown, 60, 188
Freemasonry, 134

G

Gisborne, 16, 46, 77, 79, 94, 127, 150, 160, 168, 170
Glasgow, 110, 112
Gondwanaland, 7
'Gravedigger', the 51, 75, 78; *see also* Whitmore, G. S.
Greenmeadows 109, 124
Grey, George, 35-37, 40, 68
Gummer, W. H., 115
Guthrie, Thomas, 47
Guthrie-Smith, Herbert, 12, 118, 127, 152, 157, 160
Gwavas Station, 111, 115, 118, 173, 201

H

Hallenstein's, 161

Hampden, 56, 57, 60, 61, 94, 100, 108, *see also* Tikokino.
Hapuka, 43, *see also* Te Hāpuku
Harding, John, 47, 60, 116
Harrison, H. S., 33
Haretaonga, 36, *see also* Heretaunga.
Hastings 5, 52, 60, 64, 94-96, 100-108, 111, 113, 115, 116, 120, 124, 129, 132, 133, 135-138, 141-145, 147, 148, 151, 153, 154, 157-161, 164-166, 171-174, 176-182, 185, 187-189, 195, 196, 205, 207, 211
Hatuma, 47, 48, 60, 118, 188
'Hauhau', 16, 79-80
Haumoana, 124, 182
Havelock, 50, 56-58, 60, 62, 66, 68, 104, 108, 109, 116, 124, 127, 129, 131-135, 137, 140, 143-145, 147, 151, 180, 185, 186, 188, 197
Havelock North, *see* Havelock.
Hawaii, 165
Hawke's Bay, 1, 5, 7-17, 19-23, 25-46, 48-56, 58-68, 70-83, 85-95, 97-102, 105, 107, 108, 110-133, 135-145, 150-155, 157-192, 194-198, 201-205, 211, 212
Heretaunga Plains, 10, 11, 13, 18, 24-26, 44, 49, 52, 60, 61, 71, 74, 78, 82-84, 86, 94, 103, 105, 113, 124, 127, 136-137, 142, 150, 157, 165, 166, 171
Hicksville, 101
Hitchings, Dr Thomas, 42, 56
Holland, Sidney, 171
Hyderabad Road, 54

I

Industrialisation, 21

J

Japan 116, 163-165, 167, 174.
Jervois, William, 66
Johnston, Sydney, 60, 115, 119
Joylands Cabaret, 168

K

Kahuranaki, 10, 18, 60, 188
Kaimanawa, 7
Karaitiana, see Takamoana, Karaitiana,
Karamu, 18, 52, 94, 100, 101, 124, 133, 140
Karanema's Reserve, 56
Kaweka Ranges, 7, 8, 60, 173, 188
Kawepo, Renata, 22, 25, 29, 32, 42, 81, 88
Keegan, John, 12, 13
Kennedy, Charles D., 33, 126, 130, 156, 177
Kereru Station, 60, 112, 118, 188
Kettle, Charles, 33
Kingitanga movement, 70, 72, 81
Kinross, J. G., 49, 51, 60, 64, 86, 92, 112, 114
Kirk, Norman, 191-192, 197
Koroneho, 32, *see also* Colenso, William.
Kumeroa, 118
Kuripapango, 60, 122, 157, 188

L

Latham, George, 126
Lavin, John 79-80
Liverpool, 50
Lockyer's Appliances, 160-161

M

Magdala, 54
Makaretu, 60, 188
Makotuku, 130
Manawatu River, 23, 35, 36, 60, 94, 97, 188
Manchester, 50
Maney, Richard, 72, 83, 84, 86
Mangateretere, 66, 124
Mangawhare Station, 63, 118, 129
Maniapoto, Rewi, 81
Mantell, Walter, 35
Maraekakaho, 38, 44, 49, 60, 111, 117, 188
Maraenui, 18, 177, 189, 197
Maraetotara River, 9, 10, 18, 137

Matamau. 96, 98, 100, 188
Mataruahou ('Napier Hill'), 10, 18, 24, 34, 38, 50, 53, 54, 114
Matipiro Station, 117
Maunsell, Robert, 32
Maunsell, Edward, 86
Mauriceville, 99
McDonnell, Thomas, 28, 81
McLean, Sir Donald, 21, 23, 25, 26, 34-41, 43, 44, 46, 47, 49, 50, 52, 53, 60, 63-65, 68-70, 73-79, 81, 82, 84-88, 92-93, 95, 108, 131, 134, 152, 155, 200, 211
Mellemskov, 99, *see also* Eketahuna.
Milton-on-Wychwood, 99
Modernism, 153, 207, 211.
Mohaka, 24, 37, 38, 60, 79, 80, 147, 167
Mohaka River, 173, 188, 201
'Morrie Thou', 180, *see also* Morris 1000.
Morris 1000, 180
Motor car, 116, 137, 149, 154, 165, 179, 180, 205, 207, 211
Muldoon, Sir Robert, 190, 192, 194, 196
'Muldoonism', 193
Mulgan, John, 157
Muskets, 13, 17-22, 25, 26, 31, 40, 41, 70, 71, 74

N

Napier, 5, 8, 23, 34, 42-43, 50-55, 57, 59-64, 68, 72, 74-84, 87, 89, 94-100, 102, 104-110, 112-115, 122, 124-127, 129, 130, 135-138, 143-153, 155, 156, 158-161, 164-168, 171, 173, 174, 176-178, 180-184, 186-190, 193, 195-197, 200, 204-205, 207, 211
Napier-Taihape road, 122
Napier-Taupō road, 107, 173
Naples, 167
Natusch, Guy 115, 174, 177
Nelson, William, 115, 126, 145, 148-150
Newton, Thomas Kennedy, 33
New Zealand Company, 34
Ngaruroro River, 8, 10, 11, 16, 18, 24, 32, 55, 60, 124, 155, 188
Ngata, Sir Apirana, 189
Ngatapa, 79
Ngatarawa, 86
Ngāti Kahungunu, 9, 10, 12, 14-16, 18, 23-26, 31, 32, 36, 40-43, 53, 70, 71, 73, 74, 76, 78, 81, 82, 86, 87, 89, 130, 198
Ngāti Kahungunu-ki-Wairarapa, 34
Ngāti Tūwharetoa, 18, 22, 23, 82
Niven, James J., 112
Northwood, James, 35
Norsewood, 60, 97, 99, 130, 158, 188
Nukutaurua 10, 16, 24, 25

O

Oamaru, 108
Ogilvy, Walter, 49
Oingo, Lake, 10, 16, 18, 124
Okawa, 18, 38, 41, 42
Omahu, 18, 104, 124, 131, 177, 187, 188
Ōmaranui, 18, 60, 74, 76, 77
Omatua homestead, 182
Onekawa, 176, 177, 184, 185, 188
Ongaonga, 48, 60, 188
Opotiki, 73
Orcharding, 140
Oringi, 97
Ormond, John, 47-50, 52, 56, 60, 64, 65, 68, 73, 76, 79, 81-89, 92, 94, 95, 97, 98, 100, 106, 113, 115, 125, 126, 140
Ormondville, 60, 97, 130, 188
Orua Wharo, 115
Otago, 66, 88, 92, 115
Otaki, 36
Otane, 188, 205
Otatara, 10, 11, 13, 56
O'Connor, J. J., 196

P

Pā Whakairo, 69, 74

Pakiakia, 40, 42
Pakipaki 18, 96, 124, 138
Pakowhai, 17, 18, 53, 84, 88, 94, 124, 126, 130, 187, 188
Parker, Henry, 83
Parker, Tom, 156
pastoralism 34, 47, 58, 61, 103
pastoralists 46, 49, 50, 56, 57, 63-66, 68, 88, 91, 93, 102, 107, 120, 133
Patangata, 60, 108, 188
'pavlova' lifestyle, 183, 185, 186, 211
Paxie's Café, 183
Pētane, 60, 74, 86
Pirimai, 177
Polack, Joel 28
Poppelwell, Harry, 166
Porangahau, 9, 26, 48, 52, 56, 57, 60, 61, 85, 108, 188
Porere, 81
Poriate, 15, 124
Poukawa, 10, 11, 16, 18, 19, 23, 42, 95, 141, 188, 205
Puketapu, 18, 60, 80, 124, 188
Puketitiri, 7, 9, 60, 138, 139, 169, 188, 211
Purimu Stream, 18, 124

Q

quarter-acre section, 50, 59, 157, 204

R

race-relations, 92, 131, 132
Rangitāne 10, 11, 71
Raukawa 23-25, 86
Reignier, Euloge, 32, 33
Renata, *see* Kawepo, Renata
Rhodes, Joseph
Rhodes, W. B. ('Barney'), 20, 29-30
Rhodes, Joseph, 41, 42, 46, 48, 50, 54-57, 60, 62, 63, 65, 69, 76, 92, 94
Richardson, Geordie, 51, 52, 68

Richter, Charles, 150
Riddiford, Daniel, 45, 119
Ringatū (syncretic religion), 81
Rissington, 12, 60, 75, 182, 188, 196, 199
Riverslea Station, 66, 102, 112, 113, 175
Rongowhakaata, 24
Ruahine Ranges, 7, 23, 60, 61, 138, 180, 188
Ruakituri River, 60, 78, 188
Ruataniwha Plains, 12, 23, 46, 48, 56, 60, 97, 188
Russell, Harriet, 96, 109,
Russell, Henry, 47, 49-50, 58, 64, 72, 80, 84-85, 92, 104, 115
Russell, T. Purvis, 47-48, 115, 118
Russell, Andrew Hamilton ('Ham'), 117
Russell, Andrew Hamilton ('Guy') (1868-1960), 127-128
Russell, William, 113, 115, 117, 120.

S

Santa Barbara, 153
Scandinavia 97-99
Scholefield 97
Seddon, Richard, 117.
sewerage 106, 136, 149
Shakespeare Road, 51, 57, 108, 111
Sheehan, John, 72, 86-88
Shrimpton, Walter, 117
Simla Terrace, 54
Six-o'clock closing, 182
Springbok (rugby team), 131, 190
Stafford 76, 79, 81, 85
State Theatre (Napier), 161
State housing, 189
Steiner, Rudolf, 135
Stortford Lodge, 185
Submarines (in Hawke Bay), 165, 167

T

Taenuiarangi, 10, 11, 14, 18, 24, 43

Takamoana, Karaitiana, 32, 40, 42, 69, 71, 82, 84, 85-86 88, 94, 101, 103
Takapau, 60, 96, 109, 116, 157, 188, 201
Tamatea, 9
Tamatea (Napier suburb), 178
Tanner, Thomas, 49-51, 60, 62, 66, 68, 78, 82-85, 101-103, 112-113, 115
Taradale 11, 56, 60, 67, 94, 124, 187
Taraia, 12, 14-16
Taranaki. 26, 72, 73, 77-79, 93, 97, 124, 145, 148
Tarawera, 9, 107
Tareha, 22, 24, 36, 40, 69, 74, 79, 84
Taupō, 8, 18, 22, 23, 25, 107, 109, 134, 137, 173
Tautane, 38, 56
Tavistock Hotel, 84, 108, 161, 183
Te Awanga, 10, 12, 18, 124, 188
Te Hāpuku, 14, 19, 22-26, 30-31, 35-36, 38, 41-43, 53, 70, 71, 73, 74, 84, 85, 89, 95
Te Hauke, 10, 18, 187, 188
Te Kooti, 51, 72, 75, 77-81
Te Moananui (Kurupo), 22-24, 29, 32, 36, 40-43
Te Moananui (Tareha), 79, 84, *see also* Tareha
Te Pariehe 18, 22-26, 28, 36
Te Pohue 60, 74, 138, 188, 201
Te Rangihiroa, 74
Te Roto-a-tara, 10-11, 14, 16, 18, 22, 23, 25
Te Wanikau, 23
Tennyson Street, 55, 153
Thackeray Street, 66
Thoroughbrace coach, 137
Tiakitai, 24, 32, 36
Tiffen, Frederick, 35, 47, 50
Tiffen, Henry, 56, 60, 83, 91, 93, 95, 106, 115
Tiffen Park, 50
Tiger Moths, 171
Tikokino, 56, 57, 61, 100, 108, 183, 188
Timm, Heinrich, 167-168
Tini, Manaena, 82
Titokowaru, 75, 77, 78
Tollemache, Algernon, 49
Tomoana, Henare, 32, 78, 81, 82, 84, 87, 89, 115.
Tomoana Showgrounds, 123.
Tripney, Constable 151
Tripoli, 166, 177
Tronson, Aubrey, 127
Tukituki River, 8, 10, 18, 24, 30, 47, 53, 60, 91, 117, 124, 188, 201
Tunanui Station, 66, 86
Turakina, 115
Turanga, 16
Turanganūi, 46, 77-79, *see also* Gisborne
Turton, Hanson, 85
Tutaekuri River, 8, 10, 16, 18, 30, 38, 60, 74, 106, 113, 124-126, 155, 156, 158, 174, 188, 199
Tutaekuri-Waimate River, 124
Tutanekai, 127
Tutira, Lake, 60, 80, 152, 157, 160, 188

U

U-862, 167-168
Umutaoroa, 86
Utu, 21

V

Vigor-Brown, John, 127, 137
Vogel, Julius, 89, 92-94, 97-99, 106, 110
Volkner, Carl, 73

W

Waiherere Warm Period, 10
Waikato, 18, 21-24, 31, 70, 74, 93
Waikokopu, 24, 25, 188
Waimarama, 10, 11, 18, 23, 48, 60, 65, 188, 202
Waiohiki, 18, 70, 130, 187
Waipatiki, 60, 188
Waipawa, 24, 56, 58, 60, 62, 94, 102, 103, 106, 108, 110, 111, 116, 140, 142, 158, 179, 188, 205
Waipukurau, 22, 37, 38, 46, 53, 58, 60, 62, 84,

89, 94-97, 102, 104, 108, 111, 148, 149, 158, 161, 183, 188, 205
Waipureku, 18, 38, 42, 86, 124
Wairoa, 16, 24, 39, 43, 52, 58, 60-62, 74, 78, 79, 93, 100, 108, 147, 150, 158-160, 168, 174, 187, 188
Waitangi Tribunal, 26, 31, 38, 198, 200
Wakarara, 60, 188
Wakefield, Edward Gibbon, 33
Wallingford, 52, 56, 60, 188
Wanganui, 35, 87, 97, 147, 150
Wanstead, 56, 60, 61, 188
Watt, James, 49, 51, 84, 117
Wattie, James, 160, 166, 171, 173, 195.
Weber, 94, 100, 101
Wellwood, Robert, 105
Weston, Ernest, 99, 111, 147
Westshore, 33, 124, 130, 137, 168
Whakatane, 77
Whakatu, 18, 42, 124, 138, 187, 188
Whaling, 24, 25, 27, 29, 35

Whanawhana, 60, 188
Whanganui-a-Orotū lagoon, 10, 11, 14, 16, 18, 24, 124, 130, 155, 198, 200
Wharerangi, 18, 33, 86, 178, 196
Whitmore, George S., 50-51, 60, 64, 68, 74-81, 85, 87, 136
Williams, Samuel, 44, 51, 68, 84
Williams, William 25, 29, 95-96, 98, 100, 113, 114
Woodford House, 127, 129, 131
Woodville, 97, 100, 174, 205
Woolworths, 161
Worgan, George, 72-73, 86
Wyatt, Alfred, 57

Y

Yippie, 186
Ypres, 152, 177
Yuppie, 203

www.ingramcontent.com/pod-product-compliance
Lightning Source LLC
Chambersburg PA
CBHW081152290426
44108CB00018B/2518